THE LINGUISTICS, NEUROLOGY, AND POLITICS OF PHONICS

Silent "E" Speaks Out

THE LINGUISTICS, NEUROLOGY, AND POLITICS OF PHONICS

Silent "E" Speaks Out

Steven L. Strauss

LEA LAWRENCE ERLBAUM ASSOCIATES, PUBLISHERS
2005 Mahwah, New Jersey London

Lawrence Erlbaum Associates, Inc., Publishers
10 Industrial Avenue
Mahwah, New Jersey 07430

The quoted material at the beginning of each part of the book is taken from the following sources:

Part I: Dickens, C. (1961). *Hard times.* New York: New American Library.

Part II: Einstein, A. (1954). *Ideas and opinions.* New York: Wings Books. (Reprinted from *The New York Times,* p. 37, 1952, October 5)

Part III: Dante, A. (1949). *The divine comedy 1: Hell* (D. L. Sayers, Trans.). London: Penguin Books. (Original work published 1314)

Part IV: Sheehan, H. (1993). *Marxism and the philosophy of science: A critical history.* Atlantic Highlands, NJ: Humanities Press International. (Original work published 1985)

Some of the material in the book was reworked from the following sources and appears with permission of the publishers:

Strauss, S. L. (2003, February). Challenging the NICHD reading research agenda. *Phi Delta Kappan,* 438–442.

Strauss, S. L. (2000, November). The politics of reading and dyslexia. *Z Magazine,* pp. 48–53.

Strauss, S. L. (1999, January). Phonics, whole language, and H.R. 2614. *Z Magazine,* pp. 46–50.

Altwerger, B., & Strauss, S. L. (2002). The business behind testing. *Language Arts,* 256–262.

Cover design by Kathryn Houghtaling Lacey

Library of Congress Cataloging-in-Publication Data

The Linguistics, Neurology, and Politics of Phonics: Silent "E" Speaks Out, by Steven L. Strauss

ISBN 0-8058-4743-X (cloth : alk. paper) — ISBN 0-8058-5244-1 (pbk. : alk. paper).

Includes bibliographical references and index.

Copyright information for this volume can be obtained by contacting the Library of Congress.

Books published by Lawrence Erlbaum Associates are printed on acid-free paper, and their bindings are chosen for strength and durability.

Printed in the United States of America
10 9 8 7 6 5 4 3 2 1

To my mother Selma Strauss,
and to the loving memory
of my father Seymour Strauss

Contents

Foreword

Richard L. Allington
University of Florida

I'll bet Steve Strauss and I wouldn't wholly agree on just what constitutes an "ideal" instructional plan for developing children's reading proficiencies. I'll bet our plans would diverge in the area of children's decoding development. Nonetheless, we both agree that the legislation and mandates endorsed by entrepreneurial neophonics advocates reflect little of the substantial empirical evidence concerning effective literacy instruction and even less of what scientific research has documented about how best to teach children to read proficiently. Their recommendations for developing children's decoding proficiencies fail not just to reflect the broad scientific evidence but also to reliably represent the even epistemologically and methodologically narrow findings of the National Reading Panel (Allington, 2002; Garan, 2002; Foorman & Fletcher, 2003; Shanahan, 2001, 2002, 2003; Yatvin, 2003).

Although most teachers (and probably most school administrators, teacher educators, and researchers) have not read the full NRP report, and so generally fail to recognize the systematic misrepresentations of the findings of that flawed report (Camilli, Vargas, & Yurecko, 2003; Coles, 2003; Cunningham, 2001), they do recognize that much of the current advice offered by the entrepreneurial neophonics advocates contradicts the professional wisdom that accumulates as a result of instructional experience. They recognize that, when the federal government distributes a document suggesting that independent reading at school is not supported by science but that independent reading at home is (Armbruster, Lehr, & Osborn, 2001), something is awry. When this same document offers criteria for "scientific" reading programs, criteria based more in ideology than in evidence

(Allington, 2002), teachers may wonder just what sort of science could invent such criteria.

Likewise, when policy mandates the use of a scripted one-size-fits-all reading program, teachers wonder how anyone who raised even a single child could imagine that children do not differ in their development and their instructional needs. These teachers may not be familiar with a century of research showing that "proven" programs are among the most antiscientific ideas ever promoted, but they do know that children differ and so too must the literacy instruction they receive. Some kids come to literacy with relatively little effort or anxiety, whereas others struggle. Some kids need less instructional attention, others need more, and some need much, much more. This should be considered the normal state of affairs. In every human proficiency, deviation from "normal" development is expected. Whether we look at ice skating, cello playing, video gaming, written composition, figure drawing, mathematical computation, spelling, pseudoword-decoding speed, or rapid automized naming of random objects, children differ. Even given the same quantity and quality of instruction on any of these tasks, children still differ in how easily or quickly they develop proficiency.

I worry about the current emphasis on stigmatization of children who find learning to be literate more difficult. How else is a struggling child to feel when left behind in third grade because his performances failed to meet an arbitrary institutional standard, when he fails day after day in that mandated one-size-fits-all reading program?

Every parent (and teacher) knows how important motivation is to accomplished performances. And they know how important success is to motivation (Pressley et al., 2003). Being dubbed a reading failure daily works against ever marshalling the effort needed to become accomplished at literacy. But dubbing children (and their teachers) failures seems the current policy theme.

So what is a teacher (or principal, teacher educator, researcher, or parent) to do? Jules Henry (cited in Kohl, 2003) argued for three forms of sanity.

In the first form, one believes the sham is the truth. Perhaps out of ignorance or naiveté or ideological bias, a sham simply isn't recognized as a sham.

In the second form, we see through the sham but decide to let it ride and go along with it, all the while recognizing the sham for what it is. In this case we go along with the sham when airport security demands a young mother drink from the baby's bottle of milk before being allowed to pass into the boarding area (you never know what the white milky stuff might really be!), or when grandma is allowed to bring her plastic knitting needles on board but not her aluminum ones.

In the final form, we see through the sham and fight against it as best we can. For teachers this might include ignoring mandates. For school administrators this might result in rejecting state or federal monies with too many strings attached (as a number of schools across the country have done in rejecting available Reading First funding). For teacher educators it might be documenting for education students the breadth of the fraud being perpetuated as scientifically based reading. Researchers, however, write books and articles about the fraud, which brings us to this eloquent and important book written by neurologist Steven Strauss.

Given the complexity of the topics Strauss writes about (democracy, economics, geneticism, neurology, linguistics, aphasia), I was surprised that I understood most of it and enjoyed reading all of it. My students understood and enjoyed the chapters I distributed to them for course readings. The breadth of this book is its single most striking feature. With discussions of academic imperialism, high-stakes testing, federalized education mandates, media complicity, Lysenkoism, MRI imaging, the antiscientific neophonics movement with its entrepreneurial promotion of mind-numbing skill and drill commercial kits and packages, this book cuts a broad swath through current educational fads and the pseudosciences and political and economic forces that sustain the fads.

The clear, concise, and powerful chapters on the pseudoscience that underlies the recent instructional mandates represent a major contribution to the education profession. Here Strauss illustrates just how uninformed many researchers are about the relational and marking rules of the English alphabetic system, so uninformed that they are unable to construct a reliable set of words to test their theories about decoding acquisition. They are so narrow in their training and worldview that they seem wholly unaware of the limited and parochial nature of their views of science generally, and the science of literacy acquisition specifically.

To paraphrase Harvard scholar Richard Elmore (2002), the current federal reading policy (I say "reading policy" because writing, thinking, speaking, and listening have all been somehow left behind) is based on little more than ideological gossip among people who know hardly anything about the institutional realities of classrooms and even less about the problems of improving instruction in schools. Strauss reminds us that we know better (or should) and he has elected the third form of sanity, resistance.

I hope this book finds the wide audience it deserves. I hope it moves more folks to elect that third form of sanity and begin to use both science and the professional wisdom to work to bring America's children truly evidence-based literacy instruction.

REFERENCES

Allington, R. L. (2002). *Big brother and the national reading curriculum: How ideology trumped evidence.* Portsmouth, NH: Heinemann.

Armbruster, B., Lehr, F., & Osborn, J. (2001). *Put reading first.* Washington, DC: National Institute for Literacy.

Camilli, G., Vargas, S., & Yurecko, M. (2003). Teaching children to read: The fragile link between science and federal education policy. *Education Policy Analysis Archives, 11*(15) [On-line]. Available: http://epaa.asu.edu.epaa/v11n15/

Coles, G. (2003). *Reading the naked truth: Literacy, legislation, and lies.* Portsmouth, NH: Heinemann.

Cunningham, J. W. (2001). The National Reading Panel report. *Reading Research Quarterly, 30,* 326–335.

Elmore, R. F. (2002, Spring). Unwarranted intrusion. *Education Next* [On-line]. Available: http://www.educationnext.org/20021/30.

Foorman, B., & Fletcher, J. (2003). Correcting errors. *Phi Delta Kappan, 84,* 719.

Garan, E. (2002). *Resisting reading mandates: How to triumph with the truth.* Portsmouth, NH: Heinemann.

Kohl, H. R. (2004). *Stupidity and tears.* New York: New Press.

Pressley, M., Dolezal, S. E., Raphael, L. M., Mohan, L., Roehrig, A. D., & Bogner, K. (2003). *Motivating primary grade students.* New York: Guilford Press.

Shanahan, T. (2001). Response to Elaine Garan. *Language Arts, 79,* 70–71.

Preface

In this book I explore the driving forces behind the current government-sponsored resurrection of phonics, and the arguments used to justify its legal sanctification. I show that one thing is absolutely clear: Politics has taken precedence over science, and over common sense as well.

Teachers and students today are under immense pressure, with ordnance falling from the very highest levels of government. As Washington pushes to consolidate its control over classroom curriculum, especially in the area of reading instruction, teachers and students are feeling the constraints tighten around their own independent thinking, creativity, and self-expression. The mutually invigorating joys of teaching and learning are suffocating from the smoke of burned-out teachers and learners.

To advance its agenda for reading and reading instruction, Washington has legislated a self-serving definition of *science*. It would appear that this definition has guided phonics into center stage in elementary school classrooms, and kicked meaning-centered approaches to reading off stage. In truth, though, as shown in this book, the government's distorted view of science was carefully concocted in order to justify an already-made commitment to the resurrection of phonics, even after decades of meaning-centered research had demonstrated its profound limitations.

The new phonics, or what I prefer to call *neophonics*, is a central component of the government's new curriculum. However, it did not arise in a vacuum, and would wither away overnight without the dual escorts of law and coercion, popularly referred to as *high-stakes testing* and *accountability*. Might makes right in the field of science, and it is the political right that fashions the might.

Under various undemocratically imposed accountability maneuvers, teachers are now pressured into using state-approved, commercial phonics materials, whether they agree with them or not. At the same time, they are being intimidated against using more authentic, meaning-centered materials, even when their professional judgments are on the side of real literature, written language as communication, and the cultivation of critical thinking in their students.

Students are being tested at younger and younger ages, as precious class time that should be used for meaningful curriculum gives way to test preparation. Parents are caught between the promise of a rosy economic future for a child who scores high in the new curriculum, and the reality of heightened anxiety, competitiveness, jealousy, and suspicion. The reality has not yet hit home that, given the same economic system, the future will be no less insecure than it already is, no matter how well children master phonics.

In this book I show how phonics is one element of a larger political program to remake the U.S. labor force, to equip the next generation of workers with those "21st-century literacy skills" that corporate America sees as vital to its own survival. This is corporate America's own "literacy crisis," which, true to historical form, it is trying to hand off to working people as *their* crisis. This crisis, we are told, is not corporate America's own insecurity about maintaining short- and long-term profit-making capabilities, but rather, the next generation of workers' potential inability to find decent jobs if they do not become better readers. "Raising academic standards will help your child succeed in today's increasingly competitive world," chimes the CEOs of the nation's largest corporations (Business Roundtable, 1998a, par. 2). Corporate America claims it is doing working America a favor, whipping students into line for their own good.

But phonics itself is not the brainchild of corporate America. It is the solution to corporate America's own literacy crisis that has been offered to it by certain politically well-positioned reading personalities and scientists. Still, only corporate America's extreme sense of urgency regarding its battle with overseas competitors, and its perception that winning this battle requires a new type of labor force, can explain the aggressiveness with which phonics has been dumped onto the laps of teachers and students.

Important critiques of the government's politicized phonics agenda have been on bookshelves for several years. Among these are Richard L. Allington's *Big Brother and the National Reading Curriculum: How Ideology Trumped Evidence* (2002); Gerald Coles' *Misreading Reading: The Bad Science that Hurts Children* (2002) and *Reading the Naked Truth: Literacy, Legislation, and Lies* (2003); Elaine Garan's *Resisting Reading Mandates: How to Triumph With the Truth* (2002); Richard J. Meyer's *Phonics Exposed: Understanding and Resisting Systematic Direct Intense Phonics Instruction* (2001); and Denny

Taylor's *Beginning to Read and the Spin Doctors of Science: The Political Campaign to Change America's Mind About How Children Learn to Read* (1998). Critiques of phonics itself, understood as a coherent system of letter-sound correspondences that purportedly plays an essential role in reading, have also been available, including Ken Goodman's important *Phonics Phacts* (1993). Together, these essential works take the federal government to task in exposing the faulty science, vested financial interests, and public relations gimmicks that have created the new phonics. The present work is intended as a contribution to this emerging genre. It examines the roles played by three key actors—corporate America, politicians, and state-supported reading researchers—in the formulation of the neophonics political program.

The book documents how these actors have entered into a relationship of embedded subservience. The scientists seek to satisfy the demands of the politicians, and the politicians do the same for corporate America. At each level, of course, there are individuals who only see the virtues and benefits of their own work, sincere scientists, for example, who are oblivious to any ulterior directives emanating from above. But the facts of the matter are what they are: It is not by coincidence that those scientific theories of reading that have serious problems with intensive phonics are just not drinking from Washington's funding fountain.

In the course of analyzing neophonics as a political program, I also investigate its alleged scientific bases. Proponents of neophonics have claimed that only phonics-based instruction is supported by "trustworthy" science, that linguistic science supports the notion of an alphabetic principle that "decodes" uninterpretable alphabetic writing to interpretable sound, and that neuroscience has demonstrated the brain locus where this alphabetic decoding occurs. None of these claims stands the test of empirical and logical scrutiny. Stripped of any plausible scientific ground, naked neophonics shows its true colors: It is a Trojan horse bringing an authoritarian state into the classroom in order to achieve certain political ends.

If the outcome of the brewing battle between proponents of authoritarian classrooms and those of democratic classrooms were a foregone conclusion, this book would be nothing more than a documentary of historical interest for professional educators and researchers, teachers, and students, perhaps providing some useful information to try to head off and defeat similar catastrophes in the future. But the outcome is not yet decided. Teachers know that their profession is being deprofessionalized. Students and parents are protesting high-stakes testing, rejecting the phony argument that it will improve the quality of education. Therefore, this book is also intended to be part of the armamentarium of resistance by activist educators, students, and parents.

OVERVIEW

The organization of the book is as follows. Part I discusses the central problem—an alleged literacy crisis—which is really corporate America's own crisis. It investigates the political reasons for the renewed focus on phonics, and media complicity in promoting the neophonics political program, the proposed solution to corporate America's literacy crisis. Part II examines the scientific claims of neophonics, including methodology, linguistics, and neuroscience, and exposes the flaws in its reasoning and the impotence of its arguments. Part III addresses a subject that is surprisingly absent from neophonics literature, namely, the scientific, empirical investigation of letter-sound relationships in English, of phonics itself, and demonstrates the complexity of the system and the associated benefits and limitations in the theory and practice of reading. Part IV reviews the discussions of the earlier chapters—the political nature of the supposed problem of literacy in America, the pseudoscientific solution to this pseudoproblem, and the reclaiming of an empirically adequate science of letter-sound relationships—and proposes actions to help make a return to politically undistorted science and to democratic classrooms a reality. A postscript introduces a formal analysis of the letter-sound system, using empirically based rules to convert one finite set of elements, the alphabet, into another, the phonemes of the spoken language.

ACKNOWLEDGMENTS

This book would not have been possible without the many hours of discussions I have had over the years with numerous friends and colleagues. First among these is my wife, Bess Altwerger, who has been my colleague in linguistics and reading for almost as long as we have been together. She has been a constant source of debate and encouragement, and has helped me understand what a privilege it is to have someone in your life who can take apart your arguments and still love you.

I am also immensely indebted to Ken Goodman, Yetta Goodman, Carole Edelsky, and Barbara Flores, for years of friendship and intellectual comradeship. I also wish to thank Gerry Coles, Elaine Garan, Steve Krashen, and Wayne Ross. Sue Allison's diligent work against high-stakes testing in Maryland has helped me stay abreast of developments locally and nationally in this very important struggle.

I owe my deepest thanks to the Lawrence Erlbaum Associates reviewers of my manuscript, whose questions and concerns are reflected on virtually every page, as well as Naomi Silverman, an editor with exceptional talents who helped turn some of my moments of despair into invigorating writing experiences.

Finally, I wish to thank all the teachers, students, and parents I have been fortunate to meet and address over the years at national and local conferences, who have encouraged me to continue my work, and whose perseverence in a difficult struggle has sustained my optimism for a better world.

And to Erika, Asher, Robin, Earl, Charlotte, Michael, Debbi, Logan, Austin, Stanley, Bonnie, Josh, Joanne, Bernie, Jan, Smit, Jerry, Jackie, Ann, Pat B., Pat G., Darlene, Kathy, Lynn, Bonnie, and Sue—I couldn't have done it without you either.

I take full responsibility for any and all errors of fact and logic that are in this work.

Table of Phonetic Characters

		Consonants			
p	*p*it	θ	*th*in	l	*l*it
b	*b*it	ð	*th*is	r	*r*ib
m	*m*itt				
f	*f*it	š	*sh*ip	w	*w*ash
v	*v*an	ž	mea*s*ure	y	*y*es
		č	*ch*in	h	*h*it
t	*t*ip	ĵ	*g*in		
d	*d*ip				
n	*n*ip	k	*k*it		
s	*s*ip	g	*g*ive		
z	*z*ip	ŋ	so*ng*		
Long Vowels		*Short Vowels*		*Other Vowels*	
iy	b*ee*t	I	b*i*t	R	f*ir*, f*er*n, f*ur*
uw	b*oo*t	U	p*u*t	ɑ	p*a*rt
ey	b*ai*t	E	b*e*t	ɔ	c*au*ght, s*ou*ght
ow	b*oa*t	^	b*u*t	ə	*a*bout
ay	b*i*te	a	p*o*t		
		æ	h*a*t, s*a*d, v*a*n		

In the body of the text, a sound will be denoted by square brackets, e.g., the sounds [p], [t] and [k]. The bracketed [ø] denotes silence, or the null sound.

Part I

THE PROBLEM: AN ALLEGED LITERACY CRISIS

Now, what I want is Facts. Teach these boys and girls nothing but Facts. Facts alone are wanted in life. Plant nothing else, and root out everything else. You can only form the minds of reasoning animals upon Facts: nothing else will ever be of any service to them.

—Dickens (1961, p. 11)

Chapter **1**

The Literacy Crisis According to Corporate America

During the televised debates for the 2000 presidential election, candidate George W. Bush took a stand on letters and sounds, and made phonics a campaign issue (*Transcript of the Second Presidential Debate,* ABC News, October 11, 2000):

> My friend Phyllis Hunter's here. She had one of the greatest lines of all lines. She said, "Reading is the new civil right." And she's right. And to make sure our society is as hopeful as it possibly can be, every single child in America must be educated, I mean every child. It starts with making sure every child learns to read; K–2 diagnostic testing so we know whether or not there's a deficiency; curriculum that works, and phonics needs to be an integral part of our reading curriculum; intensive reading laboratories; teacher retraining.

Candidate Bush, it appears, had been well apprised of reading as a scientific subject with potent political ramifications. Considering that his remarks took place in the setting of a public debate, his stance should have prompted a fruitful exchange with his opponent.

For example, Vice President Al Gore might have challenged Bush with any number of pointed, yet appropriate, questions. Why, Mr. Bush, is reading only now a civil right? Why not 5 or 10 or 20 years ago? Certainly the United Nations and the World Health Organization have long recognized literacy as a fundamental human right. And why is your humanistically characterized view of reading as a "new civil right" linked to inhumane psychologically and socially stressful high-stakes testing of children, replete with threats of grade retention, withholding of diplomas, funding loss, and school closures? On a more practical level, how will schools with no money for library books implement "the new civil right"?

Or, he might have asked the following: How, Mr. Bush, did you become familiar with important issues in the field of reading? Which professional teachers and educators did you consult with? Does your advocacy of phonics, so strong that you have now announced it on national television before millions of Americans, mean that you also have reservations about the results of three or four decades of scientific research, including federally funded research, on meaning-centered reading and whole language?

Of course, Gore offered no such challenge, nor any rebuttal whatsoever. Indeed, none should have been expected. The Clinton-Gore administration, like the Bush-Cheney administration, was also enamored of phonics, and had already signed into law the Reading Excellence Act (1998), which established the precedent of legislating instructional methods, by requiring phonics lessons in federally funded classrooms. On the campaign issue of phonics, the support was fully and unequivocally bipartisan.

As president, Bush linked the Clinton-Gore forced phonics legal precedent to "high-stakes testing" and "accountability." With these moves, even if teachers or students or parents do not agree with intensive phonics, they have to do it anyway, lest they jeopardize their chances at receiving a promotion, a diploma, merit pay, funding, or a job. In this way, Bush's No Child Left Behind Act (NCLB, 2001) put teeth in the Clinton-Gore snarl. And there were certainly some sharp fangs among those teeth, as the risks associated with ignoring phonics were now substantially raised.

Thus, with two strokes of the pen, first from the Democrats and then from the Republicans, decades of sound scientific research on meaning-centered reading was thrown out the window. The new, intensive phonics was now poised to intrude on valuable class time and educational experience. But to do this, it first had to be escorted into classrooms by federally supplied bodyguards and bouncers, for which the expressions "high-stakes testing" and "accountability" are just euphemisms. Meaning-centered reading, forcibly cleansed from the classroom, was relegated to the status of educational refugee.

It is extremely doubtful that a reading pedagogy based on intensive letter-sound instruction could win the hearts and minds of the majority of teachers, parents, and students simply on the basis of its own inherent scientific merit, and in such fashion be welcomed into U.S. classrooms. Clearly, the government is taking no chances. Its powerful extrascientific legal resources are indispensable for carrying through its plans for education. These resources empower it to threaten sanctions against professional teachers and educators who stubbornly refuse to abandon their belief that meaning-centered science offers the best explanation available of the nature of reading, how to teach it, and how to assess it.

Consider, for example, the summary position on reading expressed by one of the nation's largest teachers organizations, the 70,000-member National Council of Teachers of English (NCTE). In a publicly available position statement (February, 1999, par. 1–2), the NCTE conveyed its sense of decades of scientific research on the role of phonics in reading:

> Reading is the complex act of constructing meaning from print. We read in order to better understand ourselves, others, and the world around us; we use the knowledge we gain from reading to change the world in which we live.
>
> Becoming a reader is a gradual process that begins with our first interactions with print. As children, there is no fixed point at which we suddenly become readers. Instead, all of us bring our understanding of spoken language, our knowledge of the world, and our experiences in it to make sense of what we read. We grow in our ability to comprehend and interpret a wide range of reading materials by making appropriate choices from among the extensive repertoire of skills and strategies that develop over time. These strategies include predicting, comprehension monitoring, phonemic awareness, critical thinking, decoding, using context, and making connections to what we already know. (par. 1–2)

To the teachers and educators of the NCTE, phonics ("decoding") is only one of many "skills and strategies" employed by readers as they attempt to construct meaning. Consequently, an overly intense focus on phonics, or on any one of the skills and strategies, will result in the deleterious neglect of other skills and strategies, because it distorts reading as a "complex" mental act. This leads to a breakdown in the reader's capacity to construct meaning.

Can a group of 70,000 teachers and educators who have spent decades studying and debating all the complex issues in reading be converted overnight to an intensive phonics position? In the history of science, there is no precedent for such rapid change, even in the presence of overwhelmingly compelling empirical evidence. It takes time for professionals to restudy, redebate, and digest. So, insofar as the classroom teaching of intensive phonics cannot be guaranteed by the internal conviction of teachers, it must, according to the government, be elicited by the external coercion of the state.

It seems that specific forms of external coercion are a matter of ongoing government deliberation. Reid Lyon, President Bush's chief reading advisor, and variously dubbed his "reading czar" and "reading guru" by the media, testified before Congress on May 4, 2000 that "we do not yet understand the *incentive systems* that are critical in helping teachers to modify their belief systems" (*Testimony of G. Reid Lyon*, 2000, emphasis added). By the following year, Lyon was testifying in favor of one of these "incentive systems," declaring that "systems of accountability" must be "used to inform instructional practices in classroom settings" (*Testimony of G. Reid Lyon*, 2001). Of course, we are still awaiting the scientific data that will allow us to "understand" how this particular "incentive system" will modify teachers' belief systems, as opposed to just modifying what they say and do in public in order to keep their jobs.

Phonics was very much in vogue prior to the contemporary science of meaning-centered reading. Initially, phonics was the darling of behaviorist linguists, who hypothesized that letter stimuli trigger phonemic responses, and who defined learning to read as the cultivation of an "ingrained habit" (Bloomfield, 1942/1961, p. 26) to produce specific sounds when looking at specific letters. With the rise of cognitive psychology, letters were still converted to sounds, but now only in order to recognize and identify words, with recognition and identification being part of cognitive psychology's information processing machinery. As Marilyn Adams remarked, "unless the processes involved in individual word recognition operate properly, nothing else in the system can either" (1990, p. 6).

Meaning-centered reading theory and whole language transcended both of these paradigms, by viewing reading neither as fundamentally involving a sound response to a letter stimulus, nor as the informational processing of letters in order to recognize a word, but rather as the active construction of meaning. Although Noam Chomsky revolutionized linguistic theory by calling attention to the stimulus-free nature of language use, and to the insurmountable problems thereby inherent in behaviorist linguistics (Chomsky, 1959), cognitive psychology, at least in the field of reading, still did not advance very far beyond this fatal limitation. It continued to emphasize the physically observable part of written language, the letters on the page, as the fundamental building blocks of its information processing mechanisms. Alone in this regard, meaning-centered reading and whole language took Chomsky's critique of behaviorism seriously, by studying the multitude of invisible cognitive resources and strategies brought by the reader to the page during the act of reading. These include knowledge of syntax and semantics, background world knowledge and knowledge about the author and genre, and background belief systems.

At its height, phonics did scientific battle with "sight word" or "whole word" reading. Whereas cognitive psychology advocates of phonics would see letters leading a reader to sounds, and sounds leading a reader to the identification of a word, sight word advocates pointed out that many English words have complicated, if not fundamentally idiosyncratic, letter-sound relationships, and are thus better recognized "whole." But even this may have been a spurious dichotomy, because, as Richard Venezky correctly pointed out, "[a] substantial number of words are usually taught as sight words, yet within any of these most of the letter-sound patterns are regular" (1999, p. 240). Thus, a typical sight word, such as *said*, is idiosyncratic with respect to its vowel letters, but perfectly regular with respect to its consonant letters *s* and *d*.

Meaning-centered reading questioned the fundamental assumption of the cognitive psychology stance on both phonics and sight word reading, namely, that readers must *recognize and identify* words in order to comprehend. Meaning-centered reading researchers point to empirical evidence that supports the view that proficient readers often guess at words, or even ignore words on the page, as part of the normal process of constructing meaning (Goodman, 1967). But guessing and ignoring are clearly not the same as recognizing. Therefore, word recognition, even if it is a component of the reading process, plays a strictly subordinate role in the larger task of meaning construction. An overemphasis on word recognition distracts a reader away from this more fundamental task.

There is no question that this view of reading dramatically altered the landscape of reading theory and practice, in classroom after classroom, throughout the country and the world. It has been, without a doubt, the most important modern advance in our understanding of the phenomenon of reading. Furthermore, though not disavowing a role for phonics, it clarified the role that letter-sound relationships play in a reader's attempt to understand written language. It also enriched the knowledge base needed by professional teachers and educators to teach and assess reading appropriately and effectively.

But, after several decades of progress, and with productive research still running strong, the meaning-centered explosion in reading ran into an unanticipated roadblock. The roadblock, as we shall see, was set up by politicians, corporate executives, and others with a private agenda for reading education in particular, and for public education in general. The roadblock consists not of new scientific discoveries about reading, but rather of a flimsy flotsam of pseudoscientific arguments, worn-out platitudes, and frank distortions of fact, all backed up by threats of social and economic sanctions against opponents. The result is a new classroom climate, brought about by a politicized phonics, which I shall refer to as *neophonics*. More and more, politics, not science, is pushing advocates of meaning-centered reading out of the classroom.

Such has been the roller coaster rise and fall and rise of phonics. It rose initially on the tide of behaviorist linguistics, and was sustained by the cognitive reworking of the behaviorists' "ingrained habit" as information processing. It fell on its face with the discoveries of meaning-centered research, but maintained a presence through highly profitable and enticingly packaged commercial products. It is now rising again, this time with the backing of political power, not scientific argument, dealing blows to its intellectual opponents.

Where did the neophonics roadblock come from, with its cachectic coating of science on the outside, and the mighty muscle of the state on the inside? Whose idea was it? Who is building it? Who benefits from it? Who loses? And why such urgency?

Urgency is born of a sense of crisis. In 1998, the late Paul Coverdell introduced the Reading Excellence Act to his fellow U.S. Senators. "We clearly have a literacy crisis in the nation," he began, "when four out of ten of our third-graders can't read" (*Testimony of Paul Coverdell*, 1998, par. 2). The bill passed both houses of Congress, and ordered phonics into U.S. classrooms. A few years later, the No Child Left Behind Act (2001) was enacted, protecting government-imposed phonics against opponents via the use of high-stakes testing and accountability.

With these legislative moves, Washington positioned itself to radically alter the way elementary reading instruction would be carried out across the country, as well as the classroom climate under which this instruction would occur. Its actions have been virtually unprecedented in the extent to which this experiment in social engineering is transforming relationships among teachers, students, and parents. As could easily be predicted, not everyone is happy. Teachers sense the creeping deprofessionalization of their trade. Parents and students sense both the lifelessness of the new classroom curriculum, which is increasingly little more than sterile test preparation drills, and the socially unjust character of grade retention based on a poor test score.

But the public debate and discussion about whether any of this represents quality education is only now beginning, in bits and pieces, here and there. It certainly did not begin with the Bush-Gore debates. Of course, such a discussion should have preceded the enactment of the Reading Excellence Act (1998) and No Child Left Behind (2001). But it is not too late to begin now, because the government's laws are never set in stone.

The fundamental premise underlying Washington's radical plans for reading instruction is that we are experiencing a national *literacy crisis,* as Coverdell claimed, and that this crisis requires an *urgent solution.* Nothing short of this notion can explain the utterly thuggish methods being used to transform classrooms, from the falsification of government-funded research reports (more about this later, cf. Garan, 2002; Strauss, 2003), to the unprecedented Congressional legislation of a particular method of teaching reading, to the imposition on students and teachers of life-draining high-stakes testing and accountability.

And nothing short of grasping the propagandistic power of a *crisis mentality* will allow us to unravel and comprehend these devious plans. This power is of such magnitude that members of a free society, once gripped by the perception of crisis, whether real or not, may be cajoled into trading in the most precious of civil liberties for the promise, whether sincere or not, of social stability, that is to say, of the absence of crisis.

Only a crisis mentality can account for an education policy that finds something of value in punishing innocent children with grade retention and social embarrassment, when their only crime is that they did not pass an ill-conceived and socially unenlightened standardized examination. Only a nation that sees itself in crisis could be willing to discard an entire generation of professional, dedicated teachers, by transforming them into robotic test preparation machines, while waving good-bye to the ones who burn out from too much caring.

But is there really a literacy crisis? And if there is, why don't we consider that the real crisis must then lie in the notion that the richest and most privileged society in the history of the planet did not take steps to make sure that such a preventable problem would not occur?

What does it mean to say that there is a literacy crisis? Are children physically dying from insufficient exposure to the written word, just as children facing a hunger crisis die from insufficient exposure to food? Are children spiritually losing their way because they can't appreciate the epiphanies of Dostoevsky's protagonists? Are they socially maladjusted because they can't relate to Shakespeare's social elites? Just what exactly is the problem?

Suppose it were true that millions of U.S. children could not read, or could read but didn't care to, or could read and cared to read but couldn't find enough books in school libraries to keep them busy. We might want to call this a literacy *problem.* But to call it a *crisis* implies far greater seriousness—a potential for catastrophe.

So is there something catastrophic in the current state of literacy in the United States? David Berliner and Bruce Biddle, in their groundbreaking book *The Manufactured Crisis: Myths, Fraud, and the Attack on America's Public Schools* (1995), pointed to a spate of nationwide headlines in September, 1993 that reported an announcement by the U.S. Department of Education that millions of Americans were illiterate. According to Berliner and Biddle, "the basic premise put forth by the Department of Education at that conference" was "that illiteracy causes poverty" (p. 10). Perhaps this is the crisis of literacy, that it ineluctably engenders indigence.

But was there no poverty prior to the printing press? Indeed, Berliner and Biddle (1995) immediately exposed the laughable logic behind the government's bathos with the simple but crisp observation that "no one seems to have thought that the relationship between poverty and illiteracy might go the other way—indeed that good research had already been done indicating that *poverty causes low levels of literacy*" (p. 10, emphasis original). On Berliner and Biddle's account, the real crisis is poverty itself, not illiteracy, certainly a far more plausible hypothesis.

The alleged causal trajectory from illiteracy to poverty is rendered even more absurd with Berliner and Biddle's (1995) observation that the pronouncements of the Department of Education were based on a classification of individuals as illiterate if they scored poorly on a reading comprehension test. According to Berliner and Biddle:

> This sounds reasonable until one begins to think about some startling characteristics of the so-called illiterate group that the report detailed. . . . Some truly startling categories of people turned out to have been classified as among the most illiterate: 26 percent had debilitating physical or mental conditions, 19 percent had difficulties reading print because they were visually impaired, and 25 percent were immigrants whose native language was not English—the language of the test. (p. 10)

Extending the government's logic even further was Reid Lyon, Director of Reading Research at the National Institute of Child Health and Human Development (NICHD), one of the institutes of the National Institutes of Health (NIH). As noted earlier, Lyon is also an education advisor to President Bush, and was one of the chief architects of Bush's No Child Left Behind Act (2001).

Lyon (*Testimony of G. Reid Lyon,* 1998) characterized reading failure as a "significant public health problem" (par. 6), one in which "the need for informed instruction for the millions of children with insufficient reading skills is an increasingly urgent problem." This "urgency" extends to the realm of teacher preparation, where, Lyon lamented, "many teachers are underprepared to teach reading" (*Testimony of G. Reid Lyon,* 1998, par. 36).

Lyon invoked an alleged link between reading failure and other social problems. "It goes without saying," he testified in 2001, "that failure to learn to read places children's futures and lives at risk for highly deleterious outcomes" (*Testimony of G. Reid Lyon,* 2001, par. 5). More specifically, he stated:

> Of the ten to 15 percent of children who will eventually drop out of school, over 75% will report difficulties learning to read. Likewise, only two percent of students receiving special or compensatory education for difficulties learning to read will complete a four-year college program. Surveys of adolescents and young adults with criminal records indicate that at least half have reading difficulties, and in some states the size of prisons a decade in the future is predicted by fourth grade reading failure rates. Approximately half of children and adolescents with a history of substance abuse have reading problems. (p. 5)

The semantic sleight of hand in these remarks suggests illiteracy as the primary problem, and school dropout, drug abuse, and crime as its consequences. With this logic, we should also say that children who grow up speaking Mende and Temne are at risk of dying before the age of 45. This is technically true, as the citizens of Sierra Leone know only too well, but the cause and effect linkage that is implied is clearly preposterous. It is no less preposterous in the case of illiteracy, school dropout, drug abuse, and crime.

Who seriously believes that illiteracy *causes* school dropout, drug abuse, and crime? Where is the convincing, cogent argument? By what social-psychological mechanism is a child without a criminal disposition, or an inclination toward drug abuse, led from an inability to read to something far more physically destructive? Do literate people not abuse drugs? Is white collar crime caused by being *too* literate?

This Madison Avenue style chicanery insinuates cause and effect by foregrounding the problem of illiteracy against a background of social problems that are acknowledged to be serious, undesirable, and perhaps even of crisis proportions. We are finessed into concluding that illiteracy is itself a crisis problem. We should also conclude that phonics is part of the war on drugs, but no one will be surprised if illiteracy is reduced, even eliminated, and drug abuse remains a problem. In the end, Lyon's (*Testimony of G. Reid Lyon,* 2001) argument is just a Trojan horse to bring his favored method of reading instruction more into the public consciousness, and into classrooms.

Lyon's (*Testimony of G. Reid Lyon,* 1997) proposed solution to the "significant public health problem" of reading failure, a problem that he characterized as "urgent," and for which teacher preparation has been woefully inadequate, is based on an alleged "alphabetic principle." According to this theoretical underpinning of phonics, "written spellings systematically represent the phonemes of spoken words" (par. 8). But "unfortunately," said Lyon, "children are not born with this insight, nor does it develop naturally without instruction. Hence, the existence of illiterate cultures and of illiteracy within literate cultures" (par. 8). So, because illiteracy, we are told, causes poverty, and failure to learn the alphabetic principle leads to illiteracy, the solution to the global scourge of poverty would appear to be—phonics!

So powerful and persuasive must the logic of Lyon (*Testimony of G. Reid Lyon,* 1997) be that some recipients of his agency's research funds share his views to a startling degree. Thus, we read from Barbara Foorman and fellow NICHD-associated researchers that, as concerns the alphabetic principle, "unfortunately, children are not born with this insight, nor does it develop naturally without instruction. Hence, the existence of illiterate cultures and of illiteracy within literate cultures" (Foorman, Francis, & Fletcher, 1997, par. 5). According to Lyon, the NICHD's understanding of reading and literacy is supported by "the most trustworthy scientific evidence available" (*Testimony of G. Reid Lyon,* 2001, par. 15), so trustworthy, it seems, that its claims have become a dogmatic political line.

The same theme rang in the halls of Congress itself when Senator Coverdell introduced the Clinton-Gore era Reading Excellence Act (1998) into the Senate. Lamenting the poor prognosis for allegedly illiterate third graders, he stated that, "without basic reading skills, many of these children will be shut out of the workforce of the 21st century" (T*estimony of Paul Coverdell,* 1998, par. 2). He further noted:

> According to the 1993 National Audit Literacy Survey, more than 40 million Americans cannot read a phone book, menu or the directions on a medicine bottle. Those who can't learn to read are not only less likely to get a good job, they are disproportionately represented in the ranks of the unemployed and the homeless. Consider the fact that 75 percent of unemployed adults, 33 percent of mothers on welfare, 85 percent of juveniles appearing in court and 60 percent of prison inmates are illiterate. (par. 2)

As noted earlier, Coverdell (*Testimony of Paul Coverdell*, 1998) identified a literacy crisis when 40% of third graders cannot read. To support the notion of a crisis, he too insinuated illiteracy as playing a significant role in the genesis of other social problems, such as unemployment, homelessness, welfare, and crime.

Coverdell's (*Testimony of Paul Coverdell*, 1998) and Lyon's (*Testimony of G. Reid Lyon*, 1997, 2001) rhetorical style is typical and instructive. The mere association of illiteracy with other social ills says little about causality. However, to claim these associations in the course of a disquisition urging legislation that mandates phonics instruction in federally funded classrooms, without at the same time providing for independent measures to fight unemployment and homelessness, leads pragmatically to the conclusion that illiteracy is the pivotal issue, and that illiteracy *leads to* these other problems.

The sophistry goes even further. Illiteracy is also specifically identified as a *pediatric* affliction, as it makes its initial appearance in this population—children in the third grade, for example. The associated social ills, however, are specifically those of the *adult and young adult* population: unemployment, crime, school dropout, and so on. Plainly, illiteracy temporally *precedes* these other social ills. The suggested inference: It must be their cause.

But we can easily identify many social categories whose characterization of individuals predates their illiteracy, yet are also associated with illiteracy. These include being born into poverty, being born into an oppressed social minority, growing up in a household where little reading occurs, and being homogeneously tracked in school right from the start with a low test-scoring cohort. What are the causal relations now?

Clearly, a much more plausible starting point recognizes that certain social factors lead to illiteracy in the young (and obviously can persist into adulthood) as well as to unemployment, certain types of drug use, crime, and welfare in adults. What all of these social problems have in common, of course, is that they appear in groups that are most victimized not just by poverty *per se*, but also by unacceptable discrepancies in the distribution of wealth. When poverty stands alongside privilege, rather than being homogeneous across the society, the existence of *inequality* is apparent. And it is not just an inequality of income, but of *access* to both the material and cultural wealth of society. This includes access to jobs, quality education, quality health care, justice, and, not least in importance, literacy.

So far, therefore, there is simply no compelling reason to believe that a literacy crisis exists in the United States, or that it refers to something coherent and definable. The mere association of illiteracy with other social problems does not constitute a literacy crisis *per se*, as opposed to a poverty crisis or an unemployment crisis. And the appearance of illiteracy earlier in life than drug addiction and going on welfare again is a false argument. Still, Washington self-righteously forges ahead with its literacy campaign in such a way as to make one wonder why it had such harsh words for certain other governments that also saw the importance of literacy, and who instituted their own literacy campaigns, such as Cuba under Castro and Nicaragua under the Sandinistas. Washington's behavior still needs explaining.

An explanation for this behavior requires an appreciation that the current obsession with reading emanates from above, not from below, that is to say, from a wing of the presumed literate sector of the population, rather than the alleged illiterate sector. According to Berliner and Biddle, "about four out of five 'illiterates' also declared that they read 'well' or 'very well.' Only a few said that they needed to rely on family or friends to interpret prose material, and nearly half reported reading a newspaper every day!" (1995, p. 10). Thus, there is no crisis mentality among the victims themselves. The illiterates have not demanded phonics, high-stakes testing, and accountability.

This immediately suggests that the illiteracy crisis has more to do with the needs of certain literates, rather than with the needs of the illiterates. A step toward grasping this aspect of the problem can be seen in another of Senator Coverdell's comments, in which he stated that "the Reading Excellence Act will provide today's children the tools to be successful in tomorrow's workforce" (*Testimony of Paul Coverdell*, 1998, par. 7). Therefore, illiteracy may be considered a crisis because "tomorrow's workforce" will need individuals who possess certain literacy skills, so unless young people become proficient readers, they will not find good jobs in the future job market.

This formulation of the problem pretends to look out for the needs of U.S. workers, and of the illiterates among them who will not fare well in the economy. The legislation being passed to confront these needs is thereby the product of a beneficent government. But the crucial concept underlying this formulation has to do with the needs of the economy, not the needs of working people. It is the economy itself, transformed by revolutionary advances in electronic technology, that will be unable to accommodate workers who lack certain skills, including certain reading skills. In other words, and from this vantage point, the alleged literacy crisis is as much a demon for the employers as it is for the employees. Employers will find themselves unable to compete in the future economy if they lack a workforce with skills comparable to or exceeding those of their competitors. Quite simply, they will go out of business.

Indeed, the pronouncements of corporate employers make it abundantly clear that the entire notion of a literacy crisis in the United States is connected to their social Darwinian principle of self-preservation. From their perspective, there truly is a crisis, because what is at stake is their very existence as a class, and the maintenance of their coveted leading role in the international class of corporate employers.

This perspective can be seen, for example, in statements of Norman Augustine, former CEO of Lockheed Martin. According to Augustine (1997), many young job applicants "arrive at [his] doors unable to write a proper paragraph, fill out simple forms, read instruction manuals, do essential mathematical calculations, understand basic scientific concepts, or work as a team" (par. 2). He continued:

> Perhaps these examples would be less disconcerting if our economy were still based on an early industrial model where hard work, a strong back and common sense could secure a decent job for even an illiterate person. But today's global, information-based economy is defined more and more by constantly evolving technology involving, for example, fiber optics, robotics, bioengineering, advanced telecommunications, microelectronics and artificial intelligence. Countries that do not lead will be more than economically disadvantaged; they will be economically irrelevant. (par. 3)

Along with Reid Lyon, Augustine, it should be noted, has been one of President Bush's education advisors. As seen from Augustine's corporate skybox, and duly noted in the White House and Congress, illiteracy in the United States cannot be tolerated, because this will lead to "economic irrelevance," that is to say, to companies that cannot compete in the global marketplace. But the problem is not that there is a critical mass of workers who cannot read *in general.* Rather, it is that the labor force is inadequately trained in a *certain type* of reading, namely, the type required for information processing in the new, high-tech, digital economy. No matter how profoundly young people discuss poetry and modern drama, or surrealism in world fiction, there would still be a literacy crisis if they could not read "instruction manuals."

This, in a nutshell, is the real literacy crisis. It is a crisis because at stake is the "relevance" of corporate America, its survival as a global economic power, and, indeed, all the traits and prerogatives it arrogates to itself on the basis of this power. This is not only a *plausible* explanation of the crisis mentality surrounding an alleged illiteracy; it is the *only* explanation that makes any sense from among all those that have been presented to the public. Although Washington is good at giving lip service to problems like poverty, unemployment, crime, and drug abuse, especially around election time, no one can seriously argue that very much has been done about them.

In this regard, it is useful to contrast the problems that qualify as social crises for politicians and the media with those that do not. For example, Coverdell's (*Testimony of Paul Coverdell*, 1998) audience in the Senate heard him cite a figure of 40 million as an estimate of the number of adult Americans who allegedly cannot read a phone book, order from a menu, or follow directions on a medicine bottle. But the same number of people is frequently cited as lacking health insurance in this country. So why is the existence of 40 million uninsured Americans not prompting the same crisis mentality as 40 million supposedly illiterate Americans?

Politicians and the media tell us that illiteracy is a crisis because it will keep people from finding employment in the 21st-century economy. Massive numbers of workers with no health insurance is not a crisis for corporate America. True, workers need to be minimally healthy in order to go to work. But, so far apparently, they are *healthy enough*.

Indeed, public discussions of chronic medical problems typically cite time lost from work and money lost from the economy as the unfortunate social consequences of these illnesses, as opposed to, say, time lost from socializing with one's family. Migraine headaches, for example, probably affect at least 20 million Americans, and the proliferation of triptans may one day rival the proliferation of toothpastes. A typical description of its social impact can be found in a fact sheet from the National Institute of Neurologic Disorders and Stroke (NINDS), another member institute of the NIH. According to the NINDS (2001):

> Despite the fact that 1 in 4 households in the United States have someone affected by migraine headaches, migraine is still not considered by many employers and insurers to be a legitimate medical problem. Migraine, however, can cause significant disability and costs the American taxpayers $13 billion in missed work or reduced productivity annually. (par. 2)

Or, in another NINDS statement (June 8–9, 2000), "Migraine is one of the most common, and most painful of the chronic pain disorders. Its impact extends beyond the personal burden of those who suffer from migraine attacks, and impacts the national economy through an increased use of medical resources and decreased work productivity" (par. 1). Perhaps if enough sick days accumulate, we might see federal legislation requiring treatment of migraines.

In summary, the current U.S. literacy crisis is a strictly relativistic notion, not an absolute one. Despite innuendos to the contrary, it is not a third-world type of literacy crisis, in which vast numbers of people, quite literally, cannot read or write. In the United States, the literacy crisis has to do with a narrow type of reading. The crisis exists only for a small segment of society, the corporate employers, who sense that their survival as a hegemonic class in the global economy is not adequately assured.

To those who would counter that illiteracy is as much a crisis for U.S. workers as it is for employers, it should be clearly pointed out that the acquisition of cognitive labor skills merely provides the modern cognitive laborer with an improved chance of finding a job in the digital economy, but certainly no guarantee. It all depends on how the profit margins are doing. The system that today resorts to layoffs and unemployment when the margins are down will be no kinder to the 21st-century knowledge worker than it was to the 20th-century industrial worker.

Furthermore, with respect to those who claim to speak for workers and their need for secure employment, a demonstration that the views of teachers, students, and parents have been democratically consulted in the formulation of government policy would serve their argument well. Of course, teachers, students, and parents have not been consulted. To the contrary, we hear about the need to find "incentive systems" to change their "belief systems." But the protests against government policy grow daily, by teachers, parents, and students who do not agree with the attacks on teacher professionalism, or with punishing and frightening children with tests that determine their academic and vocational future.

Stated plainly, there has been no civilized, public, democratic discussion of what constitutes a well-rounded curriculum and a quality education. Therefore, what is playing out is a struggle between supporters of undemocratic government mandates and those defending democratic classrooms. From the inaccessible offices in Washington and Bethesda, all that seems to count regarding public policy on public education is corporate America's self-defined need to create the new type of literacy it feels is crucial for its own survival. In pursuit of this goal, corporate America has come up with an education reform program of its own design, and has enlisted the support of politicians and government-funded scientists to make this program a reality. To disseminate this program to ordinary citizens, and to manufacture and recruit their support, it has enlisted the willing ink of the media. This obsequious attentiveness of politicians, scientists, and the media to the corporate agenda, and to corporate America's need for an "incentive system" to change people's beliefs, is discussed in the following chapters.

Chapter 2

Corporate America's Education Reform

The special interest group that most directly and forcefully represents the views of corporate America in the areas of literacy and education reform, that has published its positions on these and related matters in publicly available papers, and that has the eager ear of Washington, is the Business Roundtable. The Business Roundtable, formed in 1972, is a coalition of CEOs of the nation's largest corporations. Now consisting of about 150 CEOs, the Business Roundtable member companies employ more than 10 million U.S. workers. Over the last decade, it has judiciously positioned itself to turn its agenda for education into public policy, at both the state and national levels. It has entered into partnerships with state departments of education, and its members sit on national "advisory" committees. Most recently, Edward B. Rust, Jr., CEO of State Farm Insurance Companies, and Norman R. Augustine, former CEO of Lockheed Martin, were appointed to President Bush's education advisory committee. Rust is the current chair of the Education Task Force of the Business Roundtable, and Augustine is its previous chair.

The positions that the Business Roundtable (1998b) takes on various social issues, from education to international trade, the environment, and health care, are in the service of its stated commitment. These involve "advocating public policies that foster vigorous economic growth; a dynamic global economy; and a well-trained and productive U.S. workforce essential for future competitiveness" (par. 1).

To achieve these ends, "the Roundtable is selective in the issues it studies; a principal criterion is the impact the problem will have on the economic well-being of the nation. Working in task forces on specific issues, the chief executives direct research, supervise preparation of position papers, recommend policy, and lobby Congress and the Administration on select issues: The Education Task Force focuses on improving the performance of our schools" (1998b, par. 2).

One of the Congressional committees that prepares legislation related to education and business, and that has taken on the Business Roundtable's agenda as if it were its own, is the House Committee on Education and the Workforce. Edward Rust recently testified before this committee, summarizing the business community's position that "schools adopt higher standards, use high-quality assessments aligned to these standards, hold schools accountable for results, and provide supports to help students and teachers reach the standards" (*Testimony of Ed Rust, Jr.*, 2001, par. 6). The House Committee on Education and the Workforce obliged the business community's wishes by first introducing the Reading Excellence Act (1998) and then introducing its successor, No Child Left Behind (2001).

The Business Roundtable's objective for U.S. education—an objective subordinate to its primary global economic commitment—is "not just to improve individual schools, but to reform the entire system of public education" (Business Roundtable, 1995a, par. 1). Augustine's (1997) approach to education reform asserts the following:

> There are, of course, many changes that would improve America's schools, including better discipline, more emphasis on ethical behavior, additional required core courses, greater financial recognition for teachers, greater parental choice, pre-kindergarten care, incentives to reward teaching achievement, day-to-day decision-making at the operating level (including authority to hire, fire, promote, reward and transfer), the lack of assurance of life-long employment, and the expectation that when customer goals are not met, you go out of business. (par. 10)

Augustine's justification for corporate America's heavy hand in education reform is that "the business community is the principal customer of the products of the educational system" ("Business Group," 1998, p. 1B). That is, schools are the factories that manufacture the skilled workers who are eventually hired by employers. More generally, the Business Roundtable (1993) sees schooling as a component of a larger "workforce development system," and claims that "there is a need for fundamental change—to establish a new workforce development system that will serve its principal customers, focus on total quality and contribute to U.S. international competitiveness" (Business Roundtable, 1993, par. 1).

These extraordinary positions of corporate America play virtually no role in partisan politics. They are hardly debated in public, if discussed at all. Indeed, the Business Roundtable (2001a, par. 4) has acted in a determined and disciplined fashion to "promote bipartisan agreement" for its program of national testing and accountability, and it has obtained it. It bragged that it "worked on education reform with former President Bush, Governor and President Clinton, and Governor Bush" and that in this work "the business community stands united" (Business Roundtable, 2001b, par. 3). In anticipation of the upcoming passage of No Child Left Behind, it praised Democratic Senator Edward Kennedy for showing "farsighted leadership in bringing us to this hopeful point" (Business Roundtable, 2001c, par. 6). And it could not contain its joy when Congress passed No Child Left Behind, stating that "we all worked to help shape the No Child Left Behind bill, and we cheered when it won bipartisan support and was signed into law last January" (Business Roundtable, 2002, par. 5).

In the 2000 election campaign, both Bush and Gore supported yearly testing from the third through eighth grades. The 2004 campaign promises identical positions from the Democrats and Republicans. Indeed, the posturing of the Democrats against the Republicans with respect to NCLB is chiefly around the former's charge that Bush is funding the bill inadequately, not that the bill expresses a corporate-inspired pedagogical assault on children.

The business community's vigorous support of high-stakes testing and accountability derives from its concerns over alleged problems in education. "Why is The Business Roundtable so committed to standards?," asked Augustine (1997, par. 2). "The simple answer is that we believe the first step to solving our nation's education problems is to substantially raise academic standards and verify achievement through rigorous testing."

But what are the education problems that so trouble Augustine and the Business Roundtable? As noted earlier, to the big business community it is "obvious that large segments of our education system are failing today," because new job applicants lack the skills necessarily to participate in the "information-based economy," placing the country at risk of being "economically irrelevant" (Augustine, 1997, par. 3). The corporate solution to this problem specifies "setting standards for our schools, putting in place the processes to meet those standards, and then testing to ensure that the standards are in fact being met" (par. 5). According to Augustine, "More and more we see that competition in the international marketplace is in reality a 'battle of the classrooms' " (par. 6).

Or, according to Rust, "So much is at stake—already many employers cannot recruit enough skilled employees to meet their needs" (Business Roundtable, 1999, par. 10). This is the real high stakes that corporate America is playing for: to "reform the entire system of public education," to turn it into a "workforce development system" by thoroughly rewriting the curriculum (called "standards") in order to create a workforce whose technological skills will preserve corporate America's coveted position as number one in the world. "In the integrated global economy, workforce quality drives national competitiveness" (Business Roundtable, 1993, par. 2).

Not surprisingly, then, the Business Roundtable (1995b, p. 7) wants "Americans [to] expect students to master the difficult substance in core academic subjects that is routinely expected of the most advanced Asian and European countries." These subjects are "basic and advanced arts and sciences, oral and written communication, mathematics, and . . . the use of computers, telecommunications and electronic data bases." The Business Roundtable threatens that "people who lack such skills will be isolated—at risk socially, economically and politically—posing dire consequences for the nation as well as the individual." That is, they will constitute a third-world sector of U.S. society that is "economically irrelevant."

Having identified the curriculum needed to outcompete the Asians and Europeans, and referring to such a standardized curriculum with the misleading term *standards* (as if a uniform, cookie-cutter, standardized curriculum inherently attains high standards), it can be more easily appreciated that high-stakes testing is but the whipping cane to mold a technologically literate and highly productive labor force out of malleable students. But testing has a whipping cane of its own, namely accountability, in which the promise of reward and threat of punishment will be based entirely on the scores, with potentially "dire consequences." As Edward Rust stated in a Business Roundtable press release entitled "Business Leaders Build Support for Tougher Tests in Schools" (Business Roundtable, 1998c), "standards, as essential as they are, are not enough. Assessment and accountability make standards real" (par. 4).

The Business Roundtable sees testing and accountability the way it sees quality control practices in business: Its "reform architecture [for education is] very much like a business improving its products and services through a process of continuous quality improvement" (1998c, par. 3). And elsewhere, "No one in business believes that testing alone will improve our schools. But you also don't get what you don't measure. Successful companies continually assess performance—both their own and their competitors" (Krol, 1997, par. 3).

The Business Roundtable advocates other coercive measures to motivate the public to support its agenda, should there be any balking at its proposals. In 1996, it declared:

> We will support the use of relevant information on student achievement in hiring decisions. We will take a state's commitment to achieving high academic standards into consideration in business location decisions. We will encourage business to direct their education-related philanthropy toward initiatives that will make a lasting difference in school performance. (Augustine et al., 1996, par. 5)

But it is only natural that the business community would prefer less confrontational means to achieve its goals. An oppositional posture could prompt some people to question its motives, not to mention the pedagogical merits of its proposals. For now, it prefers kinder and gentler "incentive systems." So the most ideal scenario from a business perspective is for students, parents, and teachers themselves to demand high-stakes testing and accountability. They might be motivated to do this in the name of quality education, and will be showered with adoration as long as quality education fundamentally refers to the quality of U.S. corporate competitiveness. Recognizing this, the Business Roundtable has been involved in a number of high-stakes media campaigns to win the public over to its program.

In 1997, the Business Roundtable announced "a new series of public service television ads. The ads feature Major League Baseball players and encourage parents to get involved in their children's education and support higher academic standards in schools" (Business Roundtable, 1997, par. 1). "The ads urge parents to 'be a big league parent' by being more involved in our schools and offer free booklets with tips on raising academic standards by calling 1-800 338-BE-SMART. The ads will be distributed by the Ad Council, the country's largest producer of public service advertising" (Business Roundtable, 1997, par. 6).

In 1998, The Business Roundtable announced the "Keep the Promise Campaign," cosponsored by the U.S. Department of Education and the Education Excellence Partnership, a coalition of the Business Roundtable, National Governors' Association, American Federation of Teachers, and the National Alliance of Business. The campaign director was Bob Wehling, of the Procter & Gamble company. The campaign used TV spots and a "fact sheet" to promote its campaign objective: "To dramatize the urgency of the need to raise standards in America's public schools and to motivate citizens to take action. A toll-free number (1-800-96-PROMISE) is provided to offer a free brochure on simple things individuals can do to help improve children's education" (Business Roundtable, 1998c, par. 5). The "target audience" is the "general public—parents, teachers, business and community leaders" (Business Roundtable, 1998d, par. 6).

Again in 1998 the Business Roundtable (1998e) announced another "hard-hitting PSA campaign to raise academic standards" (par. 1) in which:

> The Business Roundtable and its partners in the Education Excellence Partnership (EEP) launched a new radio and print public service announcement (PSA) advertising campaign imploring parents, educators, and government officials to set high academic standards for America's youth. As states and school districts are raising the academic bar by giving tougher tests and expecting higher test scores, the EEP's "Challenge Me" campaign features children of all ages asking to be challenged by all aspects of academics. (par. 1)

These, then, are the elements of the unfolding scenario of the Business Roundtable's agenda for education reform and the creation of a new "workforce development system": (a) an assembly-line manufacturing process, also called a standardized curriculum (misleadingly referred to as *standards*), to manufacture a workforce with skills that big business believes will allow it to maintain a competitive edge in the global economy; (b) quality control over the manufacturing process, referred to as *high-stakes testing* and *accountability,* to measure how well the future workforce (euphemistically called *students*) is mastering this curriculum, to make sure that none of the parts of the manufacturing machine (called *teachers, parents,* and *schools*) strays from its role in the manufacturing process, and to discard products of poor quality (students who fail), as well as machine parts (teachers and schools) that perform poorly; and (c) business propaganda (called *public service announcements*) to instill a mentality in which the object and target of this agenda, the U.S. public, sees itself as the subjective agent of change, expecting rewards for good performance, and accepting punishment for poor performance.

In its pursuit of these goals, corporate America has not been without friends and allies in positions that count: politics and the media. The role of these actors is discussed next.

Chapter 3

Political Support of the Corporate Agenda

Congress has not been blind to the "education" agenda of corporate America. In fact, it has embraced it. Its support culminated in No Child Left Behind (NCLB, 2001). But the groundwork that set the stage for NCLB had been carefully cultivated in the preceding years. The measures needed to subsequently enforce its provisions are part of the ongoing program of political support.

In 1999 Congress created the 21st-Century Workforce Commission (TWC), whose charge was to recommend policy that would help the United States create a competent, productive labor force skilled in advanced information technology. Appointed by Democratic President Clinton, its Republican director, Hans Meeder, was the co-author with Douglas Carnine of a September 3, 1997 article that appeared in *Education Week*, and that became the programmatic foundation of the Reading Excellence Act (1998), the first federal bill to mandate phonics in classrooms that receive federal funding, and the precursor to Bush's NCLB (2001). Meeder, indeed, had previously worked for the office of Congressman William Goodling of Pennsylvania, in the House Committee on Education and the Workforce.

The final report of the TWC (2000) identified a number of "core" Information Technology (IT) professions, which together represent the driving force behind advanced, globally competitive, high-tech cognitive labor. These professions are: computer scientists, computer engineers, systems analysts, database administrators, computer support specialists, and computer programmers. According to the TWC, "an IT worker [is] responsible for designing, building, and/or maintaining an information technology infrastructure that businesses and consumers use" (p. 15). IT workers learn "skills clusters," specifically: Digital Media, Database Developments and Administration, Enterprise Systems Analysis and Integration, Network Design and Administration, Programming/Software Engineering, Technical Support, and Web Development and Administration.

Commenting on the new workforce skills needed to maintain global U.S. competitiveness, the TWC (2000, p. 22) noted:

> Today, more than ever, literacy is a powerful determinant of an individual's and a nation's opportunity for economic success. Research has shown that rapidly expanding market sectors tend to have a highly literate and skilled workforce.
>
> A defining feature of the Information Economy is a new breed of "knowledge workers" who work with their brains instead of their backs. To compete, today's successful workers must have acquired "21st Century Literacy," defined by the Commission as the ability to read, write, and compute with competence, think analytically, adapt to change, work in teams, and use technology.
>
> The Commission notes that "21st Century Literacy" builds on the foundation of "20th Century Literacy." In the 20th Century, the benchmark for literacy was meeting a basic threshold of reading, writing, and mathematical computing ability. This literacy level was sufficient for the Industrial Age, but today's jobs require these basic skills as well as a higher level of academic, workplace, and technical skills. The literacy bar was raised decade by decade during the last century, and continues to rise.

With regards to the changing labor needs of corporate America, the TWC (2000, p. 23) echoed the Business Roundtable's lament: "Unfortunately, despite the importance of attaining '21st Century Literacy,' far too many high school graduates, entrants into postsecondary education, and American adults in the labor force cannot read or compute at a level adequate to complete postsecondary education and training or compete in the IT labor market."

In the special area of reading, the TWC issued the following advice:

> Community leaders concerned about meeting tomorrow's workforce needs should insist that community and school-based early reading instruction programs implement practices that are supported by the most authoritative research on reading. The research, most recently summarized by the National Reading Panel, clearly indicates what elements must be in place for a child to become a successful reader. (TWC, 2000, p. 67)

The National Reading Panel (NRP) was yet another Congressional milestone on the road to NCLB (2001). According to the *Testimony of Duane Alexander* (2000), director of the NICHD, under whose auspices the NRP operated, its charge was to "review the scientific literature reporting the results of research on how children learn to read and the effectiveness of various approaches to teaching reading" (par. 2). The panel consisted mostly of experimental scientists, with classroom reading teachers conspicuously absent from panel membership. The panel recommended that reading be taught using intensive phonics.

The role that the NRP played in Washington's support of corporate America's education reform program was to formulate the scientific recipe to overcome the literacy crisis. Interestingly, the Business Roundtable has all along refrained from proposing any particular classroom method of reading instruction, and has even given lip service to local control: "Of course, since people vehemently disagree on the best methods for teaching reading and math, [it should be left] to local educators and parents to choose the methods they believe will best produce the desired results" (Krol, 1998, par. 10). But more-than-willing scientists have enlisted in the new war on illiteracy. No doubt, they are sincere believers in intensive phonics. Some even see their scientific work as having a progressive thrust to it. Thus, a leading recipient of NICHD reading research funding, Sally Shaywitz, stated that "Society is on the cusp of a true revolution in its ability to use science to inform public policy—a revolution in which biological discoveries serve the health and education of our children" (Shaywitz et al., 1996, p. 91).

But whatever one thinks of the scientific merits of phonics in the theory and teaching of reading, there is no question that its selection as the instructional method of choice for NCLB (2001) was politically inspired. It would never have received its unprecedented level of support, to the point of being enshrined in federal law, if it was not perceived as having attributes that could serve the larger agenda.

For example, on the occasion of the presentation of the NRP report to Congress, and commenting on the panel's work, NICHD director Duane Alexander told lawmakers that "the significance of these findings for the future literacy of this nation and for the economic prosperity and global competitiveness of our people is enormous" (*Testimony of Duane Alexander*, 2000, par. 7). But the charge of the NRP did not include the economic goal of improving the literacy skills of U.S. citizens in order to enhance the competitive edge of U.S. corporations in the global economy. Unfortunately, Alexander's remarks follow from this agenda and from nothing else, because even ardent advocates of intensive phonics do not thereby automatically become cheerleaders for General Motors in its competition with Volkswagen or Toyota for a greater share of the automobile market.

In the *Testimony of G. Reid Lyon* (2001), Lyon spoke not only in support of intensive phonics, but also in support of high-stakes testing and accountability. As noted earlier, he stated that "assessments should be done yearly beginning in Grade 3 so that we know how well our schools are performing" (par. 22). This is remarkable for two reasons. First, nothing in phonics automatically turns an advocate into a supporter of coercive pedagogical practices. Second, there is absolutely no scientific evidence whatsoever that high-stakes testing and accountability lead to improved reading ability among children. So Lyon's much vaunted appeal to "the most trustworthy scientific evidence" in his support of phonics is immediately called into question by this blatant inconsistency.

Indeed, any reputable scientific testimony before Congress on the question of high-stakes testing and accountability would simply state that there is no evidence to support its use. If there was enough interest in it, the testimony could include a solicitation for funding in order to study the matter. But the appeal of phonics to those in power is not the scientific niceties of blends, digraphs, and silent *e*, nor is it whether science can justify imposing it as a regular regimen on teachers and students who would rather be doing something more meaningful. Rather, as always, it is its political utility, and the role it plays in a larger political agenda. This is *politicized* phonics, or *neophonics*.

The crucial question, therefore, is what it is about phonics that makes it so savory to those researchers and research funding agencies that enjoy a keen awareness of the political agenda of corporate America, who know that politicians want to hear that their scientific proposals will advance the U.S. "national interest," that is, U.S. corporate competitiveness, and will also adapt readily to a program of high-stakes testing and accountability. To answer this, it would do well to once again review this agenda, as it applies to education.

We have seen that corporate America wants public schools to manufacture a workforce consisting of information technology (IT) workers with 21st-century literacy skills. Their so-called "standards," which are just these skills, are manufactured via a standardized, assembly-line curriculum, which molds malleable young students, the raw material, into IT-skilled workers. In this factory model of education, high-stakes testing and accountability are the quality control mechanisms that operate along the assembly line to optimize the manufacture of a high-quality product, that is, an advanced IT worker who can maintain the competitiveness of corporate America in the global economy.

Reading is a component IT skill whose narrow function, for corporate America, is the manipulation of information—in databases, software and hardware troubleshooting, technical writing, and so on. This function of reading is regarded, fundamentally, as just another labor skill, albeit a complex psychological one that needs to be rigorously taught and rigorously tested, and built up over the school years from more elementary skills.

Thus, in its support of the education agenda of corporate America, the purpose of NICHD research is to provide corporate America with a practical, that is, teachable, and quantifiable, that is, testable, approach to reading instruction, one that incorporates the notion of reading as a complex skill whose function is to manipulate information. The qualitative pole of the research, reading as information manipulation, becomes one of the standard cogs in the assembly line. The quantitative pole, testability, becomes a feature of the quality control.

In this context, phonics is the ideal model of reading, practically begging to be of service. First, it satisfies corporate America's *conceptual* requirements for its projected new and improved U.S. labor force, because it expresses the germ of the idea of reading as a complex, information-manipulating skill. The cognitive operations of decoding letters to sounds and segmenting words into phonemes can be thought of as the fundamental, molecular skills, which together constitute the most elementary act of information processing in reading. With time, and faith, the elementary skills of reading become more complex, information manipulation more skillful, and we witness the creation of an IT worker.

Second, phonics satisfies corporate America's *practical* demands for quality control in the manufacture of its new labor force. Phonics skills are easily quantifiable, perhaps more so than any other aspect of reading. Response times, measured in scalar seconds, and response accuracy, measured in binary "right" and "wrong," are the dependent variables. Thus, phonics readily lends itself to quantitative assessment, hence to high-stakes testing and accountability.

Third, but not least in significance, phonics is ideally adaptable to the *pedagogy* that is required for imposing an authoritarian, top-down, externally defined "standards" curriculum on classrooms. Intensive phonics lessons in no way derive from the otherwise natural inquisitiveness of children. Nor do scripted phonics lessons promote teacher spontaneity in response to children's real learning interests. As long as there is a preconceived score that must be attained, and adverse consequences for not attaining it, there will be unrelenting pressure to conform to the script. Then, teachers truly become mere thespians, playing the role of representative of the state.

Furthermore, to the extent that intensive phonics classrooms employ linguistically vapid, "decodable" reading materials, rather than authentic literature, meaning-based thinking is squelched. Students thus learn to value externally defined right and wrong behavioral responses, which is, of course, a precondition for a disciplined, subservient workforce. In this manner, a virtual censorship of authentic literature and critical thinking enters the classroom through two back doors, which bear the mislabels *science* and *standards*.

The NICHD's narrow-minded emphasis on intensive phonics reflects a narrowness in its view of the functions of reading. Contrary to the assertions of the TWC, the bar in literacy is lowered under this approach, not raised, and it is lowered substantially. The NICHD is content with a theory of reading that sees it as mere information manipulation, the special form of labor that characterizes an advanced IT worker, a "knowledge worker." To the NICHD's way of approaching reading, good literature consists of "information manuals." Thus, although the NICHD talks about high standards, its sights are set rather low. And though it talks about "the most trustworthy" science, there is no less trustworthy and lower quality science than that which allows a political agenda to define its theoretical categories and constructs.

But the neophonics tarantella does not stop here. To the extent that it is serious about its goals, the government will not be content with mere passage of legislation related to phonics. The legislation carries no weight unless it is also enforced. This, of course, was the Business Roundtable's admonition, discussed earlier, and well appreciated by its friends on Capitol Hill. But there is a frightening, totalitarian logic to the scenario that has been set in motion.

High-stakes testing and accountability are corporate America's proposals for enforcing the federally mandated reading programs. The enforcement is achieved, in part, by means of the various threatened psychological and material consequences of failure. Should any students, teachers, or schools balk at the required curriculum or perform poorly on tests, they will face retention, loss of funding, and other punishments.

But the federal legislation also refers to phonics as the classroom practice most supported by scientific research, and to science itself as the arbiter of competing claims among alternative practices. Indeed, it is this special appeal to science that provides phonics, and its associated legislation, with its neutral veneer.

But if the federal legislation cites "science" as its justification, and if the government is serious about enforcing its own laws, then it will need to enforce this aspect of the law as well. It will need to maintain surveillance over the scientific integrity of reading programs sent into the classroom, granting visas only to those that satisfy its criteria. That is to say, to defend and enforce its own laws, the federal government will need to create a science police.

Such a measure is indeed in the works. In *The New York Times* Education Life Section of November 10, 2002, reporter James Traub wrote about Congress's newly established Institute of Education Services, headed by Grover J. Whitehurst, Assistant Secretary for Research and Improvement at the Department of Education. As Traub explained, Whitehurst is currently setting up the "What Works Clearinghouse, a body that will establish standards for research" (section 4A, p. 24). Whose standards? It would be an inconsistent omission if the federal government failed to create a science police. The logic of its own program demands it.

One can speculate about the reasons behind the omission of a special science police from the actual education bill itself. Perhaps legislators understood that the added controversy would frighten the public, making it more difficult for them to publicly support the larger package. This would entail that the science police be created via a mechanism utilizing far less public debate, as has indeed been the case. Or perhaps the need for a science police to enforce Bush's education bill was simply not yet recognized or appreciated. Still, whatever process created the "What Works" science police, it is the logic of the government's own policy that necessitated its appearance.

In light of this dramatic move to the right in education policy, it is worth recalling its bipartisan support. The Reading Excellence Act (1998), for example, was introduced by Republicans William Goodling and Paul Coverdell, and signed by the Democratic Clinton administration. Leading Democrats, such as Senator Edward Kennedy, lauded phonics in the hearings that preceded the vote. When Bush unveiled his No Child Left Behind Act (2001) proposal, replete with phonics, high-stakes testing, and accountability, the loyal opposition limited its meek criticism to the issue of vouchers, which was, at the time, just a smokescreen and a diversion, as nobody expected vouchers to pass anyway, and even Bush himself abandoned any serous fight for it shortly after it was proposed.

Thus, whatever differences may exist between Democrats and Republicans on this or that detail cannot hide their fundamental agreement when it comes to serving corporate America's goal of retooling the labor force in the name of education reform.

Chapter 4

Media Complicity in Promoting Neophonics

The role of the mass media in pushing education policy to the right has been nothing short of utter complicity with the corporate agenda. In some cases, outright deception has been employed. Consider the case of *The Baltimore Sun,* the only major newspaper in this major metropolitan city.

For several years, *The Baltimore Sun* (hereafter, *The Sun*) has been running a daily column on the teaching of reading. The series has inundated its readers with "scientific evidence" highlighting the virtues of phonics and the failings of whole language. Its message has been that the rejection of phonics, in the name of whole language, has resulted in a crisis in literacy in Maryland and the nation. This crisis, we are told, lies at the very heart of such social problems as unemployment and crime. The magnitude of the crisis is such that nothing short of an invigorated state control over teacher-training and classroom curriculum can hope to carry us into the 21st-century adequately armed to deal with the social challenges that lie ahead.

But, as *The Sun* sees it, some ordinary citizens are rising to the challenge posed by this crisis. In one of its front-page articles in the series (November 19, 1997, p. 1B), *The Sun* featured a "Howard [County] father" with "concerns about his daughter's reading," and about how reading was being taught in her kindergarten classroom. What Hans Meeder, the concerned father, saw in that classroom was, he thought, so "crazy," that he "literally couldn't sleep one night" (p. 1B).

According to *The Sun* (1997) Meeder's concerns prompted him to seek out Reid Lyon, as if that would be the natural next move of any concerned father. Meeder then approached the Howard County P.T.A. to help arrange a public talk for Lyon on reading and reading instruction.

What was it that so passionately shocked Meeder's educational sensibilities and compelled *The Sun*'s editors to treat his torment as particularly newsworthy? According to *The Sun*, it was that his daughter's teacher was using a principle of whole language in the classroom, according to which the children were encouraged to "guess at words based on context" (p. 1B). The teacher did not use the seemingly more rational and scientific principles of phonics, "which teaches students to decode sounds and groups of letters to figure out words" (p. 1B).

Nowhere in the article is the teacher given an opportunity to explain and defend her own professional choice of teaching strategies for Meeder's daughter. The subtext, already promoted throughout *The Sun* series, is that many of our children's teachers are poorly trained, and that these poorly trained teachers are promoting illiteracy by encouraging kids to "guess" at words, even incorrectly, rather than rationally "decoding" words to arrive at their correct identification.

But it seems that our concerned father Meeder is, as we know, no neophyte to the reading scene. Not found anywhere in *The Sun* piece is relevant background information on Meeder, including that he was chief of staff to William Goodling's House Committee on Education and the Workforce, the committee responsible for drafting House Bill H.R. 2614 (1997), the House version of the Reading Excellence Act (1998), and the very same committee before which Reid Lyon gives his periodic testimonies about NICHD reading research. Nor do we learn that it was Meeder's co-authored article in *Education Week* (Carnine & Meeder, 1997) that formed the programmatic basis for H.R. 2614.

We do not learn that Meeder left his position with Goodling's office to head up Horizon Consulting Services, a policy research firm based in Columbia, Maryland. *The Sun* article did mention that Meeder was "a consultant specializing in education issues and an aspiring politician" (1997, p. 1B). But it did not mention that Meeder's consulting firm was funded, in part, by the Bradley Foundation, which has also funded the "research" of Charles Murray, co-author with Richard Herrnstein of *The Bell Curve* (1994), the 1990s version of the argument for the racial inferiority of African Americans.

Meeder, the specialist in education issues, and a University of Maryland graduate, had never taken even a single course on education (as he personally told me). Still, this did not detract from his apparently more weighty credentials as a factotum for corporate America, for which he earned an appointment by President Clinton to head up the TWC, charged with making policy recommendations on how to keep corporate America's shelves well stocked with advanced IT workers.

Today, this concerned father is Deputy Assistant Secretary of Vocational and Adult Education in the U.S. Department of Education. The Department's "Biography of Hans Meeder" notes that "Meeder is responsible for directing research and dissemination activities in support of career and technical education in high schools and colleges, and adult basic education and English language acquisition" (U.S. Department of Education, Office of Vocational and Adult Education, November 6, 2001, par. 3). It notes that "Meeder is also responsible for policy development in the administration of the Carl Perkins Vocational and Technical Education Act and the Adult Education and Family Literacy Act" (par. 3). It describes Meeder as having "a background in education public policy [that] includes a broad expertise in workforce trends, research on effective practice, and education accountability systems" (par. 4). It states that Meeder "is currently pursuing a Masters in Business Aministration through the University of Maryland" (par. 8). Quite plainly, business credentials outweigh education credentials in U.S. public education policy.

After his departure from the House Committee on Education and the Workforce, Meeder's responsibilities there were taken over by Robert Sweet, president of the National Right to Read Foundation. Sweet understands the corporate literacy crisis as well as Meeder does. In 1996, he wrote: "Unless we change the way our children are being taught to read, we run the risk of becoming a nation of illiterates, unable to compete in the international marketplace, and with increasing dependence on government support at home" (Sweet, 1996, par. 101). The "change" that Sweet advocates of course, is in fact the "sole purpose" for the existence of the National Right to Read Foundation, which "is to eliminate illiteracy in America by returning direct, systematic phonics to every first-grade classroom in America" (par. 101). According to the National Council of Teachers of English, Sweet has also been associated with the Christian Coalition and with Hooked on Phonics ("Reading Bill," November, 1997).

If *The Sun* had given Meeder's daughter's teacher an opportunity to explain her professional opinion about how reading should be taught to kindergartners, she might have pointed to *The Sun*'s misleading reference to the term *guessing*. From the point of view of a phonics advocate, guessing at words would appear to be a license for an anything-goes tolerance of inaccurate and sloppy word identification. From the point of view of a whole-language teacher, however, guessing at words is a strategy that promotes meaning-based thinking. As understood by advocates of whole language, this is an eminently justifiable method, based on 30 years of scientific research on reading.

The fact that whole language believes in critical thinking, and that it has no materials of its own, suggests what really lies behind the media "smear campaign" (Meyer, 2002, p. 1) against it. It is the chief ideological obstacle to neophonics, and is therefore a potent weapon when grasped by teachers and parents. Whole language is a threat to those forces in society that fear critical, self-confident, independent-minded thinking. It is a threat to those forces that care only about reading as the manipulation of information. It is a threat to those forces that do not want young people to explore their own beliefs and ideas. It is a threat to corporations that divert billions of dollars of school funds to their profit ledgers through the sale of phonics materials.

But why would *The Baltimore Sun* care one way or the other about the outcome of this battle? The answer to this question is contained in another of *The Sun*'s articles on reading and education, which identifies The Maryland Business Roundtable for Education as "[t]he behind-the-scenes force that is wielding the influence in school reform" in the state of Maryland ("Business Group," 1998, p. 1B).

The Maryland Business Roundtable for Education (MBRT) was formed in 1992 by 53 companies who came together to support "high standards and rigorous assessments" in schools (MBRT, 1996, p. 3), with "consequences for schools and school employees based on demonstrated performance" (p. 12). It was initially organized and founded by Norman R. Augustine.

At the time of *The Sun* ("Business Group," 1998) article, the Maryland Business Roundtable for Education's Board of Directors included CEOs and other executives from Legg Mason, Potomac Electric Power Company, Lockheed Martin, Travelers Group, Baltimore Gas and Electric, Bell Atlantic-MD, Bethlehem Steel, Colliers Pinkard, Commercial Credit Corporation, Crown Petroleum, KPMG Peat Marwick, Manor Care Inc., Maryland Chamber of Commerce, and Signet Bank. Other members include Apple Computer Inc., Group W Television Inc., GTE Government Systems Corporation, IBM Corporation, Johns Hopkins University Inc., Kaiser Permanente Medical Care Program, Marriott Corporation, Merrill Lynch and Company, NationsBank, Northrup Grumman Corporation, Perdue Farms, Procter & Gamble, Sylvan Learning Systems, T. Rowe Price Associates, United Parcel Service, University of Maryland System, USF&G Corporation, W. R. Grace and Company, Whiting-Turner Contracting Company, and Xerox Corporation. Lockheed Martin also provided Buzz Bartlett to serve on Democratic Governor Parris Glendening's Maryland State Board of Education.

The MBRT for Education has been a major force in Maryland behind the push for new state tests, mandated teacher-training requirements at the college level, and the restructuring of school curricula via its participation in School Improvement Teams. In 1998, a public outcry involving scores of angry parents was provoked when the School Improvement Team of a prominent public high school proposed eliminating a unique feature of the class scheduling policy, one that had allowed its students greater access to "nonacademic" courses in drama, music, and art. The new proposal was designed to promote greater emphasis on the "core" academic courses.

Three teachers at the school were "involuntarily transferred" after they protested the scheduling changes.

The MBRT for Education is also behind the annual Teacher of the Year award. Award celebrations have been cosponsored by Northrup-Grumman, First National Bank, *The Baltimore Sun,* and WJZ-TV, and broadcast on Maryland Public Television, which sits on the Public Policy Committee of the Maryland Business Roundtable for Education.

The MBRT for Education surveyed Maryland businesses "to identify skills employees will need in the future" (*MBRT,* 1997, p. 1). They found the following:

> 73 percent of companies hiring high school graduates reported employees lack adequate communications skills; 69 percent report inadequate writing and reading skills.
>
> 93 percent of responding firms considered improved or expanded technical training in high school to be important.
>
> 80 percent of firms that hire manufacturing or skilled trades workers report difficulty in finding qualified workers. (p. 1)

Their worry, however, is not over students' abilities to think critically about the etiology of society's ills. The material interest of corporations in the public education system is that it produce a skilled, disciplined workforce. MBRT for Education director June E. Streckfus succinctly characterized education reform this way: "The [high school] diploma will have value to businesses statewide. If a business is hiring a young person who has a Maryland diploma, [the employer will know] they will have a high level of basic skill" ("Business Group," 1998, p. 4B).

What a curious formulation this is of the goals of an education system: to develop in students skills that are simultaneously "high level" and "basic." The two concepts can only be juggled together if they refer to an education whose goal is solely the raising (to a high level) of (basic) labor productivity. Any mention of critical thinking for participation in a democratic society is mere lip service, intended for public appeasement.

The Sun's interest in this matter is immediately apparent from the fact that it too is a member of the MBRT for Education, *though this fact appears nowhere in the article.* So, in its own words, and quite literally, it belongs to the "behind-the-scenes force that is wielding the influence in school reform" ("Business Group," p. 1B). Indeed, how much more behind-the-scenes can a print media outlet get than to report about the deeds of an organization, of which it is a member, without informing its readers of this membership? Anything more behind-the-scenes would have to be called a conspiracy.

Part II

THE NEOPHONICS SOLUTION: A CASE OF CONTEMPORARY PSEUDOSCIENCE

Teaching should be such that what is offered is perceived as a valuable gift and not as a hard duty.

—Einstein (1952/1954, p. 67)

Chapter 5

The Variety of Scientific Methodologies

Officials of the NICHD defend the institute's research and recommendations on reading by glorifying its alleged scientific character. Referring to its National Reading Panel (NRP) Report (2000), NICHD Director Duane Alexander stated that "for the first time, we now have research-based guidance from sound scientific research on how best to teach children to read" (Bock, 2000, par. 3). And, as already noted, Reid Lyon repeatedly testified before the U.S. House Committee on Education and the Workforce that NICHD reading recommendations are based on "the most trustworthy scientific evidence available" (cf., e.g., March 8, 2001, par. 14).

Alexander's (Bock, 2000) remarks are truly amazing. If the NRP's meta-analysis was performed on "sound scientific research" studies from the previous three decades, the only conclusion one can draw from his remarks is that this research was not being used to guide instruction in the best possible way. But why not? Were advocates of intensive phonics barred by federal legislation from presenting their findings at scientific conventions? Did McGraw-Hill and other publishing outfits just not have the proper marketing savvy to persuade school districts of the virtues of intensive phonics? Were teachers misled, misguided, and ultimately beguiled by clever whole-language tricksters, being at bottom unable to think for themselves?

The sad truth is that the NRP's meta-analysis added no new research to the field of reading, and its conclusions were far from original. According to James Cunningham (2001, p. 327), the NRP "first denigrates, then ignores, the preponderance of research literature in our field" (p. 327). The only thing that could be legitimately claimed to have been accomplished "for the first time" was the government's judicious selection of a tiny group of unrepresentative studies to meta-analyze in order to promote as scientific a view of reading instruction that was becoming increasingly discredited scientifically by advocates of meaning-centered reading.

Even worse, the NRP contradicted its own meager "scientific" assertions when it signed off on the summary version of its comprehensive report. As Elaine Garan (2002) meticulously demonstrated, whereas the mass distribution short summary version touted the virtues of phonics, the much longer, and far more cumbersome, full report claimed nothing of the sort. It stated instead that "there were insufficient data to draw any conclusions about the effects of phonics instruction with normal developing readers above first grade" (Garan, p. 57). It is not without interest that the summary report was prepared, in part, by the firm of Widmeyer-Baker, a public relations outfit that counts McGraw-Hill as one of its clients.

Faced with this and numerous other relevant revelations about NICHD trustworthiness, NRP "technical advisor" Barbara Foorman acknowledged that "the National Reading Panel executive summary is intended for a general audience, and anyone who only reads the summary is likely to be misinformed" (Foorman, Francis, & Fletcher, 2003, p. 720). This, unfortunately, is nowhere to be found in the summary report. *Caveat lector.*

Although he may trust NICHD science, Lyon surely does not trust the teachers and teacher educators who are to carry it out in practice. They need to have their "belief systems" changed by various "incentive systems." Among such incentive systems, of course, are coercive high-stakes testing and accountability. Perhaps a more potent incentive system was suggested by Lyon (2002) in a presentation he delivered on November 18 at a forum in Miami, Florida sponsored by the Council for Evidence-Based Education. This ordinary public functionary, and advisor to our terrorist-fighting President Bush, baldly declared; "If there was any piece of legislation that I could pass it would be to blow up colleges of education" (p. 84). Perhaps to paraphrase: Teachers have been irreparably miseducated. We need to start from a new ground zero.

Of course, the mere mixing of politics and science does not entail that the science itself is poor. And just because the main impetus for neophonics is the narrow political agenda of corporate America, for whom public schools are merely factories for workforce development; and just because the methods being employed to promote this agenda are undemocratic, insofar as teachers, students, and parents have virtually no effective voice in the design and implementation of curriculum and assessment; and just because the most powerful government on the planet has taken the side of corporate America against the overwhelming majority of its own citizens, and permitted its most esteemed medical and scientific institutions to misinform the American people under the guise of being disinterested generators and repositories of useful knowledge—just because all these legitimate *political* reasons exist to question neophonics, does not entail that its basic *science* is also misguided and flawed. But it is.

The basic scientific foundations of neophonics, as they have been presented by its proponents, can be divided into three categories. The first deals with scientific methodology, or how studies of reading and reading instruction should be carried out. The main questions that arise in this category have to do with the advantages and disadvantages of experimental versus nonexperimental studies.

The second category concerns linguistic science, and how our understanding of written language bears on our understanding of reading. The main questions that arise here have to do with the nature of alphabetic writing and its role in the process of interpreting a piece of written text.

The third category falls under the general rubric of neuroscience, and, more specifically, deals with contemporary high-technology brain imaging studies that allegedly shed light on the nature of reading, and on how best to teach it. The main questions that arise in the category of neuroscience, as they bear on neophonics, involve the limitations of the technology itself and the role of phonological processing in reading. These three categories will be discussed in turn, beginning with the question of methodology.

The particular brand of scientific method trumpeted by the NICHD is referred to as *experimental*. Hypotheses are formulated. Certain known input variables are controlled by holding them constant across test conditions. Others are allowed to vary. Outcomes that distinguish one test condition from another can then be correlated with the input variables. Statistical analysis can decide whether the correlations are significant. Repeated trials can demonstrate whether the findings are reliable. And implicit in the whole enterprise is a set of assumptions about the validity of the variables, their presumed correspondence to real aspects of the reading process.

For example, a group of beginning readers may be given *x* hours of instruction on phonics rules *y* and *z*. A control group, matched for age, reading level, gender, and so on, is not given this instruction. The two groups are tested on the speed and accuracy of their oral readings of a list of words. There are two test sessions, one immediately before instruction, and one shortly afterwards. The responses of the two groups are compared.

The study group is found to score significantly higher than the control group on oral word readings following instruction, though both groups scored equivalently on the pretests. The researchers conclude that teaching phonics improves reading ability.

According to the NICHD, any study of reading and reading instruction that does not use this method and design is not "trustworthy." So, the NICHD only funds studies with this type of experimental characteristic. And its National Reading Panel, charged with evaluating scientific research on reading instruction, only reviewed studies that used such an experimental design.

But the NICHD's research program on reading can at best only be a caricature of science, because it reduces science to a method. And the mirror image of this reductionism is the elevation of method itself to a status above that of understanding the phenomenon of reading. One need look no further than to the linguistic stimuli used as variables in NICHD studies, including phonemes, real words, and pseudowords, to realize that these are entities defined by linguistic theory, and that this theory is based on a wholly nonexperimental scientific methodology. Thus, the NICHD's experimentalism requires the results of nonexperimental research in order to proceed.

But even if it were true that experimental design were the only appropriate scientific methodology for studying reading, one still needs to base the experiments themselves on justifiable premises. However, virtually all of the NICHD research on reading assumes the correctness of the alphabetic principle, according to which "written spellings systematically represent phonemes of spoken words" (*Testimony of G. Reid Lyon*, 1997, par. 8). Lyon, in fact, referred to this principle as "nonnegotiable." True to this rigid characterization, nowhere does the NICHD critically examine it, though it is obligated to do so on scientific grounds, because there are clearly many intricately spelled words that, at the very least, raise questions about its integrity. Instead, the NICHD acts in the wholly unscientific manner of presuming that the alphabetic principle was firmly established long ago, that the matter has been settled once and for all. However, should empirical investigation of the alphabetic principle demonstrate that it is fundamentally flawed, then the entire research enterprise upon which it is built falls apart, no matter how pretty the experimental design.

The simple truth of the matter, which escapes the NICHD's blinders, is that there are several distinct methods of empirical, scientific investigation, all of which play an important role in advancing our understanding of reading and how reading should be taught. The appropriateness of any particular method depends on the phenomenon under study, the information sought, and the logistics and practicality of the study.

In fact, the existence and utilization of distinct research methods in linguistic science is so well established that the only reason to elevate one particular method to a privileged status above all others is to promote a view of reading that relies on that method, and downplay, if not downright denigrate, views of reading that do not. This is precisely the effect of the NICHD's deification of experimental design, because such design is the primary method used in research on phonics, whereas descriptive design is the primary method used in meaning-centered approaches to reading, such as whole language.

Even the NICHD's public presentations of its views on experimentalism betray this motive. It does this by means of a rhetorical *double entendre.* For example, in his presentations before Congress, Lyon (*Testimony of G. Reid Lyon,* 1997, 2000, 2001) routinely emphasized how the work of the NICHD on reading is based on research that is "valid" and "reliable." But these terms are simultaneously technical, having special scientific meanings, and nontechnical, having certain colloquial meanings. The two sets of meanings are not the same.

When used technically, validity and reliability refer to aspects of an experimental research study. Vaidity refers to the notion that a particular variable under study bears a real relationship to the actual phenomenon of interest. In phonics, for example, studying how readers turn letters into sounds could legitimately be called a study of reading, the phenomenon of interest, if the conversion of letters into sounds were a demonstratable component of the reading process.

Similarly, reliability refers to the notion that the findings of a controlled experiment are the result of the experimental design itself. Thus, in a reliable study, repeated trials would continue to generate the same, or equivalent, results.

The colloquial usages of these terms are quite different. They show up in expressions like "Oh, that's a valid point of view," and "She's a reliable friend." Here, the terms have a distinctly positive connotation. A "valid point of view" refers to an opinion or belief that rests on some real facts or experiences. A "reliable friend" is someone you can count on in a time of need.

The scientific meanings have distinctly *negative* connotations. The reason an experimenter even discusses the validity of his or her experiment is because the experiment is *not* fully valid, and *never* can be, as long as the phenomenon of interest is not the object of study in the experiment. That is to say, validity expresses not only how much a certain variable reflects the phenomenon of interest, but, at the very same time, how much it does not. Converting a letter to a sound is patently *not reading.* Therefore, any study of letter-sound conversion that calls itself a study of reading must be able to demonstrate a valid relationship between the two.

On the other hand, the nontechnical meanings have distinctly *positive* connotations. One would prefer to hold a valid, rather than an invalid, point of view. And one would prefer to have a reliable, rather than an unreliable, friend.

The technical notions of validity and reliability are not applicable to a purely descriptive study. This is because the phenomenon of interest in a descriptive study is not broken down into presumed component parts. Instead of looking at how certain letters are pronounced, a reader is given an authentic piece of written language to read. From the very outset, the phenomenon under study is nothing more and nothing less than reading itself, the phenomenon of interest. In other words, we simply don't need to ask whether, or to what degree, the study validly represents reading.

Unfortunately, Lyon (*Testimony of G. Reid Lyon*, 2000) added obfuscation to onslaught on this matter. He stated, "It remains to be seen whether the extensive qualitative and descriptive education research literature used predominantly over the past decade or more to guide instructional practices contains studies that adhered consistently to the basic principles of reliability, validity and trustworthiness of the data" (par. 7).

Thus, advocating valid and reliable research is really just code for advocating experimental design. But in not clarifying the technical meanings of these terms to a lay audience, such as the Congress of the United States, the additional message is conveyed, based on the nontechnical meanings, that such research design is the only one that is truly trustworthy.

But nothing can be further from the truth. Experimental design is only one of several recognized scientific methodologies. It is appropriate in certain research settings, and inappropriate in others. Other methodologies, including the descriptive methodology that underlies meaning-based approaches to reading, also have their own conditions of appropriateness.

This point can be clarified by considering a further aspect of Lyon's (*Testimony of G. Reid Lyon*, 1997, 2000, 2001) Congressional testimonies, namely, that he applied the notions of validity and reliability only to research involved in the development of measures of assessing reading proficiency and the effectiveness of instructional materials. For example, in the *Testimony of G. Reid Lyon* (2001) he spoke on behalf of:

> The critical need to provide support to states and local educational agencies to identify and/or develop the most reliable and valid screening and diagnostic reading assessment instruments that can be used to identify at-risk children and to document the effectiveness of the instructional material, programs, and strategies. (par. 16)

But nobody questions that experimental design is appropriate for answering these types of questions. What is significant is the omission from his statement, and from numerous others, of just what counts as the appropriate methodology for developing a scientific, empirically based model of reading itself, of how readers interact with print to construct meaning, apart from any question of how it is to be assessed or taught. Although experimental, quantitative research may be appropriate for evaluating the effectiveness of screening and instructional techniques, it is simply not appropriate for studying the phenomenon that is actually being screened and instructed, namely, reading.

The phenomenon of reading defies strict experimental study because it is fundamentally a form of *purposeful* linguistic behavior, where the reader's purpose is the construction of meaning. Purposeful behavior cannot be tampered with by using experimentally designed stimulus materials or test conditions, without at the same time altering the very purpose of the event. An experimental study of letter-sound behavior turns the subject's purpose for reading into sounding out letters, not the construction of meaning. These are qualitatively different phenomena.

Advocates of the neophonics reading agenda have finessed this fundamental problem by *defining reading* as the set of phonological processes that convert letters of the alphabet to the sounds of speech. We are told that these processes are automatic, or must be made automatic by intensive instruction. This nonpurposeful automaticity renders such processes entirely appropriate for experimental investigation. Then, having maneuvered automatically across the threshold from written language to oral language, via the engine of phonic decoding, all of the reader's purposeful mechanisms of meaning construction can now come into play. But, strictly speaking, these are aspects of an already familiar oral language facility, not reading.

Advocates of a descriptive approach to reading hold the view that the translation from written to oral language is *not* a necessary aspect of the construction of meaning, though it of course plays a role, alongside other psycholinguistic processes. Reading begins immediately and right away as a purposeful event, not as the decoding of print, which is not to deny that it contains automatic elements. Likewise, walking to the mailbox is a purposeful event that contains unconscious, automatic elements like muscle contraction and postural reflexes.

A sizeable research literature clearly demonstrates that an overemphasis on letter-sound conversion distracts a reader from understanding the text (cf. Weaver, 2002). Changing the purpose of the event has deleterious consequences. As a fundamentally purposeful language act, the reading event cannot be broken down into presumed component parts without altering the capacity to construct meaning. Therefore, it must be studied as a whole event, and described using proven observational techniques.

The maneuver of extracting out letter-sound conversions from the larger phenomenon of meaning construction, and calling these letter-sound conversions automatic (even when it is really a grinding, purposeful instruction that makes them automatic), identifying these conversions with reading, and thereby justifying a strict experimental approach to the study of reading, can be pictured as in Fig. 5.1.

The role of letter-sound conversion in Fig. 5.1 is to propel the reader from written language to oral language, one word at a time. Pronouncing a word is then supposed to allow the reader to retrieve associated properties of the word, including its meaning, from the reader's mental lexicon. This meaning can now be manipulated along with the meanings of other pronounced words in whatever ways occur naturally in the construction of

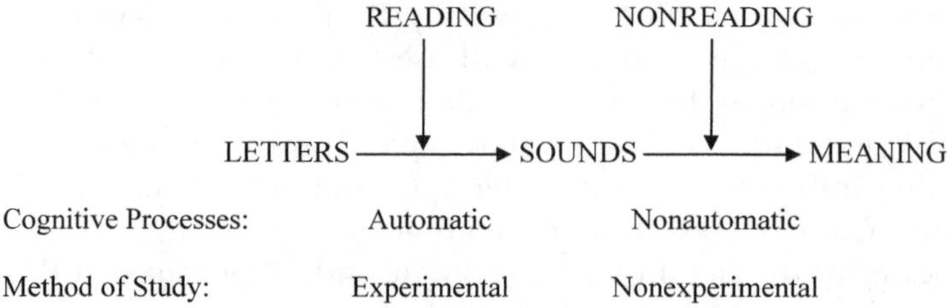

FIG. 5.1. Neophonics view of reading.

complex meanings in oral language use. (Whether oral language users construct meaning by listening to one word at a time, in succession, has not been addressed by the neophonics school.) But the entire enterprise therefore stands or falls on the correctness of the alphabetic principle, and on the capacity of this principle to generate a printed word's pronunciation *without a prior identification of that word.* As I demonstrate more fully later, the alphabetic principle cannot be maintained in a form sufficient to uphold the neophonics model of reading. It is indeed rather interesting that advocates of neophonics have actually refrained from undertaking an empirical investigation of the principle.

The purposeful, open-ended, and fundamentally uncontrollable nature of meaning construction in the use of oral language has not been seriously questioned, except by the most hardened behaviorists. By considering the interpretive principles involved in oral communication, which are not themselves dependent on the oral medium, we can gain insight into the general mental processes of meaning construction that are no less applicable to reading.

Consider a simple example. John and Mary are at the dinner table together, whereupon John, pointing, says to Mary, "Please pass the wine." Mary reaches for the decanter, and hands it to John. John then says, "Thanks."

John and Mary, being fluent speakers of English, execute this exchange in a matter of seconds. This simple observation underscores the speed with which various complex, yet very routine, mental operations occur, a phenomenon no less humbling to our imagination than the speed of complex chemical reactions.

What has transpired in these few seconds? Let us say that John has a communicative intention, namely, to convey to Mary that he wants some wine, and that he would like her to aid in his retrieval of the nearby bottle. Of course, we cannot actually observe this mental intention *in situ*, so to speak. But we can analyze John's observable behavior and infer its existence as an explanation of what we observe. I may use introspection to assist with this analysis, because introspection tells me that I have a specific communicative intention whenever I speak to someone, and I therefore infer that John has one as well, assuming that John and I are similar in possessing this human trait. To say that John has an intended message is to attribute a physically invisible purpose and goal-directedness to his otherwise observable behavior.

Now, John's observable behavior is of an acoustic-visual nature: He produces sounds, as well as certain visible postural movements. There are numerous other features of his observable behavior—eye movements, head turning, food chewing—but we do not necessarily attend to all of these. If the communicative event is to be successful, we must, at the very least, attend to those aspects of the observable behavior that convey meaning.

But human vocal sounds are, in and of themselves, meaningless. Indeed, modern linguistic science incorporates de Saussure's (1922/1966) famous "arbitrariness of the sign," according to which the sounds of any individual word are arbitrarily related to the word's meaning. The word *see*, for example, means whatever it means, but not because it begins with a voiceless spirant and ends with a high, front vowel. The fundamental truth of this dogma can be found in the fact that a variety of sounds may be employed to convey an identical meaning: *arbre*, *Baum*, *tree*, and so on.

By analogy, visible postures and movements, which we might interpret as conveying certain meanings, are also inherently meaningless. Extending an index finger in the direction of an object is an observable event, absolutely without meaning at the physical level. But it functions in a system of communication to reference, or index, the object pointed to.

So Mary's task, at one level, is to attend to those physically observable events that are inherently meaningless. The selectivity of Mary's attention to certain inherently meaningless physical events, and not to others, underscores the important linguistic principle that listening is as purposeful and goal directed as speaking. Mary's goal as a listener is to figure out John's communicative intention, in other words, his intended meaning.

Therefore, John and Mary both have communicative goals. Their behavior at the physical level is driven by, and guided by, these goals. It is the existence of communicative goals that renders their behavior purposeful. And to say that their behavior is purposeful is to say that it is not entirely automatic.

What is nonautomatic about John's behavior is his carrying out of the desire to communicate an intended meaning. His particular selection of words, syntax, and posture is also not entirely automatic. He must choose the latter from among the available possibilities on the basis of what he is capable of choosing (e.g., the words he knows and the sounds he can produce), and on the basis of what he believes Mary is capable of perceiving, attending to, and interpreting.

What is nonautomatic in Mary's behavior is her selective attention to John's behavior, as noted earlier, as well as certain aspects of the interpretation she comes up with, not least of which is her decision to either accept or reject an interpretation. She chooses to attend to those salient physical features that she is capable of attending to, in virtue of her grammatical knowledge and the integrity of her auditory and visual sensory systems, among other things. And the interpretation that she accepts must be based on her best judgment of John's communicative intention.

That Mary's behavior is not automatic can also be appreciated from the observation that there is more than one possible interpretation of John's communicative behavior. For example, if someone else were seated at the table besides John and Mary, John's verbal utterance and bodily posture could just as easily have been expressed to convey the message about passing the wine to that third person. Mary's task would therefore have to include the utilization of other available information to decide which meaning was more likely, if she is to be successful. John may or may not provide this information. If he does not, Mary might take into account, say, the age of the third party to assist with her interpretive task. If the third person were their infant son, John most likely intends the wine for himself.

Therefore, a complete characterization of what has transpired in the few seconds of interaction between John and Mary must recognize phenomena at two levels, the mental and the physical, as shown in Fig. 5.2. Both the productive (John) and receptive (Mary) participants in the communicative event operate at the two levels. Each has a meaningful communicative goal, and each has an inherently meaningless motor or sensory action.

Now we must ask what the relationship is between the mental level and the physical level. In some sense, the mental level is the more important of the two, because we would say, for example, that John had succeeded in his communicative goal if Mary understood his intended meaning, even if he was relatively unsuccessful at the physical level (for example, if he spoke with food

Mental Level:

John: convey intended meaning to Mary

Mary: interpret John's communicative behavior

Physical Level:

John: selectively produce sounds and visible postures (MOTOR)

Mary: selectively perceive sounds and visible postures (SENSORY)

FIG. 5.2. Communicative goals.

in his mouth and thereby muffled the sounds). We would say that Mary had succeeded in her communicative goal if she understood John's intended meaning, even if she had difficulty perceiving the acoustic information (and so relied more on the finger pointing). But the communicative event would remain unconsummated if John's vocalizations and postures were performed perfectly, yet Mary still did not understand his intended meaning.

Therefore, we can say that the physical level is subordinate to the mental level in linguistic communication. The physical level serves the goals of the mental level. And this is true for both the productive and receptive participants.

For both John and Mary, the physical level contains the clues to the communicative goal. The clues are put there by John, and perceived by Mary. They are both auditory and visual, but only as a matter of sensorimotor efficiency, as the existence of tactile clues (e.g., Braille writing) demonstrates.

Therefore, John's role in the communicative event is to produce physical clues to his underlying communicative intention, whereas Mary's role is to search for and interpret these clues. In a sense, John formulates a communicative puzzle, and Mary attempts to solve that puzzle. Thus for both John and Mary, this is a problem-solving task. John's task is to come up with a particular selection of words, syntactic structures, bodily postures, and so on, that will be recognized by Mary, and will successfully lead her to formulate a thought that represents John's intended meaning. Mary's task is to identify the linguistic and postural clues, and to try to solve the problem of why John selected these particular clues. Her solution to this problem is a mental hypothesis, a thought, which, if John has been successful, is roughly the meaning he intended to communicate. Thus, in identifying the linguistic and postural clues, in this case the utterance "Please pass the wine" and the posture of finger pointing, Mary is enabled to reason that John uttered this sentence and pointed his finger because he wanted her to give him the decanter of wine. John's saying "Thanks" is not merely an expression of gratitude; it is, perhaps even more so, confirmation to Mary of the correctness of her reasoning.

Therefore, the phenomenon of linguistic communication is far from being a simple, direct deposit of John's intended meaning into Mary's brain. John's meaning is not even released into the physical setting: only *clues* to meaning are. John must instead induce Mary to think the thought that is his intended meaning. He does this by setting up a problem for her to solve, namely, why he said what he said, moved the way he moved, and so on. If Mary's solution to this problem is the desired thought, then John was successful in attaining his communicative goal.

Both John and Mary are constrained by a principle of communicative efficiency. If John sincerely wants his message to be understood by Mary, then he must make her problem-solving task as uncomplicated as possible. His clues must be salient and straightforward, not hidden and obscure.

Likewise, Mary's task is rendered easier if she seeks out those clues that most perspicaciously encode John's intended meaning. Even if John's message is somehow encoded in, say, the rhythm of his chewing on the dinner salad, Mary does better to attend to his linguistic utterance and symbolic postures, because these, unlike the chewing, contain conventionally agreed-upon meanings that are mutually known, and thereby expedite the exchange of meanings.

Insofar as participants in the communicative event mutually adhere to certain principles of behavior, such as the principle of efficiency, the event that occurs must be considered an act of tacit social cooperation. Linguistic communication is therefore akin to a game, except that the rules are not necessarily spelled out on a conscious level.

The cooperative nature of linguistic communication has often been noted, and is a fundamental principle of modern linguistics. Its profound significance was first pointed out in a highly influential paper by H. Paul Grice entitled "Logic and Conversation" (1975). Grice made the observation that the "Cooperative Principle" of linguistic communication is not just a social principle; simultaneously, it functions as a logical premise on the basis of which individual conversational participants draw logical inferences. Grice defined the Cooperative Principle as follows: "Make your conversational contribution such as is required, at the stage at which it occurs, by the accepted purpose or direction of the talk exchange in which you are engaged" (p. 45).

Grice (1975) also defined four "maxims," which may be thought of as specific cases of the Cooperative Principle. Simplified versions of these maxims are as follows:

Maxim of Quantity: The conversational contribution is to be not more and not less informative than is required.

Maxim of Quality: The conversational contribution is to be truthful.

Maxim of Relation: The conversational contribution is to be relevant.

Maxim of Manner: The conversational contribution is to be clear and concise.

In my example, Mary might take John's utterance as violating the maxim of quantity, because his linguistic expression literally does not specify to whom he wants Mary to pass the wine. But as long as she adopts the Cooperative Principle, and assumes John's acceptance of it as well, she must assume that the maxims are adhered to, and that any violation is only an apparent one. Thus, she must assume that John's communicative intention itself is not underspecified, even though his lexical and syntactic choices may be. Therefore, she must come up with other premises that allow her to draw a logical conclusion that can represent John's communicative goal. In the absence of other clues, she is entitled to the default conclusion: The object of John's request is himself.

In order for all of this to work, John must intentionally omit additional clues to the object of his request. Thus, John and Mary both know what the default case is. This an example of mutual knowledge.

Mutual knowledge may be topical as well, as when John and Mary, in discussing political matters, use the expression "the current U.S. president" to refer to George W. Bush. Their mutual knowledge represents a pool of unstated premises that can figure into their conversational reasoning. Another such pool is their mutual beliefs and convictions, such as, say, their common desire for world peace, which figures as an unstated premise in the following conversation:

John: Whom do you plan to vote for in the upcoming election?

Mary: Well, both Green and Brown support increased funding of weapons of mass destruction and oppose the principle of self-determination.

John: Then I guess we'll have to pick either Smith or Jones.

It can now be appreciated that linguistic communication involves the presentation and perception not of meaning *per se*, but rather of clues to meaning. Clues, furthermore, are not the same as behaviorist stimuli. Meanings are figured out, or constructed, by thought processes that use the clues. Meanings do not automatically appear as a response to some overt stimulus.

Some of the clues are overt and observable, such as linguistic sounds and bodily postures. Other clues are tacit and unstated, such as mutual knowledge and mutual beliefs. Thus, linguistic communication is the exchange of meanings via the selective production and perception of clues from a variety of overt and covert cuing systems. But the relative proportion of clues from the various cuing systems is not fixed, and can vary dramatically. Indeed, given sufficiently great mutual knowledge and beliefs, a particular instance of linguistic communication may require only an overt wink, nod, or other posture to convey a message, without any overt linguistic utterance. That is to say, the phonological or syntactic cuing system is not always needed or used.

On the whole, this may seem like a very inefficient way of exchanging meanings. But a moment's reflection makes it clear that it really cannot proceed in any other fashion. The essence of the meanings that are communicated is not in their physical properties, whatever these may be: the particular time of their occurrence, the neuronal synapses that underlie their existence, and so on. Rather, meanings are abstract conceptual structures, defined by formal properties and the relations of these formal properties to one another. Their essence is, in a sense, metaphysical, not physical. Yet exchange of anything between individuals must occur in a physical medium. The riddle of linguistic communication is how humans exchange abstract conceptual entities through a concrete, physical medium. The solution to the riddle is the existence of symbol systems, which associate the abstract conceptual structures of meaning with acoustic, visual, or other physical entities that can pass through a physical medium.

A number of common variations of the normal communicative scenario are imaginable. For the speaker, I have already suggested the possibility of varying the proportions of overt and covert clues, so that in some cases the majority of clues are linguistic and postural, whereas in other cases the majority of clues are components of unstated mutual knowledge and beliefs.

An interesting variation occurs when the listener anticipates a speaker's intended meaning before the speaker has presented all of his or her clues. Suppose John and Mary have a mutual friend Sam, whom they both know has recently taken his licensing exam to practice pet psychotherapy. John and Mary are each anxiously awaiting the day when Sam will hear from the examining board. Finally, Sam calls John to tell him that he has received the letter informing him that he has passed. John quickly telephones Mary. Their conversation proceeds as follows:

Mary: Hello.

John: Hello, Mary. This is John. Listen, I just got great news from Sam. He—

Mary: He passed his exam! Wonderful news!

Clearly, this case of the very common phenomenon of anticipatory discourse is based on Mary's recruitment of mutual background knowledge to assist in formulating a guess as to John's intended meaning well before he has provided all of his intended clues. Perhaps because of her excitement, she interrupts John to express her guess.

Now, suppose Mary were more self-restrained, and continued listening until John finished his utterance. As the existence of anticipatory discourse shows, such self-restraint does not entail that the listener actually needed all of the speaker's clues to come up with a satisfactory meaning. At the point where Mary has already entertained a guess as to John's intended meaning, John continues to deliver symbolic clues from his cuing systems. What does Mary do with these additional clues?

In the first scenario, Mary might simply ignore these clues if John had the opportunity to express them. But in the second scenario, Mary could use the subsequent clues to confirm or disconfirm the guess she has formulated on the basis of the earlier clues. We know this occurs when we hear a speaker say something that seems to conflict with earlier meanings, at which point we interrupt the discourse to ask for clarification. Under this view, the listener, on the basis of a purposeful selection of clues, constructs meaning by formulating a tentative hypothesis as to the speaker's intended message, and then uses subsequent clues to confirm or disconfirm, and thereby refine, this hypothesis. Coming up with a speaker's intended meaning is thus a case of hypothesis formation and hypothesis testing.

Certain situations may be regarded as exhibiting restrictions on the availability of cuing systems. These restrictions can apply to both overt and covert systems. For example, an adult attending the symphony who acknowledges and acquiesces to the social constraint to whisper is limited in his or her utilization of the linguistic cuing system, more specifically, of the subsystem that transforms linguistic representations into phonatory motor programs.

Telephone conversations are situations that render the postural cuing system unusable. Or an adult listening to a lecture about the complexities of contemporary politics may understand all of the speaker's words, yet still lack the background knowledge necessary to formulate the speaker's intended meaning.

In such situations, speakers and listeners routinely compensate for the unavailability or inutility of certain cuing systems by increasing the recruitment and utilization of other cuing systems. For example, the whispering adult may rely on additional postural information, or perhaps make explicit some of the background information required to interpret his or her message. In telephone conversations, indexical expressions often referred to by pointing may need to be made more explicit, and intonational variations may make up for the inability to express emotional meanings with facial postures.

Compensatory mechanisms exist precisely because of the cooperative and purposeful nature of linguistic communication. If the restricted availability of a cuing system renders successful meaning exchange more difficult, additional clues can be provided by the remaining, still available cuing systems, in order to minimize this difficulty. As the previous examples indicate, the situational restrictions on available cuing systems, and the consequent reliance on compensatory mechanisms, are a normal part of linguistic communication.

It should be more than obvious that the forces that guide conversational structure and reasoning cannot be adequately studied with experiments. How could one conceivably control for the maxim of quantity? And who has claimed that, despite the extensive descriptive methodology, such linguistic analysis is not trustworthy? In order to adequately study such purposeful linguistic behavior, the event must be allowed to unfold naturally. A scientific analysis of it involves meticulous observation, formulation of hypotheses, and reobservation.

Experimental and descriptive methodologies do not exhaust the broad study of language. At least three distinct methodologies have been utilized, the third being introspective judgments of well-formedness. Each has its own appropriateness and feasibility characteristics.

Experimental design is entirely appropriate, and logistically feasible, for the study of biochemical processes in tissue cultures, the orientation of ions in magnetic fields, and, in general, automatic events of the physical universe. Experimental design is appropriate for investigating these types of questions since the laws that govern the phenomenon under study are not changed by placing that phenomenon in a controlled setting. In such a way, therefore, relevant factors can be teased out and isolated, and studied independently of their natural environment.

Experimental design is not appropriate in those situations where altering the natural environment of a phenomenon, for the purpose of isolating one variable for study, qualitatively changes the nature of the phenomenon itself. In such a situation, descriptive design is more appropriate, and often the only logistically feasible one. In descriptive design, the researcher does not take the event apart. Rather, the researcher observes the whole phenomenon of interest, in its pristine form, formulates empirically falsifiable hypotheses about the patterns and regularities observed, and then goes back to observe again, in order to assess the hypotheses.

The renowned cultural anthropologist Margaret Mead (1961) referred to such practice as "interpretive science." She noted that "the student of the more intangible and psychological aspects of human behaviour is forced to illuminate rather than demonstrate a thesis," noting that such illumination is "based upon a careful and detailed observation" (p. 260). In describing how she set about observing the behavior of adolescent Samoan girls, Mead pointed out that "the type of data which we needed is not of the sort which lends itself readily to quantitative treatment. The reaction of the girl to her stepmother, to relatives acting as foster parents, to her younger sister, or to her older brother,—these are incommensurable in quantitative terms" (p. 260). Ultimately, purposeful human behavior defies strict experimental study.

Advocates of descriptive research in reading argue that reading is also fundamentally a purposeful language event. Unless a reader is reading with the express goal of trying to understand the written material—reading for meaning—the phenomenon of reading has simply not occurred. Everyone knows that merely sounding out a letter does not automatically lead to meaning. And this is obviously true in experimental studies in which subjects are asked to sound out letters that are part of nonsense words. Therefore, no matter how insistent its supporters may be, a cogent argument can be made that studying letter-sound conversion in isolated, artificial, experimentally controlled settings, where the subject is not reading for meaning, is, in the end, not a study of reading.

Put another way, sounding out a letter as an isolated task is a fundamentally distinct phenomenon from sounding out the same letter when it occurs in the setting of a piece of written material that a reader is reading for meaning. These are two distinct language acts. One is not simply a component of the other. This is what descriptive researchers mean when they advocate phonics *in context.*

The third type of method, introspection, has been used to great advantage, and with spectacular results, in the study of mathematical systems and linguistic structures. This method relies on subjective intuitions about the well-formedness of abstract mental structures. This research, in principle, can be done in one's head. In mathematics, the "researcher" reflects on the "grammaticality" of strings of terms, such as $y = ax + b$, and their logical relationships. In syntactic research, *well-formedness* refers to the grammaticality of sentences. The researcher reflects on the acceptability of strings of words such as "John eats potatoes," and the unacceptability of strings of words such as "eats John potatoes," and devises rules that can correctly distinguish the two types of strings. Underlying patterns are sought, and are incorporated in the formulation of the rules themselves. The complete set of such rules is called the *grammar* of the language. Crucially, the subjective nature of the method does not at all mean that it is arbitrary. It is constrained by empirical data and laws of logic.

All three types of methodologies have well-established track records in linguistic and nonlinguistic disciplines. Intuition-based research forms the basis for work in mathematics, the study of "abstract objects" (Katz, 1981). Experimental design forms the basis for work in the natural sciences, the study of the laws describing automatic behavior in the "objective world." Descriptive, ethnographic, qualitative analysis is the preferred method in cultural anthropology.

With regard to the study of language, all three methodologies have been widely applied. Intuitions about well-formedness constitute the data of grammatical analysis and theory, as noted. Experimental design has illuminated characteristics of sound and word identification in various acoustic environments, and of letter-sound conversion. Descriptive analysis has been applied to the study of language development in children, and to the role of dialect choice in different social settings. Table 5.1 shows how research in language makes use of methodologies that are routinely accepted in other disciplines.

Despite parochial views to the contrary, no one methodology holds a higher claim to scientific trustworthiness than any other. The distinct methodologies merely correspond to distinct aspects of the phenomenon under

TABLE 5.1
Methodologies in Language Research

Scientific Method	*Representative Areas of Study*
Subjective intuitions of well-formedness	Mathematics, grammatical theory
Experimental design	Natural sciences, real-time letter and word identification
Descriptive design	Cultural anthropology, language development and sociolinguistics

study, ultimately, to distinct questions we ask about these phenomena. Indeed, many research situations require the complementary use of distinct methods. The study of language variation in social settings, for example, uses descriptive methodology to identify contextual features that favor the use of certain linguistic forms, but the internal nature of those forms is explained by grammatical theory, itself developed using intuition-based methodology.

Reading is a complex enough phenomenon that all three methodologies have a place in its scientific investigation, as long as their relative importance is understood. Intuition-based methodology helps us understand the grammatical system that readers utilize. Experimental methodology helps us understand automatic processes such as letter and word identification, to the extent that they are recruited in reading. Descriptive methodology helps us understand the purposeful construction of meaning. In fact, it is precisely in virtue of the purposeful and intentional nature of meaning construction, in which mental representations of interpretation do not follow as an automatic consequence of a given set of conditions, that descriptive methodology is rendered the quintessential methodology for research in this area.

An analogy can be made with the phenomenon of walking. Walking is a goal-directed, purposeful motor activity. In addition to the spatial goal, which guides direction of movement, there is a temporal goal, which guides pace. Obstacles must be anticipated, and compensatory twists and turns made if any are encountered, or if the terrain changes unpredictably. Certainly walking could not occur without the automatic biochemical processes involving changes in actin and myosin filaments in muscle fibers. But these automatic processes are variably recruited in the service of the larger purposeful act. They acquire their significance in the context of the larger act. A physical therapist helping a trauma or stroke patient learn to walk would hardly fare well if the focus of therapy was restricted to increasing the strength, speed, and accuracy of movement of individual muscle groups, and not on the goal of ambulation itself.

Advocates of intensive phonics explicitly argue that letters of the alphabet encode the sounds of speech, and that the conversion of print to sound is a prerequisite to comprehension. Furthermore, even if the study of meaning construction in oral language requires descriptive, nonexperimental methods, reading itself is fundamentally a "core" task of "phonological processing" (Shaywitz et al., 1996, pp. 79–80) that is, or must become, a set of automatic mental processes that operate accurately and quickly. These automatic processes must be studied experimentally, to see how they operate in letter and word identification, and to tease apart which ones a young reader has mastered, and which ones he or she has not. Having isolated phonological processing as the "basic functional cognitive unit underlying reading and reading disability," scientists could "focus" on this, "rather than simply and broadly studying reading" (Shaywitz et al., p. 80).

And indeed, as long as reading is just the automatic conversion of letters to sounds, it can be thought of as a subject requiring experimental investigation. The complex and open-ended principles of meaning construction, which require descriptive methods of study, are not technically part of reading *per se*, but rather part of a more broadly defined field. Reading merely gets the reader from print to sound, at which point all the interpretive variation inherent in meaning construction will follow from the reader's use of ordinary conversational abilities.

In other words, written language must first be translated into oral language. Then, the mechanisms that construct meanings in oral language can be activated, and the reader can "comprehend." This is the essence of the neophonics model of proficient reading, namely, the automatic processing of unnatural and culturally created letters in order to convert them to the "natural" sounds of oral language, which thereby gains for the reader entry into a realm of nonautomatic linguistic processes with which the reader is already fluent and familiar, although this new realm is not itself technically part of reading. From this conception it follows immediately that the experimental analysis of automatic processing is the only legitimate methodology for studying reading, that the neurology of reading can proceed on the basis of utilizing only those tasks that tap into phonological processing, and that the focus of reading instruction needs to be explicit and intensive phonics and phonemic awareness, in order to develop the desired automaticity in the processing of artificial alphabetic letters.

However, numerous studies, carried out over the past several decades, have demonstrated that reading for meaning does not presuppose a prior translation of print to sound, that guessing at words based on nonorthographic information and even ignoring words are part of the normal process of reading (cf. Weaver, 2002, for an extensive review). I will not go over this extensive literature, but will concentrate instead on demonstrating the inability of the alphabetic principle to effect the necessary translation.

However, for the sake of briefly addressing problems with the neophonics print-sound translation model, consider a reader who enounters the sentence fragment "The man married the —," with the final word not appearing until the very next page. Does a proficient reader really need to see the letters on the next page before feeling confident that that word is *woman*? One would have to literally turn off the brain's normal thought processes in order to prevent syntax, semantics, and knowledge of social norms, including the Cooperative Principle and conversational maxims of linguistic communication, from triggering a guess as to how the sentence continues. Scanning letters from the word *woman* as the reader turns the page would then only need to be done in order to confirm or disconfirm that guess. And this does not require a full identification of the word. A proficient reader might feel entirely comfortable scanning only the initial letter *w* in order to conclude that guessing that the next word was *woman* was indeed correct. And if the guess was incorrect, a reader who was reading for meaning would note a semantic inconsistency, go back to the previous page, and make the necessary semantic-based correction.

In intensive phonics classrooms, eliminating the ordinary and natural syntactic, semantic, and social cuing systems may force a compensatory increase in the use of the phonic cuing system, perhaps even a reliance on it. This might occur if a word appeared alone on an otherwise blank page. It certainly would occur if all other cuing systems were entirely eliminated by presenting the reader with isolated, individual nonsense words that have no conventional meanings. What else can a reader do when encountering *glig*, *phiph*, *sklen*, and *trave*, other than to sound them out? In such isolated forms, there is no morphologic, syntactic, or semantic information that can be recruited. But this is hardly the norm. And just because a reader has been forced into sounding out a word, by depriving him or her of every other linguistic, psycholinguistic, and sociolinguistic resource, does not mean that what has now occurred is normal reading.

Ultimately, the fatal flaw for advocates of the neophonics view of reading is twofold. First, neophonics advocates study reading as a phenomenon that is extracted from a communicative act, thereby changing the nature of the process inself. Second, it cannot even be maintained that converting letters to sounds is what allows a reader to identify a word. As a serious investigation of the alphabetic principle demonstrates, many ordinary words need to already be identified *before* the phonics rules can be set in motion. And even when sounding out can be accomplished without prior word identification, and a word's pronunciation can be achieved, this still does not guarantee an automatic, subsequent word identification. To the extent that these problems exist, the entire rationale for the neophonics program is undermined and, having no legs to stand on, it can do nothing but implode.

The next chapter begins a look at this problem.

Chapter 6

Problems With the Alphabetic Principle

The strictly scientific component of neophonics is based entirely on the premise that there exists an "alphabetic principle," and that children need to be taught this in order to become readers. The alphabetic principle is "nonnegotiable" (*Testimony of G. Reid Lyon,* 1997, par. 11). It asserts that "written spellings systematically represent phonemes of spoken words" and, "unfortunately, children are not born with this insight, nor is it acquired without instruction" (*Testimony of G. Reid Lyon,* 1997, par. 8; Foorman et al., 1997, par. 5).

What is truly unfortunate, however, is that we never find out from Lyon, or from other NICHD personalities, just what the system looks like. According to Foorman et al. (1997), the system is "elegant," but we get little more than a single, unrepresentative example of this from them:

> Pause for a minute and consider the simple elegance of arranging subsets of these 26 letters so that you can read the word "box" and explain why the inverse order of letters, "xob" does not yield a word of English. In so doing, you have demonstrated the alphabetic principle, the insight that written words are composed of letters of the alphabet that are intentionally and conventionally related to segments of spoken words. (par. 5)

Indeed, Foorman et al. acknowledged that a computer would need about 2,000 phonics rules to turn written English into sound.

Of course, merely demonstrating that there is a systematic and elegant alphabetic principle stills says nothing about whether this has to be taught in order for a child to become a reader. There is a systematic and elegant physics behind fastballs, curves, and sliders, but which pitching coach is seeking out physics prodigies for the local traveling team?

In order to make the claim that the alphabetic principle must be taught in order for someone to become a reader, there must at least exist an alphabetic principle. It is rather remarkable, therefore, that neither Lyon, nor Foorman, nor any other neophonics advocate, as far as I can tell, has elaborated on this system, investigated it empirically, and shown teachers what it is that they are supposed to be teaching. In the end, the floating definition of *phonics* is merely some vague, old-fashioned notion of letter-sound correspondences, with the significant ones being those that make it to production as a piece of K–3 merchandise.

But is there really nothing more to learn about letter-sound relationships than that some of them are regular, that there are a bunch of blends and digraphs, and that mixed into the pot are a whole lot of exceptions? Of course, the only way to answer this question is to seriously investigate the matter, but this risks discovering properties of the system that raise serious questions about whether it needs to be, or even can be, taught at all. Before pursuing this aspect of the investigation, however, some problems with the alphabetic principle need to be pointed out.

More than half a century ago, the well-known behaviorist linguist Leonard Bloomfield wrote about the importance of letter-sound relationships in learning to read. In one passage, he discussed a handful of examples:

> The accomplished reader of English, then, has an overpracticed and ingrained habit of uttering one phoneme of the English language when he sees the letter p, another when he sees the letter i, another when he sees the letter n, still another when he sees the letter m, still another when he sees the letter d, and so on. In this way, he utters the conventionally accepted word when he sees a combination of letters like pin, nip, pit, tip, tin, nit, dip, din, dim, mid. What is more, all readers will agree as to the sounds they utter when they see unconventional combinations such as pid, nin, pim, mip, nid, nim, mim. (1942/1961, p. 26)

These examples merit reflection.

At the outset, Bloomfield's (1942/1961) claims are factually incorrect, even if his behaviorist notions are accepted. So whether a reader produces a phoneme as a habitual response to a letter stimulus, or instead conjures up the right sound via some other psycholinguistic mechanism, the alignment of one sound with each letter is empirically false. This is well known, of course. Bloomfield's letters *p*, *i*, and *n* have different pronunciations in the words *Phil*, *ice*, and *hymn*. But granting that Bloomfield's examples are typical cases, and that the exceptions can be easily explained, his point is that in the *ideal* phonics rule, one letter corresponds to one sound. Perhaps it is this ideal that makes letter-sound relationships "elegant," on Foorman's (Foorman et al., 1997) view.

The notion of a one-to-one ideal is implicit in the way Bloomfield (1942/1961) presents his examples. The pairs *pin-nip*, *pit-tip*, and *dim-mid* hint that the phonics rules that turn single letters into single sounds do so no matter where in the word the letters appear. The rules even apply when the letter sequence does not spell an actual word of the language, as in *nim* and *min*. Thus, the ideal phonics rule is one that turns a single letter into a single sound, without having to take into consideration any other aspects of the letter's alphabetic or lexical environment.

Bloomfield's (1942/1961) selection of the vowel letter *i* also buttresses the notion of an ideal system. With the lone exception of words ending in *r*, the pronunciation of the vowel *i* in a three-letter word of the form C*i*C (C = consonant) is perfectly uniform and regular, always the short [I] sound. In *fir* and *sir*, the vowel is *r*-controlled, as it is in *her* and *fur*. Interestingly, Bloomfield does not include C*ir* sequences in his list of examples.

There are no words of the form C*iw* or C*iy*. In other words, the vowel letter *i* does not permit an immediately following *w* or *y*. But this is simply a restriction on how words can be spelled in English. It cannot be due to a phonics violation, because a conventional pronunciation could be applicable to C*iw* and C*iy* as easily as it is for C*ey* and C*ew*. Notice, again, that Bloomfield (1942/1961) did not include *piy* or *tiw*, or similar C*iy* and C*iw* nonwords, in his list of nonword examples. Thus, his examples implicitly respect *spelling rules*, in addition to phonics rules.

Once any other vowel is used, exceptional pronunciations and relaxed spelling patterns are more likely. Thus, we have *pan*, *par*, *pay*, and *paw*, each with a distinct vowel sound. We also have *hen*, *her*, *hey*, and *hew*, also with distinct vowels. Alongside regular *con*, *Don*, and *Ron*, we have exceptional *son*, *ton*, and *won*. Curiously, the Chinese loan words *won* and *ton* are pronounced with the regular phonics pattern. The pronunciation of *ow* in "how now brown cow" contrasts with "grow slow" and "low blow." The words *fun*, *guy*, and *put* all have different vowel pronunciations.

Compared to all the other vowels, *i* is the most regular and unexceptional in words of the form CVC (V = vowel). So, via a judicious selection of examples, Bloomfield (1942/1961) conveyed the idea that the ideal phonics rule applies to single letters, creating single sounds, no matter what other letters appear in the word or nonword. But the ideal is only an ideal, and begins to break down as soon as we leave the narrow set of words that are spelled with a consonant letter surrounding the letter *i*.

Still, even though the ideal breaks down, there are regular, letter-based patterns to the new pronunciations. Thus, a final *y* in the single-syllable words always induces a long sound when the preceding vowel is *a*, as in *bay*, *day*, *hay*, *jay*, *lay*, *may*, *nay*, *pay*, *ray*, *say*, and *way*, or *e*, as in *hey*, *grey*, and *whey*. An ideal phonics rule, such as "letter *a* is pronounced short" or "letter *e* is pronounced short" must be supplemented with "unless the final letter is *y*, in which case it is pronounced long."

In general, and again in simple, single-syllable words, a final *r*, *y*, or *w* induces a change in the vowel pronunciation from that which is seen in the Bloomfieldian (Bloomfield, 1942/1961) ideal. Interestingly, Bloomfield's ideal is a short vowel pronunciation, not long, therefore not the pronunciation that shows up in the name of the letter. Indeed, the long pronunciations of *a*, *e*, *i*, *o*, and *u* typically appear only in a more narrowly defined alphabetic environment, such as when followed by *y*, by a silent *e*, or by certain vowels. Thus, we not only have *pay* and *grey*, but *pane* and *pine* (silent *e*) as well as *reed*, *food*, *rain*, *road*, and *lien* (following vowel).

Yet even these categories subdivide further. For example, silent *e* words in which the main vowel is separated from silent *e* by two consonant letters may or may not be pronounced with a long vowel. The vowel is long when the two letters are *ng*, *th*, and *st*, as in *range*, *strange*, *bathe*, *writhe*, *taste*, and *haste*, but short when the two letters are *nc*, *ng*, *ns*, *rc*, *rg*, or *rs*, as in *dance*, *dunce*, *hinge*, *lunge*, *tense*, *rinse*, *farce*, *barge*, and *parse*. If the word contains the sequence *ie*, which is otherwise pronounced long, this long pronunciation takes precedence over the short vowel pronunciation before two consonants, as in *pierce* and *fierce*. If the word contains *e*, *i*, or *u* immediately before *r*, the *r*-controlled pronunciation takes precedence over the short vowel pronunciation, as in *terse*, *dirge*, and *curse*. If the word contains the sequence *ea* before *r*, the *r*-controlled pronunciation takes precedence over the long vowel pronunciation, as in *hearse*.

The phonics rules that would apply to the words thus far discussed include at least the following:

The letter *p* is pronounced [p].
The letter *f* is pronounced [f] (etc.).

A vowel letter is pronounced short in words where it is the only vowel letter, and surrounded by consonant letters, unless:

1. it is immediately followed by the letter *r*, in which case it is (a) *r*-controlled if *i*, *e*, or *u* (as in *fir*, *her*, *fur*), (b) [ɑ] if *a* (as in *car*, *far*), or (c) [ɔ] if *o* (as in *for*).
2. it is immediately followed by the letter *y*, in which case it is (a) long if *a* or *e* (as in *say*, *hey*), (b) [a] if *u* (as in *buy*, *guy*), or (c) [ɔ] if *o* (as in *boy*, *coy*).

3. it is immediately followed by the letter *w*, in which case it is (a) [uw] if *e* (as in *new, grew*), (b) [ɔ] if *a* (as in *paw, saw*), or optionally [æ] if *o* (as in *how* vs. *low,* and *bow* [bæw] vs. [bow]).

The revised Bloomfieldian (Bloomfield, 1942/1961) system is already highly complex, and this on the basis of only a handful of single-syllable words. Imagine the proliferation of rules as the set of words expands to include multisyllabic ones, where pronunciations will depend on the presence or absence of an accent, as in *atom* versus *atomic,* or where a consonant pronunciation depends on which syllable it belongs to, as in *latex* vs. *later* (cf. Kahn, 1978).

The sheer complexity, in and of itself, does not argue against the existence of a systematic and elegant phonics system, but it must raise questions about its role in teaching reading. There are at least two important questions that need to be addressed by researchers who advocate intensive phonics instruction in elementary classrooms. First, of all the phonics rules that can be described, on what empirical basis do we determine which ones need to be taught, assuming, as seems reasonable, that we are not going to subject little children to a barrage consisting of 2,000 rules? Second, from what general theory of language learning does it follow that the special case of language learning called "learning to read" is explained on the basis of teaching a select, and usually unrepresentative, sample of the full, and large, complement of phonics rules? As far as I can tell, these questions have been neither raised nor answered.

Still, none of the phonics rules developed thus far violates the general rationale behind the use of phonics rules in the teaching of reading, which is to allow a reader to recognize a word by first identifying its pronunciation, and then presumably associating this pronunciation with syntactic and semantic properties that are stored in the mental lexicon. They are therefore legitimate candidates for an intensive phonics program. But it is also legitimate to wonder whether their complexity renders them less than teachworthy.

Additional examples complicate the matter even further. Consider words that begin with the letters *th* immediately followed by a vowel letter. This letter combination can be pronounced with either a voiced *th,* as in *the, this,* and *that,* or voiceless *th,* as in *thin, thick,* and *thank.* A more expanded list of *th*-initial words reveals that it is pronounced voiced when the word is a grammatical function word, and voiceless otherwise (Venezky, 1999, p. 166):

Voiced *th*: '*that*', '*the*', '*them*', '*then*', '*there*', '*these*', '*thine*', '*this*', '*thither*', '*those*', '*thou*', '*though*', '*thus*', '*thy*'

Voiceless *th*: *thank, Thelma, thick, thin, thought, thud, thyroid.*

Clearly, an accurate formulation of the phonics rules that describe this pattern must state that initial *th* followed immediately by a vowel is pronounced voiced in grammatically functioning words, and voiceless in content words. But in order to know whether the word is a function word or a content word, the reader must have already identified it. And it must have been identified on the basis of information other than letter-sound correspondences, such as syntax, semantics, and background knowledge. Because the reader must already have identified the word in order to sound it out correctly, the rationale for phonics as instruction is undermined in these cases.

Or consider the pronunciation of final *s* in *as* and *is*, compared to *bus* and *yes*. Again, the distinction is grammatically based, with a voiced [z] sound appearing in function words (except direct objects and demonstratives, e.g., *us, this*) and voiceless [s] appearing in content words (Venezky, 1999, p. 45):

Voiced [z]: *as, has, is, his, was*
Voiceless [s]: *bus, Gus, pus, Wes, yes*

Similar examples abound. The letter *s* is voiceless when *house* is a noun, but voiced when it is a verb. The letter *g* immediately following *n* and immediately preceding *er* is pronounced if the *er* is part of the stem, as in *finger* and *linger*, but is silent if *er* is a separate suffix, as in *singer* and *ringer*, unless that suffix is the adjectival comparative, as in *longer* and *stronger*. The initial *s* of stems such as *sist* and *sult* is voiced if the preceding prefix ends in a vowel, as in *resist* and *result*, but if the prefix is the iterative *re*, as in *remake* and *retell*, then the stem must be a real word, and its intial *s* will be voiceless, as in *reserve* (serve again vs. Army reserve) and *resort* (sort again vs. beach resort). And virtually all of the so-called sight words exhibit such word-level phonics, as can be readily appreciated in a simple example such as *said*, where the phonics rule "*ai* is pronounced [ɛ] in the word *said*" clearly shows that the word must already be identified in order for the correct sounding out to occur.

The only way an advocate of intensive phonics can support using rules such as these is to formulate them in such a way that there is no appeal to the identity of the word itself, or to any higher level information. For example, the rule for initial *th* can read: "Initial *th* is pronounced voiceless unless it is found in the *spellings the, then, this, that, there, those,* and so on." Or, the rule for final *s* can read: "Final *s* is pronounced voiceless unless it is found in the spellings *as, is, was, has, his,* and so on." Or the rule for *said* can read: "letter sequence *ai* is pronounced [ɛ] when it is found in the larger letter string *said*."

It should be obvious that such formulations of phonics rules leave unexpressed the empirical generalizations that underlie them, that function words, for example, form the basis for the set of forms that receive a voiced pronunciation, or that sight words exhibit phonic behavior peculiar to that word, and not to the letter string that constitutes the visual form of that word (*one* is idiosyncratically pronounced [wʌn], but *cone, done,* and *gone* are not pronounced [kwʌn], [dwʌn], and [gwʌn]). From the standpoint of scientific analysis, formulations of phonics rules that avoid reference to the identity of the word fall very far short of empirical adequacy. In the case of the rule for initial *th,* it is only by accident that a non-word-level formulation correctly identifies words with voiced consonants. It does so simply by listing them. But the list could just as easily and just as arbitrarily be *the, then, thin, than,* and *thank.*

It is only when phonics rules are thought of as tools to decode written language, turn it into sound, and thereby lead to word recognition, that they must be formulated against their empirical grain. It is only in order to satisfy a preconceived notion of what phonics rules are supposed to do that they must, in many cases, be scientifically distorted.

Even though it may be possible in certain cases to use empirically distorted phonics rules to still create accurate pronunciations, other cases do not fare as well. Consider homographs, words that are spelled alike, but have distinct pronunciations, such as *lead* (lead singer, lead pipe), *read* (like to read, it was read), *bow* (tie a bow, take a bow). Here it is clear that it would be patently absurd to formulate pedagogically friendly phonics rules on the basis of the full word identity, as in "*bow* is pronounced [bow] if it's something you tie, and [bæw] if it's bending at the hips." Once the word is recognized, the goal supposedly achieved via phonics rules has already been accomplished.

But the only way to avoid this scenario is to formulate a phonics rule that leaves open more than one possible pronunciation. Thus, the rule for 'ow' is: "The letter sequence 'ow' is pronounced either [ow] or [æw]." Then, the phonically well-trained reader, on encountering 'bow', will produce both [bow] and [bæw]. The problem with this solution, though, is that the phonics rules, even if a necessary tool for word identification, are clearly not a sufficient tool. Something else must assist the reader in the identification process.

And it may not be only with homographs that we encounter this problem. Consider the virtually astronomical metaphorical proliferation of word uses that is part of the ordinary life of language. Like a budding yeast cell, a qualitatively new word eventually breaks loose from repeated and highly adaptable word use extensions, producing, for example, the new word *window,* used to refer to the space where a bank teller encounters a customer, even when an actual physical window is no longer present. Or consider the word *key,* used to refer to the clue that unlocks the mystery, or *tongue* used to refer to the flap of a shoe.

What does it mean to say that a reader has identified the word *window* or the word *key* or the word *tongue*? Which word *window*, which word *key*, and which word *tongue*? In principle, phonics cannot narrow down the identity of the intended word in these, and probably tens of thousands of cases, even if it produces accurate pronunciations.

In summary, therefore, the phonics rules that are needed to generate pronunciations for even the most simply spelled words very quickly run into problems. There are, from the outset, very many rules and subdivisions of rules. The rules are complex. Some rules are not even empirically accurate when formulated for instructional purposes, but rather take on a certain form only in order to satisfy the assumption that a reader must first turn a written word into sound before the word can be recognized. Finally, phonics rules, in general, are not sufficient by themselves to identify all words, even when the pronunciations are accurately determined. And to make matters even worse, pronunciations themselves are frequently also not sufficient to narrow down the identity of a word.

Given all these problems, a scientific approach to understanding reading must question one of the underlying, fundamental assumptions of phonics, which is that letters of the alphabet systematically represent the sounds of the language. In fact, it can be easily shown that only part of this system represents sounds directly, whereas other parts represent other aspects of language, including word structure and syntax.

Consider the phenomenon of homonyms, words that are spelled differently, but have the same pronunciation. One might ask, as the centuries of spelling reformers (cf., e.g., Hart, 1569/1968; Pitman, 1969) indeed did, why such words are not spelled alike. This is tantamount to asking whether there is any advantage to keeping the spellings of homonyms distinct, and the answer seems quite obvious, because English orthography clearly tolerates them. When *right* and *rite*, *meat* and *meet*, *rain* and *rein*, and *mints* and *mince* are spelled differently, what is thereby conveyed is that these are different words. The spelling system permits a flexible, nonunique letter-sound system in order to encode not only sounds, but word identity as well.

A preference for lexical and grammatical integrity over phonic purity can also be seen in the letter-sound relations that hold for various syntactically functioning suffixes. Consider the plural suffix *-s*, which is pronounced voiceless in words that end in a voiceless consonant, as in *laps*, *books*, and *lots*, and voiced in words that end in a voiced consonant, as in *labs*, *bags*, and *beds*. Notice that the uniform spellings cannot be due to the unavailability of a letter to represent the voiced sound, because *z* is clearly available, and could readily be used to spell *labz*, *bagz*, and *bedz*. But such spellings would annihilate the information that is conveyed by using the letter *s* in all words, namely, that despite different pronunciations, the suffix is the same.

And it is not only the plural suffix *s* that behaves this way. The same phenomenon is seen whenever *s* functions as a grammatical suffix. We thus have third-person singular *asks* and *hums*, and the possessive and contracted copula *Pat's* and *Bob's*. The past tense suffix *ed* retains its uniform spelling whether it is pronounced voiceless, as in *looked* and *topped*, or voiced, as in *begged* and *rubbed*.

Stems demonstrate the same preference for lexical integrity over phonic purity. Consider the pairs *music-musician*, *part-partial*, and *beast-beastial*. These exemplify a robust pattern in English, which is that the stem spelling remains invariant even when its pronunciation changes under the influence of a suffix. Thus, *music* ends with a [k] sound, which becomes a fricative before *ian*. The word *part* ends with a [t] sound, which becomes a fricative before *ial*. And *beast* ends with a [t] sound, which becomes an affricate before *ial*.

These points were noted by Venezky (1999). He observed that "morpheme identity [is] usually preserved in prefixing and suffixing," and that "visual discrimination of homophones . . . is encouraged through different spellings" (pp. 9–10). These examples demonstrate that the spelling-sound system in English is governed not just by an alphabetic principle, but by a type of logographic principle as well, in which the integrity of stems and affixes is maintained via invariant spellings, despite variant pronunciations, whereas the distinctness of stems and affixes is brought out by distinct spellings, despite identical pronunciations. But once this is acknowledged, it is impossible to insist that phonics is the *sine qua non* of reading, that words must be identified by converting their spellings to sounds.

Indeed, and most significantly from a scientific standpoint, once a logographic principle of English orthography is recognized, there is no reason not to acknowledge the empirically greater adequacy of grammatically conditioned rules over alternatives, such as was observed in the case of *th*-initial words and *s*-final words. Then it becomes fundamentally impossible to assert that phonics is a system of letter-sound relationships that is needed for written word identification, by turning the written word into sound. This is impossible because the word must first be identified in order to then know how it is pronounced. It is only by empirically distorting the rules to eliminate the higher level information that this role can be maintained. But what are these rules now, if not just a mountain of misleading misinformation about how letters relate to sounds? They are no more scientifically based phonics rules than are statements such as "nouns are people, places, and things" grammatical rules. So the ultimate question that every teacher and parent is entitled to ask becomes: How is it that children learn to read by being fed misinformation about letters and sounds?

The existence of a logographic principle in English spelling is hardly a theoretical embarrassment. Indeed, it is a welcome empirical result, because it explains patterns of spelling-sound correspondences in numerous words of English on the basis of a type of symbol-sound correspondence that is already known to exist in other languages. In other words, it is not a bizarre peculiarity of English, but rather an established precedent among writing systems.

In contrast to alphabetic writing, the individual symbols of a logographic writing system represent whole words or morphemes, not discrete sounds. It was the form of writing of the oldest known writing system, ancient Sumerian Cuneiform. It is found today in modern Chinese. Examples from the latter are shown in Fig. 6.1. In the examples in Fig. 6.1, there is no individual brush stroke that represents the sound [f] or the sound [s] or the sound [ei]. Rather, the symbol as a whole represents the word, whose pronunciation happens to be [fu] or [si] or [mei].

Therefore, if we were to imagine a rule that connected the logographic symbol to sound, it would have to be one that referred to the entire symbol, not to its component strokes. And the entire symbol itself, representing as it does a whole word of the language, is thereby a unit of higher level grammatical structure rather than a mere sound. It is in just this sense that we can say that the symbol-sound correspondence obeys a logographic principle.

Similarly, any spelling-sound rule of English that refers to a written symbol of lexicosyntactic structure is thereby logographic in character. The rule for sounding out initial *th* must note the word's part of speech, or syntactic category, in order to correctly assign a voiced or voiceless pronunciation. The rule for final *s* must determine whether or not that *s* is a separate suffix. If not, as in *as, was,* and *gas,* then the pronunciation will again depend on the part of speech, becoming voiced in certain grammatically functioning words, and voiceless otherwise, as we have seen. These rules can be thought of as phonics rules with a logographic character.

Every so-called sight word of English undergoes a phonics rule that has a logographic character. The rules that sound out the word *said*, for example, include one that turns *s* into the sound [s], another that turns *d* into the sound [d], and still another that turns the letter sequence *ai* into the sound [ɛ] *when that letter sequence appears in the written word said.* Whereas the rules for *s* and *d* are ordinary phonics rules, in which an identified letter is related to a sound, the one for *ai* is a phonics rule with a logographic character, because it must identify the whole word in which it resides in order for the correct sound to be assigned.

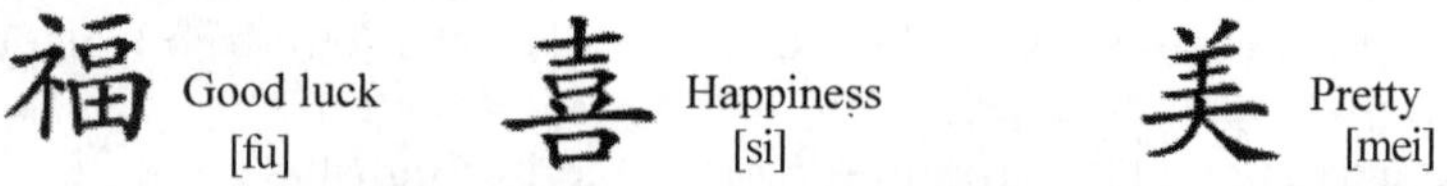

FIG. 6.1. Chinese symbols.

Likewise, the letter sequence *steak* undergoes a rule that turns the subsequence *ea* into the sound [ey], precisely because it lies in the *word steak*. The *word do* idiosyncratically connects its vowel letter *o* to the sound [uw]. The *word pint* idiosyncratically connects its vowel letter *i* to the sound [ay]. It is in its reference to the whole word that the letter-sound phonics rule functions logographically, even though only a part of the word undergoes a conversion to sound.

Of course, there is a big distinction between a logographic system, like written Chinese on the one hand, and an alphabetic system that behaves logographically, like written English, on the other. The former consists of symbols that individually represent morphemes and words, that is to say, lexicosyntactically functioning units. The latter consists of symbols that individually do not stand for whole morphemes or words, or any other lexicosyntactically functioning unit, but where the scanning of a word's full spelling in order to properly carry out a letter-sound rule confers on that rule a lexicosyntactic character. Thus, English writing has alphabetic structure, but can exhibit logographic functioning. It is a hybrid system.

It is interesting to observe that systems that are structurally logographic may also exhibit alphabetic functioning. Therefore, they are hybrids as well.

Consider, for example, the representation of foreign loanwords in Chinese. By definition, these do not have preexisting logographic symbols in the language. The convention on creating logographic "spellings" for these words is to select logograms whose pronunciations figure into the pronunciation of the loanword. These are then appropriately concatenated together to represent the desired loanword.

For example, the names *Reagan* and *Lenin* are written in Chinese as in Fig. 6.2. Notice that the symbols which spell *Reagan* have the meanings "inside" and "roots," which clearly have nothing to do with the referent of the word *Reagan*. However, their pronunciations are, respectively, [li] and [gen], and these are similar enough phonetically to the sounds contained in the target word.

Similarly, the word for *Lenin* in Chinese is written with symbols whose meanings are "series" and "quiet," again with no implied connection to the referent of the word. But the pronunciations are [lie] and [niŋ], and it is for these pronunciations that the logograms are selected.

In the examples in Fig. 6.2, a system that is otherwise logographic, where a symbol represents a whole word, extends itself so that symbols can be used to represent sounds. In this sense we can say that a symbol that has logographic structure can nevertheless have alphabetic function.

The alphabetic functioning of logographic symbols is therefore rooted in the need to represent new words, though it is not absolutely and uniquely determined by this. In principle, logograms could be selected on

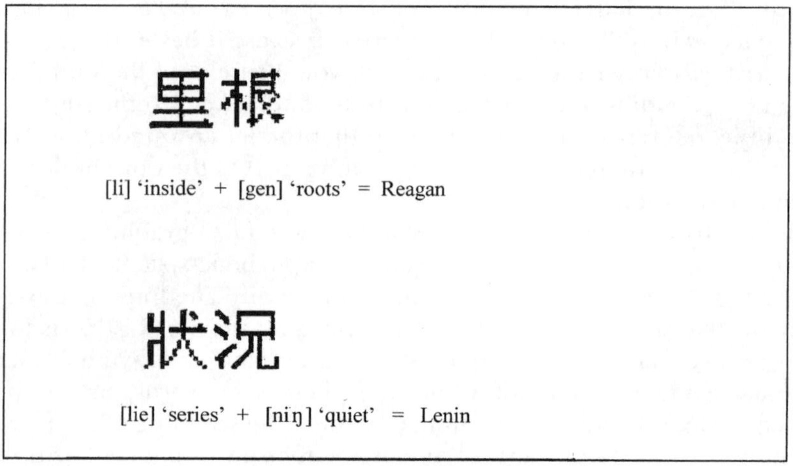

FIG. 6.2. Chinese symbols for *Reagan* and *Lenin.*

the basis of the meanings they represent, rather than pronunciations. But a logogram's pronunciation exists, and is thereby available to be exploited.

Similarly, even if we grant that letters represent sounds, once a word's spelling is agreed upon, that word as a whole can now be identified by scanning and identifying the whole sequence of letters that constitutes its spelling. There is, in principle, no reason why this lexicosyntactic unit cannot now condition letter-sound correspondences.

The logographic functioning of alphabetic letters is rooted, in part, in the failure of the phonics system to obey Bloomfieldian (Bloomfield, 1942/1961) simplicity, because such a system would require that sounds be derived only from individual letters. But we have already seen that Bloomfieldian simplicity is bound to fail, and for reasons having nothing to do with logographic writing systems. For example, it fails as a result of the existence of phonological alternations in the spoken language, variant pronunciations of morphemes that work their way into the phonic system. Therefore, it is noteworthy that the complex rule types created in the phonics system as a result of a violation of Bloomfieldian simplicity give the system a new, logographic function, which happens to be the primary function of other writing systems.

Consequently, we are too quick to dismiss English spellings on the grounds that they are overly complex, because a function of the complexity is to mediate the logographic behavior of letters. To claim that complexity is a problem is therefore equivalent to stating that the logographic functioning of letters is a problem. But logographic behavior is a natural function of writing systems.

Written English exhibits logographic behavior in still other ways. One has to do with the spelling of loanwords, especially names. It is customary for English to leave essentially unchanged the spellings of those foreign names, written natively anyway with Roman letters, even when they contain spelling sequences that are not native to English. Thus, we have *Sartre, Goethe, Lloyd, Czech, Bologna,* and *van Gogh.* As Venezky (1999) put it, in English spelling, "Etymology is Honored" (p. 7).

Now, if English were governed strictly by the alphabetic principle in its maximally simple form, letters should uniquely represent sounds. We should then somehow require that such loanwords undergo a change in their spellings when incorporated into English texts. Or, at the very least, we should expect that, if left unchanged, they would pose a serious problem for readers. But we in fact recognize a word as a nonnative name precisely by its unusual spelling pattern, and this becomes part of the spelling landscape for English. Therefore, the letters and their arrangement in such words signify a logographic category: foreign names.

In some cases, this type of phenomenon exploits the presence of gaps in English spelling patterns. The gaps may be filled only by words recognized as belonging to a certain nonphonological category. For example, it is unusual for English words to be written with a final vowel pair, though certain productive patterns do indeed exist. Thus, we have the fairly productive *ee* in *bee, free, glee, see, tee, tree,* and *wee,* and the somewhat less productive *oo* in *boo, coo, too,* and *zoo, oe* in *hoe, toe, roe, shoe,* and *ea* in *tea, sea, flea, pea,* and *yea.* For other vowel pairs, examples are even harder to come by, such as *Mae, pia, Cleo, boa, you,* and *duo.* And some vowel pairs make their way in only as obvious, isolated foreign words, such as (*My*) *Lai* (Vietnamese) and *roi* (French).

But notice the curiously regular pattern we find in words that end in *ao,* an absolute black hole of English spelling, unless representing words of Chinese origin: *Chao, Kao, Lao, Mao, Pao, Tao.* Indeed, should another word with this spelling pattern be added to the language, say, *Fao,* it would immediately be recognized, whether correctly or not, as Chinese. Therefore, these spelling sequences come to be associated with a specific morphological category, once again producing logographic behavior.

Abbreviations are an accepted and very common phenomenon in written English, posing no special obstacle to reading. Such representations depart from a strict alphabetic functioning of letters, and, to that extent, behave logographically. Consider abbreviations for names of states. In spellings such as *WI* (Wisconsin), *MI* (Michigan), *CA* (California), and *IA* (Iowa), the double letter sequence signifies a larger word. It may appear to do this by representing the initial syllable of the word. In fact, however, these syllables are illusory. The abbreviations are not even intended to be sounded out, whether as syllables or anything else, as the unnatural and nonexistent pronunciations [wI], [mI], [ka], and [ayə] make perfectly clear. Other state abbreviations make this point more clearly, as a sounding out of the abbreviation produces a syllable that is found nowhere at all in the full pronunciation. This is the case for *MO* (Missouri), *ME* (Maine), *GA* (Georgia), and *LA* (Louisiana). The abbreviations therefore directly represent the whole word.

Other types of abbreviations seem to argue more plausibly for a syllabic behavior of letters. Consider the *acronyms CIA, NIH, HIV, FBI, PTA, DOE, M.D., B.S., M.A., Ed.D.*, and *Ph.D.* These are pronounced with syllabic letter names, and so appear to represent a syllabary functioning of letters. But the syllabary behavior is again illusory. The central function of the letters remains logographic, because the pronounced syllables are actually *names*, that is, the names of the letters, another lexicosyntactic feature. So, when reading these abbreviations aloud, it is the letter name that is first identified, and the syllabic pronunciation follows as a consequence. Evidence that this is the empirically correct analysis comes from abbreviations that contain letters whose names are not a single syllable. There being only one of these in English, namely *w*, we can see from examples such as *www.com, WWF*, and *WHO* that it is that letter name itself that is read aloud.

Consider abbreviations such as *Sgt., Dr., Cpt., Cpl.*, and *Mr.* These, and numerous others of this sort, represent whole words via the consonants that correspond to sounds in their ordinary pronunciations, and that are present in their conventional spellings. They can be thought of as a type of consonantal spelling, neither purely alphabetic nor purely logographic.

Consonantal spellings are found in Semitic languages (Sampson, 1985), where symbols for the vowel sounds are absent (words are conventionally written right to left), as seen in Fig. 6.3. Whereas in Arabic (and Hebrew) the vowels that eventually show up in pronunciation are determined by morphological and syntactic patterns (noun class, verb inflection, and so on), in English there is no way to predict from the abbreviation's consonantal sequence which vowels will appear in the spoken form of the word. This must be determined simply by identifying the whole word that corresponds

جبل [l][b][g]	[gabal]	Mountain
تل [l][t]	[tal]	Hill
نهر [r][h][n]	[naher]	River

FIG. 6.3. Arabic examples.

to the consonantal sequence. Thus, these consonantal examples represent a function of letters that is still subordinate in behavior to the logographic function.

Formally, we can accommodate the behavior of these abbreviations in a phonics system with rules that turn the entire abbreviation into a pronounced word, such as "*Mr.* is pronounced [mIstR]," "*Sgt.* is pronounced [sɑrĵInt]," "Dr. is pronounced [daktR]," and so on. Such conversions unfortunately do not reveal in a direct way that a word's pronunciation includes some sounds that correspond by ordinary phonics rules to letters in the abbreviation. For example, *Mr.* is indeed pronounced with [m] and [R]. As an alternative, we could consider a rule of the form "*Mr.* is pronounced by inserting [Ist] between the *M* and the *r*," leaving the *M* and *r* to be sounded out by ordinary phonics rules. Either way, the letter-sound connection is complex.

In either case, we need rules that look at the entire abbreviation, because there is no smaller piece of the word that will allow us to predict the remaining sounds. But a rule that identifies the entire spelled input as its domain of application, rather than a smaller component part of the input, is precisely the characteristic that defines logographic writing.

Indeed, what formally distinguishes logographic writing from nonlogographic writing (consonantal, alphabetic) is just that the former routinely contains rules that look at the entire input symbol, whereas the latter routinely contains rules that operate on the input's component parts. In the Chinese examples in Fig. 6.1, each individual symbol stands for a whole word, and consequently is sounded out as the full pronunciation of that word. In the Arabic examples in Fig. 6.3, each word is spelled with symbols that represent the component consonant sounds only, and not the vowel sounds. In English, individual consonant and vowel sounds are all represented.

Therefore, the special phonics rules that apply to abbreviations like *Dr.*, *Mr.*, and *Cpt.* have a logographic quality insofar as the entire word string is scanned, and a consonantal quality insofar as letters representing vowel sounds are absent. Similarly, as we have seen, sight words, such as as *said, steak, great, one, plaid,* and *broad,* are hybrid representatives of the English written lexicon. They require logographic, whole-word identification, though they may make alphabetic conversions in only part of the word.

The unscientific stance of merely asserting an alleged systematicity and elegance of phonics rules, without at the same time exploring their characteristics, leads advocates of neophonics to be totally unaware of the contradiction between the nature of the phonics system and the purported pedagogical purpose of the rules, which is to allow a reader to turn the written word into sound, and thereby identify the word. In a variety of ways, the system must first identify a word before it can be sounded out. Therefore, if word identification plays a role in reading, it cannot be claimed to proceed uniformly, nor perhaps even typically, on the basis of first reconstructing the word's pronunciation. Instead, word identification must be made on the basis of nonphonic information.

Furthermore, to the extent that logographic features permeate the phonics system, it simply cannot be maintained that letter-sound relationships constitute its fundamental characteristic. Although the alphabetic principle expresses only one part of the phonics system, it does not tell the whole story. Indeed, it may only represent one short chapter.

But this is a devastating story for neophonics, given that its entire scientific raison d'être is the primacy of the alphabetic principle. Without the alphabetic principle there is no neophonics model of reading, nor is there a rationale for intensive phonics in the classroom. And the grand high-tech field of the neuroimaging of reading, which is really just the neuroimaging of sounding out letters, is left holding a limp baton, as the next chapter discusses.

Chapter 7

Functional Neuroimaging and the Image of Phonics

Besides a linguistics and psychology of self-proclaimed trustworthiness, the scientific arsenal of neophonics also includes a growing stockpile of high-tech images of the brain. The media has deemed this highly newsworthy. In a front-page headline on November 3, 1997, *The Baltimore Sun* announced, "The Brain Reads Sound By Sound" (p. 1A). Beneath the headline was a photograph of Reid Lyon standing before a picture of the brain taken with a magnetic resonance imaging machine. The article itself referred to the work of Yale researchers Bennett and Sally Shaywitz on the neuroimaging of reading. It claimed that phonics is supported by brain research, and meaning-centered programs have distracted us from scientifically defensible teaching.

But there is, in fact, no research at all that has ever demonstrated that the brain reads sound by sound. This is because no brain-research subject has ever actually read anything closer to authentic language than a word or short phrase. Typically, subjects stare at false letters, real letters, and sequences of letters, the latter constituting both nonwords and real words. Taking a picture of the brain while a subject is performing a task of letter-sound conversion, and even finding the part of the brain where this occurs, does not mean that the brain reads sound by sound. It only means that the reader performed a sounding-out task, and the MRI machine could find the part of the brain that was activated for that task.

The most that one can conclude from research on the neuroimaging of reading is that, in using this sophisticated technology, an active area of the brain can be identified when a subject is given a task that requires phonological or other psycholinguistic processing. But the task itself must be a demonstrable component of the reading process in order to conclude that this is a study of reading, and this simply has not been done for most, if not all, of the tasks used in neuroimaging. Without satisfying this condition, neuroscientists who study "reading" have really only studied how neuroimaging can track some potentially insignificant and meaningless cognitive operation.

Shaywitz et al. (1996) noted that the claim of the centrality of phonological processing in reading is a hypothesis generated from psychoacoustic and psycholinguistic research carried out many years ago, prior to the advent of neuroimaging, citing, in particular, the work of Alvin Liberman (Liberman, 1971; Liberman, Shankweiler, & Liberman, 1989). Shaywitz referred to the "discovery" of phonological processing of written words as "an essential prerequisite" to neural investigations of reading (p. 79).

In other words, the hypothesis that "the brain reads sound by sound" really contains two intertwined notions, only one of which is rooted in contemporary neuroimaging studies themselves, whereas the other is rooted in an older science, arguably discredited. The neuroimaging-based notion is that the brain can perform phonological processing tasks when presented with orthographic stimuli, and that we can identify special areas of the brain involved in such phonological processing using neuroimaging technology. But the further assertion that this finding demonstrates that the brain reads sound by sound is derived exogenously, from nonneurologic studies, and is in and of itself not supported by the neuroimaging research. Taken at face value, the neuroimaging data demonstrate only that neuroimaging technology is sensitive to phonological processing, and can provide us with pictures of it. We can conclude that phonological processing occurs in the brain.

The point can be driven home even further when we consider that neuroimaging has been used to look at other aspects of psychological processing besides phonological ones. For example, a number of scientists have studied semantic processing, independent of phonological processing, and have found specific brain regions where this occurs. In their extensive review of neuroimaging and language processing, Demb, Poldrack, and Gabrieli (1999, p. 263) concluded that "imaging studies have consistently reported left-prefrontal activation during tasks of semantic processing."

On the basis of neuroimaging alone, there is no more reason to select phonological processing as the "core" component of reading than there is to select "semantic processing," or any other type of processing whose neural basis can be demonstrated. The selection of a privileged, core operation occurs instead on the basis of prior nonneural theoretical considerations. A generous interpretation of the neuroimaging data could justify a newspaper headline that states, "Scientists Demonstrate that Reading Occurs in the Brain," but nothing more.

An interesting instance of this type of problem can be found in the field of "neurotheology." The May 7, 2001 issue of *Newsweek* featured an article (Underwood, 2001) about scientists at the University of Pennsylvania who used neuroimaging to study subjects undergoing intense, "religious" experiences. The scientists wanted to find out if there is a specific part of the brain that is dedicated to such experiences. The subjects were practicing Buddhists and Catholic nuns, experienced at meditating and fervent praying. During moments of heightened emotional experience, a picture was taken of the brains of these subjects, using single photon emission computed tomography (SPECT). The authors of the study claimed that certain frontal and temporal regions of the brain consistently lit up, demonstrating that there are areas of the brain where such intense experiences occur.

So what does the study demonstrate? At best, it demonstrates that specific regions of the brain are activated during a certain type of emotional experience. Or, because this was never in doubt anyway, another interpretation of the data is that neuroimaging technology is a sensitive tool to identify those areas.

But how do we interpret this finding? One of the scientists referred to in the *Newsweek* article stated that there are two possibilities. According to Andrew Newberg, we can either say that the human brain can be activated to produce a particular type of subjectively intense emotional experience, which we can then interpret *post hoc* as religious in nature, or we can say that the activation itself produces a state of mind that allows the subject to perceive an external spiritual reality: "There is no way to determine whether the neurological changes associated with spiritual experience mean that the brain is *causing* those experiences . . . or is instead *perceiving* a spiritual reality" (p. 55).

Both of these options bring in notions from outside the study itself to aid in its interpretation, an unavoidable and entirely legitimate move, as long as we understand what it is that is being imported into the explanation. The former is perhaps a more conservative interpretation. But to call the experience "religious," as opposed to "emotionally intense," or to invoke an external spiritual reality, as opposed to a "new way of perceiving material reality," is simply not supported by, nor does it arise from, the neuroimaging data alone.

An even more striking claim about reading and the brain appeared in an April, 2002 issue of *Neurology*, the main journal of the American Academy of Neurology. The authors of the study (Simos et al., 2002), including NICHD personalities Jack Fletcher and Barbara Foorman, claimed that their neuroimaging study found that the "brain activation profile" of poor readers "becomes normal following successful remedial training" consisting of 80 hours of intensive phonics (p. 1203).

The study used magnetoencephalography to take pictures of the brain of both good and poor readers during tasks of phonological processing. Images were obtained on poor readers both before and after "treatment." The posttreatment images looked like those of the good readers.

Now, even the editors of *Neurology* had a difficult time with the authors' (Simos et al., 2002) conclusions. In a separate comment that appeared in the same issue (p. 1139), Peter Rosenberger and David Rottenberg (2002) declared their support for phonics in general, noting, in their opinion, that the 1930s neurologist and phonics luminary Samuel Orton (1937) was right in proposing a defect in phonological processing as the key to understanding dyslexia. But they also stated that "reservations may be in order regarding [the] conclusion" that "a 'deficit in functional brain organization' has been 'reversed' by remedial training," because "it appears that as a result of remedial training the dyslexic children are doing what normal readers do naturally" (p. 1139). That is, the study may simply show "that the subject is doing something different (or differently)." They concluded, "Why don't the dyslexic children do it naturally? It is not clear that the study . . . brings us any closer to the answer" (p. 1139).

Neuroimaging is a field of study that blossomed in the last decade of the 20th century, and so it might be called one of the success stories of the federal government's self-proclaimed "decade of the brain." Certainly, 10 years is ample time to achieve some spectacular results in a domain of scientific research. But it is also long enough to influence public opinion, if state policy and priorities are the real issue, for example, if the public's embrace of phonics were one of the goals behind the neuroimaging of reading.

Neurology and neuroimaging have taken on political attributes, and there is no question that the neuroimaging of reading has been used as a tool to pump up the importance of phonics. For example, Shaywitz et al. (1996) have suggested that brain imaging of phonological processing may one day represent the pinnacle of reading assessment:

> The discovery of a biological signature for reading offers an unprecedented opportunity to assess the effects of interventions on reading in nonimpaired readers as well as in individuals with dyslexia. It is reasonable to suggest that brain activation patterns obtained while subjects engage in tasks that tap phonological processing represent the most precise measure of phonological processing. By using activation patterns obtained while individuals perform phonological tasks, it is possible to determine the functional organization in the brains of individuals with dyslexia, impose interventions, and measure the effects of those interventions on the brain. If measurable effects on brain organization are seen after the intervention, it is possible to repeat the fMRI to determine whether these differences persist after the intervention ends. (p. 91)

Unfortunately, what is missing from this proposal is some plausible way of determining whether the measurable effects on brain organization represent a positive or negative impact of intervention. This can only be assessed clinically, and it is such assessments, not brain activation patterns, that must remain the gold standard. It would serve no one's interest to say that we have corrected an abnormality on a picture of the brain without having also corrected it in the brain's owner.

The awesome potential of brain imaging maneuvers its way into other areas of neuropsychological dysfunction with a similar line of reasoning. A recent study of a homosexual pedophile using brain imaging (Dressing et al., 2001) purportedly demonstrated a specific part of the brain that was activated when the subject viewed provocative photographs. A different pattern of activation was seen in normal controls. The authors suggested that future research investigate whether the effectiveness of treatment of homosexual pedophilia could be assessed by comparing brain images before and after the intervention. But certainly one would consider such individuals to have been helped only if their behavior changed, no matter what happened to the brain images.

The digital culture that we now live in is in obsequious awe of the power of high technology. Televised images of high-technology warfare have demonstrated its capacity to inflict death and destruction at the mere push of a button hundreds of miles from the target. Neuroimaging itself uses the most advanced software and hardware technology available to study the brain during various cognitive activities. In fact, as pointed out by Vicente Navarro (1993, pp. 25–26), the same corporations that manufacture high-tech medical equipment, including neuroimaging machines, also manufacture high-tech military equipment. In particular, General Electric, at the time of Navarro's writing, ranked number 6 in contracts with the Pentagon, and number 2 in production of nuclear reactors, and was one of the leading manufacturers of neuroimaging scanners. Conceptually, it is as if the equivalent of satellite-guided smart bombs were searching out areas of the brain of interest to cognitive scientists. Almost by might-makes-right default, such impressive power casts high-technology research as valid simply in virtue of the strength of the technology itself, regardless of what is studied, or how it is studied. This intimidating aspect of the technology, which is appreciable, no doubt contributes to the illusion that it can one day replace basic, real-life clinical assessment.

Thus, when mainstream media outlets, such as *The Baltimore Sun* (1997), show front-page pictures of NICHD personalities pointing to neuroimages of reading, and have headlines that proclaim "The Brain Reads Sound by Sound" (1997), its impact on lay opinion should not be underestimated. Powerful technology props up the image of "science."

But the government, insofar as its representatives are among those forces pushing a "scientific" approach to reading, is in a very curious predicament. Consider its "decade of the brain," announced via presidential proclamation 6156 on July 17, 1990 by former President George Bush, Sr. Bush began by stating that "the human brain, a 3-pound mass of interwoven nerve cells that controls our activity, is one of the most magnificent—and mysterious—wonders of creation" (par. 1). Most biologists and neuroscientists, however, would instead refer to the human brain as the most advanced achievement of biological evolution. Bush's spin betrays a sensitivity to his perceived constituency, and therefore a more subtle political message. The message is the ironic, inherently contradictory need to boost the public's acceptance of "science," while at the same time making sure that this is an unquestioned, uncritical, that is, unscientific acceptance. Such scientific fundamentalism can be stimulated by massaging other fundamentalist ways of thinking, such as that which underlies adherence to creationism. So we have Bush's allusion thereto, as well as another *Baltimore Sun* headline, which read, "Phonics Paves Christian Way" (1998).

Government interest in high-tech studies of the human brain was already present in 1989, a year before Bush's proclamation, when, "in response to a request from the U.S. Army Research Institute (ARI), a National Research Council (NRC) committee was formed to undertake, over a one-year period, a study of new technologies in cognitive psychophysiology, particularly with respect to potential applications to military problems" (Druckman & Lacey, 1991, p. 5). The ARI was specifically interested in "develop[ing] measures of brain activity during cognition, already studied under laboratory conditions, to be used as indices in personnel selection and training in the military context" (p. 2). In its report, it noted that "promising possibilities exist in the monitoring of the direction of attention, in the measurement of mental workload, and in monitoring performance in missions of long duration" (p. 2).

The committee reviewed a number of high-tech instruments for studying human cognition, including positron emission tomography (PET), functional magnetic resonance imaging (fMRI), evoked response potentials (ERP), and magnetoencephalography (MEG). It recommended "the simultaneous and complementary use of the technologies" and "that data be obtained on the range of variability in functional and structural maps across and within individuals" (Druckman & Lacey, 1991, p. 2).

Most interestingly, the committee also recommended that "any major agency involved in personnel training would be well advised to participate in research programs that either contribute to or keep them abreast of advances in the field" (Druckman & Lacey, 1991, p. 1). In this regard, it is not hard to imagine corporate drooling over the possibility of neuroimaging studies of reading and other cognitive activities being used to solve problems of "personnel selection and training," by assisting in finding individuals who possess cognitive traits that promise to yield the most advanced levels of brain labor productivity.

The Army Research Institute's committee consisted of the following scientists: John I. Lacey, Emanuel Donchin, Michael S. Gazzaniga, Lloyd Kaufman, Stephen M. Kosslyn, Marcus E. Raichle, and Daniel Druckman. Among the more prominent of these members was Marcus Raichle, a neurologist at Washington University and seminal researcher in high-tech neuroimaging studies of the human brain. In 1994, Raichle and his colleague Michael Posner, from the University of Oregon, published *Images of Mind* (Posner & Raichle, 1994), which won the American Psychological Association's book of the year award.

In this book, Posner and Raichle (1994) reviewed their work, and that of others, in using positron emission tomography (PET) scanning to study human cognition. The book is actually a wonderfully readable account of their research and is filled with stunning artwork and photography. The main cognitive activity discussed by Raichle and Posner is what they refer to as "reading."

For Raichle and Posner, *reading*, at least operationally, is the identification of letters and words. But their main concern is what parts of the brain are used in these activities. To this end, their studies relied on a well-known physiologic property of the human brain, that blood flow varies according to the brain sites being used. Thus, by injecting the blood of a subject with a tracer chemical, one that can be detected by PET technology, pictures can be taken that show the location of the tracer during specific cognitive acts. Technically, then, such pictures are really of blood flow, but what is inferred is that the site of this blood flow contains an area of special cognitive interest.

Because tracer chemicals used in PET scanning pose some potential health risk, PET is no longer the technology of choice to study the brain localization of cognitive acts. Instead, functional magnetic resonance imaging (fMRI) is used. This technique relies on the machine's ability to detect changes in oxygen consumption in brain tissue, which varies in location, depending on the current brain task. Because the oxygen is naturally present in the blood, no radioactive tracer or other foreign agent need be injected. And the magnetic field generated by the machine is thought to be without significant health risk. Therefore, fMRI has become widely used in research studies, especially among pediatric-age subjects.

The principles underlying the methodology used in both PET and fMRI, and in virtually all neuroimaging, are identical. It is crucially important to understand that, in using the technology, it is not enough to simply ask a subject to read something, whether a word, sentence, or other input stimulus. The picture taken by PET scanning will show where the tracer travels during this activity, and the picture taken by fMRI will show where oxygen is consumed. But both the itinerary of the tracer and the consumption of oxygen occur in far more parts of the brain than just the sites where reading supposedly occurs. This is because the brain simultaneously performs other activities while it reads. It performs these, in fact, to support reading. For example, it regulates level of arousal, attentiveness to task, and general aspects of visual perception and processing that underlie any visual task. Indeed, even when the brain is resting, many areas still light up. Therefore, PET and fMRI images of reading simultaneously highlight other areas of the brain as well.

This phenomenon is depicted in Fig. 7.1, a rough, schematic rendition that I have drawn, adapted from the PET image generated by Posner and Raichle (1994, p. 80) from subjects reading real words aloud, such as *ant, razor, dust, furnace, mother,* and *farm.* Darkened areas indicate brain regions undergoing increased blood flow during the performance of the task. In Posner and Raichle's PET scan images of the oral reading of single words, both the left and right hemispheres of the brain are activated, with a predominance seen in the posterior part of the left hemisphere. But since reading the words aloud requires that the brain simultaneously regulate a certain level of arousal, attention to the task, and general visual processing, all of these functions will also generate brain areas that light up on the imaging scan. Therefore, mere inspection of the scan does not yet tell us which area is uniquely devoted to reading.

Even comparing a task-related image to some resting state is not unproblematic. This problem has been nicely summarized by Krasuski, Horwitz, and Rumsey (1996, p. 34):

> When a complex task (e.g., a complex language task demanding focused attention, reading, verbal generation, changes in categorical set, signaling with button presses) is compared with a resting state, it is not clear which variables or mental operations account for the differences in images. As a result, as experimental designs associated with brain imaging have become more sophisticated, the challenge has focused on methods for fractionating tasks into individual components that can be manipulated systematically one at a time.

In other words, identifying a reading-specific area requires finding a way to cancel out from the complex brain images just those areas that are felt to not specifically represent reading, which only support reading. Then, at least logically, what is left over is a picture of that part of the brain dedicated to reading. The technique used to accomplish this feat is called *subtraction methodology.*

This is not as easy as it might appear. In order to subtract out the extraneous images, what we really need, at the very least, is a picture of just those

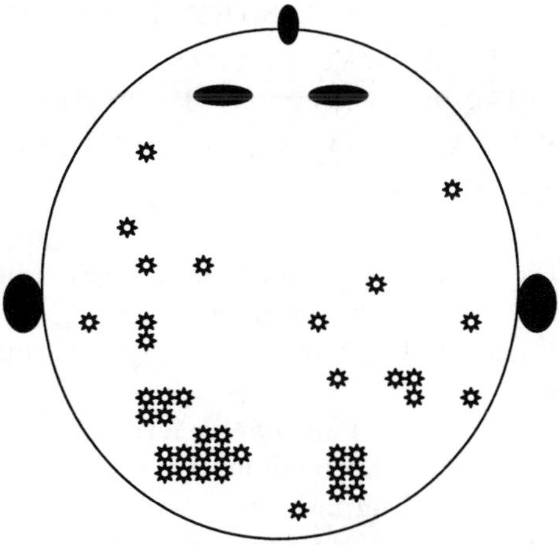

FIG. 7.1. Brain image for real words.

parts of the brain that are activated during arousal, attentiveness, and general visual processing, that is, of everything else the brain is doing during reading. In principle, erasing the latter image from that obtained during reading will show where reading occurs.

However, it is simply not possible to have a subject perform a cognitive task that only involves a certain level of arousal, with a certain level of attentiveness, and with general aspects of visual processing, without actually doing something specific. Indeed, attentiveness means paying attention to a specific task. Arousal, attentiveness, and general visual processing are recruited in the service of particular acts.

In other words, it is not possible to directly generate the second of the two neuroimages needed to solve the following subtraction equation:

$$\begin{array}{rr} & \text{READING} + \text{AROUSAL} + \text{ATTENTION} + \text{VISUAL PROCESSING} \\ - & \underline{\text{AROUSAL} + \text{ATTENTION} + \text{VISUAL PROCESSING}} \\ & \text{READING} \qquad\qquad\qquad\qquad\qquad\qquad\qquad\qquad\qquad \end{array}$$

Although we may be able to generate a neuroimage for the first line, we absolutely cannot for the subtrahend in the second line, because there is no such thing as isolated arousal, attention, and visual processing. Thus, our desired image of reading is not yet producible.

What is needed, therefore, is a subtrahend that constitutes a specific task. But this creates yet another problem, for if the task performed during reading and the task performed when not reading are sufficiently different, then their respective levels of arousal attentiveness, and general visual processing may be significantly different:

READING + AROUSAL 1 + ATTENTION 1 + VISUAL PROCESSING 1
– TASK 2 + AROUSAL 2 + ATTENTION 2 + VISUAL PROCESSING 2
(READING – TASK 2) + (AROUSAL 1 – AROUSAL 2) + (ATTENTION 1 – ATTENTION 2) + (VISUAL PROCESSING 1 – VISUAL PROCESSING 2)

For such distinct levels of arousal, attention, and visual processing, distinct areas of the brain may be activated, and it will once again not be possible to obtain an image of reading simply by subtracting out arousal, attentiveness, and visual processing.

Therefore, what we need is a *subtractible* level of arousal, attentiveness, and visual processing. To be subtractible, it must be essentially equivalent to that obtained on the reading task. In practice, this means that the task whose neuroimage will be subtracted from that of the reading task must be as close as possible to the reading task itself. Then, as a consequence of this psychological propinquity, and by hypothesis, this second task will recruit equivalent levels of arousal, attentiveness, and visual processing.

So now we have two tasks, roughly equivalent in arousal, attentiveness, and visual processing. We will be able to subtract the arousal, attentiveness, and visual processing of the second task from that of the reading task. The neuroimage of the reading task will show areas of the brain that represent activated reading, along with arousal, attentiveness, and visual processing. The neuroimage of the second task, needed in order to generate a subtractible image, will show areas of the brain that represent that task, and its associated arousal, attentiveness, and visual processing as well. If AROUSAL 1 = AROUSAL 2, ATTENTION 1 = ATTENTION 2, AND VISUAL PROCESSING 1 = VISUAL PROCESSING 2, then the subtraction problem becomes the following:

READING + AROUSAL 1 + ATTENTION 1 + VISUAL PROCESSING 1
– TASK 2 + AROUSAL 2 + ATTENTION 2 + VISUAL PROCESSING 2
READING – TASK 2

In this way, we can successfully subtract out arousal, attention, and visual processing. But now, how do we interpret READING – TASK 2?

This is a potentially serious problem, because the interpretation of READING – TASK 2 will make no sense whatsoever if the tasks are sufficiently distinct, even when they recruit equivalent levels of arousal, attention, and general visual processing. For example, what does <READING *ANT, FARM*>$^{\text{Task 1}}$ – <THINKING ABOUT CHESS MOVE>$^{\text{Task 2}}$ mean?

The solution to this problem is to devise two tasks for the subject, both of which are presumed to recruit the same levels of arousal, attention, and visual processing, thereby allowing these to be subtracted out of the neuroimage, but which differ in that one task is thought to represent a component subtask of the other. Then, subtracting the subtask from the main task, or the "control task" from the "target task," will reveal a definable cognitive operation. This cognitive operation is the one that allows the brain to distinguish between the control task and the target task. And, if the two tasks are claimed to play a role in reading, then the cognitive operation that distinguishes the two also plays such a role.

For example, suppose identifying a real, written word involves, in part, the identification of the component letters of the word's spelling. As reiterated earlier, this will require a certain level of arousal, attention, and general visual processing. Now suppose further that identifying letters involves a cognitive operation that determines that the letters are not false fonts, such as ˥, ⊥, and ¬. These tasks, for the sake of argument, involve equal amounts of arousal, attention, and general visual processing. Then, we can subtract the neuroimage obtained by having a subject "read" false fonts from that obtained by having the subject "read" real letters:

REAL LETTERS + AROUSAL 1 + ATTENTION 1 + VISUAL PROCESSING 1
– FALSE FONTS + AROUSAL 2 + ATTENTION 2 + VISUAL PROCESSING 2
____
REAL LETTERS – FALSE FONTS

The derived neuroimage, obtained by subtraction, represents some presumed cognitive operation that allows a reader to distinguish real letters from false fonts.

Similarly, having identified real letters, a string of real letters, such as *zyhv*, can be distinguished from another string, such as *zorp*, in that the former is an essential orthographic nonword, whereas the latter is a possible orthographic word, or pseudoword. Then, neuroimages formed by having a subject read nonwords can be subtracted from neuroimages formed by having subjects read pseudowords to identify the part of the brain that plays a role in the presumed cognitive operation that allows this distinction to be made. The next step in this type of research would be to subtract images obtained by having a subject read pseudowords from those obtained by having a subject read real words, in order to identify the part of the brain that plays a role in the presumed cognitive operation that allows this distinction to be made.

Posner and Raichle (1994) present neuroimages based on precisely this paradigm. The schematics in Figs. 7.2 through 7.4, in conjunction with the schematic in Fig. 7.1 for real words, are based on their PET images and correspond to the four types of visual stimuli used in their experiments (p. 80). Posner and Raichle pointed out that, as revealed by their PET images, the oral reading of both single words and pseudowords preferentially recruits

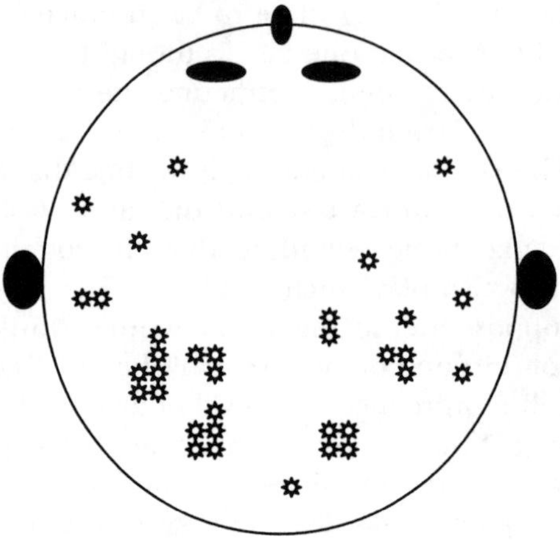

FIG. 7.2. Pseudowords.

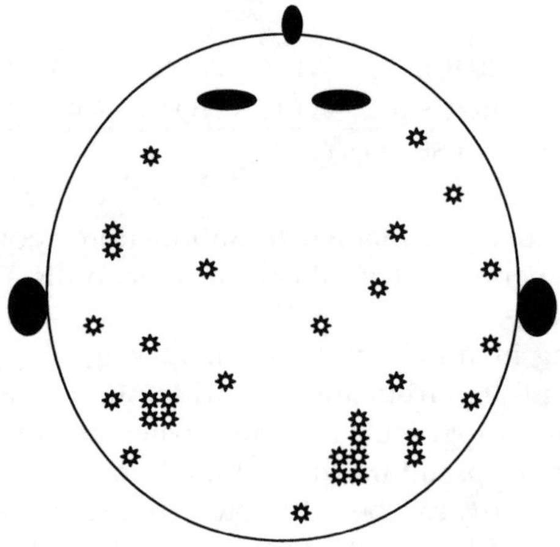

FIG. 7.3. Letter strings.

the left hemisphere, whereas that of letter strings and false fonts preferentially recruits the right.

Now, if we were to subsequently subtract the activated areas of one image from that of another, a purely manufactured and artificial image could be created, itself not generated from the real-time performance of a single task by an actual subject, but that logically may represent the cognitive operation that allegedly distinguishes the task associated with the one image from the task associated with the other. For example, a hypothetical subtraction of the scan for pseudowords from that for real words will reveal the

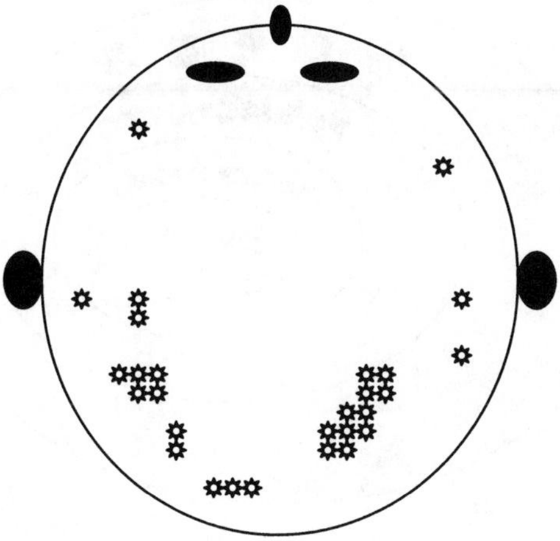

FIG. 7.4. False fonts.

parts of the brain that are specifically recruited in the cognitive operation that distinguishes the former from the latter. A rough approximation of this is shown in Fig. 7.5. The actual complexity and problems involved in performing these maneuvers have been discussed by a number of authors (cf., e.g., Krasuski et al., 1996). A focal brain region may participate in a number of different circuits, and activated areas may actually be inhibiting other areas. These problems notwithstanding, by judiciously selecting subtraction sets, or stimuli that lie successively within one another, a sequence

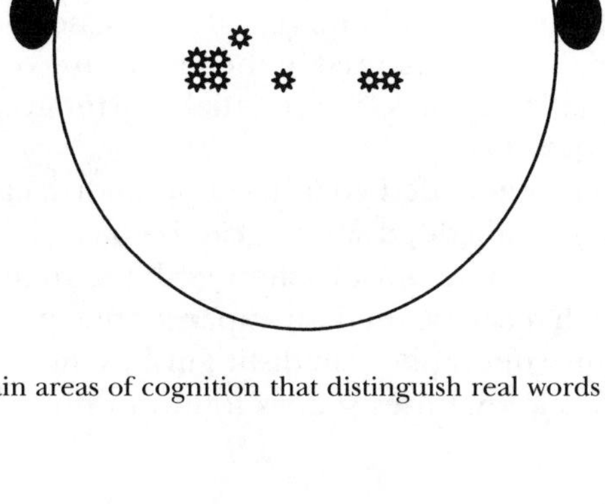

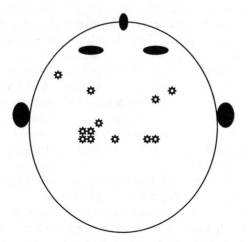

FIG. 7.5. Brain areas of cognition that distinguish real words from pseudowords.

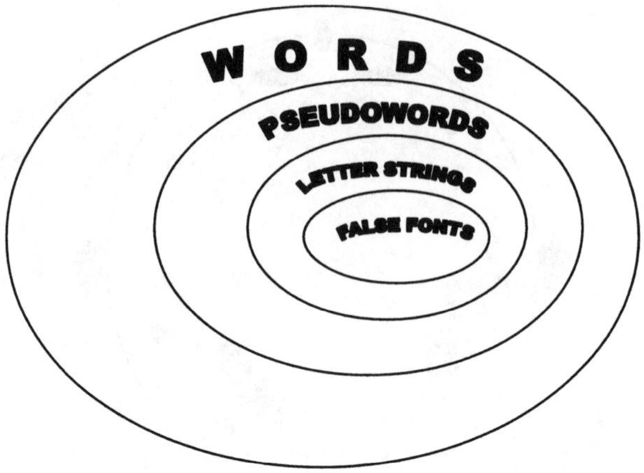

FIG. 7.6. Stimuli for generating brain images.

of microcognitive operations can be reconstructed that, it is claimed, leads to word recognition.

The successively embedded sets of stimuli used by Posner and Raichle (1994) can be depicted as in Fig. 7.6. Each ring in Fig. 7.6 represents a set of stimuli, as well as a brain image produced by that stimulus type. Cognitive processes allow passage from one ring to the next.

In a similar manner, Shaywitz et al. (1996, p. 89) employed the subtraction methodology to study a set of concentrically embedded stimuli in order to identify brain regions involved in cognitive operations that purportedly play a role in reading. Distinct stimulus types, we are again told, "engage" specific types of cognitive "processes." For example, the sequence of lines / / \ / engages "visuospatial" processes. The image showing brain regions identified in the processing of such stimuli can be subtracted from the image identified in the processing of stimuli that engage "visuospatial + orthographic" information, such as strings of mixed upper and lower case letters, such as *BtBT*. This image can be subtracted from the one obtained in the processing of a stimulus such as *LETE*, which allegedly engages "visuospatial + orthographic + phonological" processes. And this image can be subtracted from the one obtained in the processing of a stimulus such as *CORN*, which allegedly engages "visuospatial + orthographic + phonological + semantic" processes.

These successively embedded cognitive operations, each one tapped by means of successively embedded stimuli, can be pictured as in Fig. 7.7. Notice, though, that there is no obvious limit to the number or type of sets of subtraction stimuli that can be used for experimental purposes. Why not investigate the cognitive operation that distinguishes the processing of an impossible false font, one that uses shapes found in no orthographic system

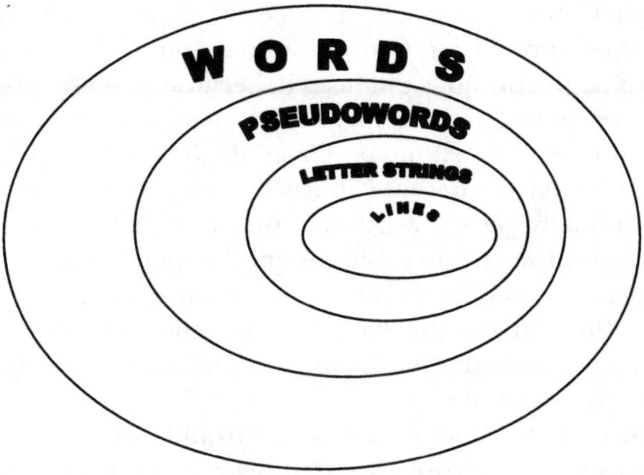

FIG. 7.7. Embedded cognitive operations (adapted from Shaywitz et al., 1996).

(such as representations of three-dimensional cubes or spheres) from possible false fonts? The potentially unconstrained proliferation of sets of subtraction stimuli immediately raises the question of whether the presumed cognitive operations corresponding to them are indeed central to reading, or simply products of a researcher's clever imagination. Indeed, it demands that this question be addressed.

Deciding whether a subtraction set corresponds to some real aspect of the reading process, or is merely a piece in an otherwise irrelevant mental puzzle, can only be based on evaluating it against an independently developed, empirically grounded theory of reading. If such a theory of reading can point to evidence that real readers need to know how to recognize false fonts, for example, then this would lend some validity to the subtraction set in which such fonts are found. But without an independent theory that is firmly grounded in studies of real readers reading authentic texts, a model of reading that is based solely on the methodology demanded by some technology will merely recapitulate that methodology, and represent nothing more than an illusion of theory. The bottom-up, or inside-out, method of data collection will be confused for the nature of cognitive processing. Students of linguistics will immediately recall that what passed for theory in the days of the behaviorist-inspired, structuralist taxonomic classification was really nothing more than a description of the methodology used to obtain data, not really a theory about how language works. It was rejected in favor of generative grammar, which understood the distinction between the method of data collection and the theory of grammar that could then generate the data (Halle, 1959; Harris, 1951).

Unfortunately, this is precisely the theoretical problem with subtraction sets. It should be appreciated that the subtraction methodology is a necessary artifact of the technology that uses it, because brain functions that support but are not themselves reading, such as maintaining wakefulness or attending to a task, must be eliminated from the image if we are to ultimately obtain a picture that represents "pure" reading. Successive subtractions must occur to finally get to "word identification." Thus, the technology is really suitable only for studying cognitive microoperations, because the narrower the microoperations, the closer is the subtrahend to what it is subtracted from, thus further justifying the hypothesized, and methodologically necessary, equivalence of arousal, attentiveness, and general visual processing in the two tasks.

Larger processes are bound to run into trouble sooner or later. For example, the presumed macroprocess that ties pronouns to their antecedent referents across a text may be identified using stimulus pairs such as the following:

Task 1: John went shopping. Then John went home.
Task 2: John went shopping. Then he went home.

But in larger and larger texts, with numerous uses of the pronoun, and variable lengths separating them, the confounding interaction between the target macroprocess and other micro- and macroprocesses, not to mention qualitative and quantitative differences in arousal, attention, and visual processing, will surely render difficult, if not impossible, the determination of the cognitive operation that presumably distinguishes the processing of one text from another.

As a consequence of these methodological contingencies, Posner and Raichle (1994), along with other neuroimaging researchers, constructed experimental paradigms that identify finer and finer grades of phonological and other linguistic processing, so that image subtraction is akin to shaving off successive layers of cognitive activity. In their studies, Posner and Raichle identified the layered cognitive operations involved in word identification via phonological processing, and showed how neuroimages obtained from tasks given to subjects can be subtracted one from the other. Each successive task is designed to get at a finer grade of cognitive processing, so that embedded in more complex tasks are the simpler ones. At the very simplest level of processing, we have the visual determination of false fonts. At the next higher level, we have the visual processing of real letters. Higher still, we have the visual processing of essential nonwords, followed by pseudowords, and then, finally, real words.

But, as pointed out earlier, the methodological contingencies of the technology rule out the possibility of studying larger macrocategories of reading, such as aspects of connected text processing. This is because, with increasing complexity of the text, it becomes more and more difficult, indeed impossible, to identify the single cognitive operation that distinguishes that text's processing from the processing of some simpler text, and so on until we reach the level of false fonts and letters, all the while preserving equivalent levels of arousal, attention, and general visual processing.

We have seen that it is precisely the confounding problem of arousal, attention, and general visual processing, and the desire to eliminate their contribution to PET and fMRI images, that leads to the subtraction methodology. Arousal, attentiveness, and general visual processing constitute a type of background noise in the system, which needs to be filtered out in order to identify the signal of interest.

The signal that is left over once the background noise is eliminated has a definable characteristic to the extent that the control task and the target task are conceptually related to each other. But the subtraction of one from the other can only occur if their respective levels of background noise are equivalent. And this is more readily achieved the briefer the control and target events are, as we have seen. In this way, the technology of neuroimaging studies only very brief events, each of which is thought to represent a component subprocess of reading.

Looked at still another way, we can say that neuroimaging technology is, in effect, a highly advanced camera that takes still pictures of the active brain, where picture clarity is achieved only insofar as the exposure time is shortened. The shutter speed must be very fast, not longer in duration than several hundred milliseconds. If the exposure time is increased, the pictures become more and more fuzzy.

When a technology continuously monitors a cognitive event, one that may proceed over seconds, minutes, or even longer, we say that such technology is engaged in on-line processing. It is apparent that neuroimaging technology, despite its sophistication, is incapable of studying reading online. Instead, it takes snapshots. At best, an illusion of on-line monitoring can be obtained by splicing together a series of neurosnapshots, each one representing a successive microevent. The cognitive operations that identify false fonts, real letters, pseudowords, and real words generate pictures that can be sequenced this way:

FALSE FONTS → REAL LETTERS → PSEUDOWORDS → REAL WORDS

And an even better illusion might be created if we identify finer and finer layers of cognitive activity. So, the distinction between false fonts and real letters might be accomplished by series of cognitive operations that successively identify impossible false fonts, then possible false fonts, then partial English letters based on lines and curves, then actual English letters.

In this manner, an even more "realistic" motion picture of word reading can be constructed:

> IMPOSSIBLE FONTS → POSSIBLE FONTS → PARTIAL LETTERS → REAL LETTERS → PSEUDOWORDS → REAL WORDS

As with motion pictures, such a sequence is not a true continuous event, though it perceptually appears to be. The close sequencing of neuro-snapshots creates the illusion of on-line monitoring.

As observed earlier, however, there is no limit, in principle, to the distinctions that can be made in identifying cognitive operations that can be studied with neuroimaging. Actually, the limit is only that of our imaginations. What is fundamentally lacking in this pseudoscience is any empirical argument that the task of distinguishing false fonts from real fonts, or pseudowords from real words, plays a fundamental role in reading.

It is therefore entirely premature to proclaim neuroimaging the new gold standard in reading assessment. Neuroimaging technology is inherently and fundamentally limited, insofar as it can only study very brief events. It cannot study events of relatively long duration. And it absolutely cannot study reading on-line. In other words, it is physically incapable of "simply and broadly studying reading."

Yet, whereas it is one thing to use neuroimaging to study phonological processing, all the while understanding and acknowledging its inherent technical limitations, it is quite another matter to identify the narrow constraints of the technology with the fundamental cognitive operation of reading, and to imply that simply and broadly studying reading, an enterprise that would necessitate an alternative to neuroimaging, is just a distraction from the gold standard.

In other words, the NICHD proceeds as if it does not matter that the technology it uses to study reading has severe, inherent limitations. Phonological processing is the core process, neuroimaging is the best measure of phonological processing, and we therefore do not need to study anything else. Instead of acknowledging that its methodology is incapable of simply and broadly studying reading, the NICHD acts as if there is no theoretical reason for simply and broadly studying reading.

Thus, whereas we earlier identified an essential distortion of NICHD reading theory as due to its misguided adaptation to a political agenda, as well as to a misguided bearhug embrace of a supposedly nonnegotiable alphabetic principle, we now can identify a further distortion that is due to the misguided adaptation of the theory to the physical limitations of one of its research tools. The tool cannot simply and broadly study reading, so its proponents declare that does not need to be studied, that such study is a distraction. Nowhere else in science is the theory no more advanced than the tools used to study it.

For those interested in microprocesses, neuroimaging is truly a fascinating technique, one whose inherent limitations are the mirror image of its virtues, curiously similar in this way to human nature. But for those who are also interested in macroprocesses, its inherent limitations render it a purely subordinate, ancillary technique, to be judged against reading that is, indeed, simply and broadly studied.

Part III

RECLAIMING THE SCIENCE OF PHONICS

By that hid way my guide and I withal,
Back to the lit world from the darkened dens
Toiled upward, caring for no rest at all,

He first, I following; till my straining sense
Glimpsed the bright burden of the heavenly cars
Through a round hole; by this we climbed, and thence

Came forth, to look once more upon the stars.
—Dante (1949, pp. 288–289)

Chapter 8

Three Definitions of *Phonics*

The centerpiece of neophonics, its alleged scientific raison d'être, is the alphabetic principle. Though described as a principle that connects letters of the alphabet with sounds of the spoken language, the alphabetic principle actually underlies three distinct ways of defining and understanding phonics: (a) as an abstract system of rules that converts letters to sounds, which may or may not be known (epistemology); (b) as a system of rules that must be learned in order to become known (psychology); and (c) as a system of rules that must be taught in order to become learned (pedagogy). Despite being interrelated, these are conceptually and empirically distinct notions.

It may be possible to characterize some abstract cognitive system by identifying its properties and governing principles, without in any way implying that the system needs to be either learned or taught. It may be present, for example, as innate knowledge, perhaps in an immature form requiring exposure to a sufficiently rich environment in order to grow. This, in fact, is the philosophical understanding of Chomskyan grammatical systems (Chomsky, 1965, 1975).

We may be able to characterize some abstract cognitive system, and even argue compellingly that it does not develop from an innate endowment, but must rather be learned in order for it to become known. But this does not entail that it must be taught in order to be learned. Again, appropriate exposure to the system, or its real-life manifestations, may trigger ordinary learning mechanisms that promote its acquisition.

Finally, we may be able to characterize some abstract cognitive system, and argue compellingly that it is not innate, and furthermore, that the only way to learn it is for it to be explicitly taught. Clearly, these are three distinct empirical scenarios.

Though distinct, however, the three scenarios are hierarchically interrelated. Obviously, the existence of the abstract cognitive system must be assumed in order to validly argue that it must be learned, or both learned and taught. And, just as obviously, if it does not need to be learned, it certainly does not need to be taught.

These three scenarios underlie the real intent and meaning of Lyon's (*Testimony of G. Reid Lyon*, 1997, par. 11) assertion that the alphabetic principle, the systematic connection between the letters of the alphabet and the sounds of speech, is "non-negotiable." The principle, which identifies an abstract system, operates purely at the level of epistemology. The fundamental claim of the neophonics community is that letter-sound relationships must be known in order for someone to be a reader. But by itself, this says nothing one way or the other about whether it needs to be learned or taught. These are empirical questions, and represent supplemental claims that are not part of the actual formulation of the alphabetic principle.

But Lyon (*Testimony of G. Reid Lyon*, 1997) extended the notion of nonnegotiability of the alphabetic principle from epistemology to psychology and pedagogy. He asserted that letter-sound relationships must not only be known in order for someone to be a competent reader, but, in addition, they must be learned in order to be known, and taught in order to be learned. And the argument for doing this is based on the premise of the supposed "unnaturalness" of both the alphabetic principle and learning to read.

Thus, in order to make the case that phonological processing must be explicity and directly taught, Lyon (1998) argued that it cannot be acquired naturally:

> Programmatic research over the past 35 years *has not* supported the view that reading development reflects a *natural process*—that children learn to read as they learn to speak, through natural exposure to a literate environment. Indeed, researchers have established that certain aspects of learning to read are highly unnatural. Consider the linguistic gymnastics involved in recovering phonemes from speech and applying them to letters and letter patterns. Unlike learning to speak, beginning readers must appreciate consciously what the symbols stand for in the writing system they learn. . . . Unfortunately for beginning readers, written alphabetic symbols are arbitrary and are created differently in different languages to represent spoken language elements that are themselves abstract. If learning to read were natural, there would not exist the substantial number of cultures that have yet to develop a written language, despite having a rich oral language. And, if learning to read unfolds naturally, why does our literate society have so many youngsters and adults who are illiterate? (p. 16)

Thus, for Lyon (1998), there are at least two aspects of learning to read that demonstrate its unnatural character, and that thereby necessitate formal instruction. The first is phonemic awareness, the notion that skilled readers must be conscious of the component sounds of words, in order, ultimately, to connect them to letters of the printed form. The development of such conscious knowledge is not a natural phenomenon, and must be explicitly taught. The second is the alphabetic writing system itself, which is a late human invention that has found its way into many, though not all, cultures.

Lyon (1998) offered an indictment of advocates of natural reading development:

> Despite strong evidence to the contrary, many educators and researchers maintain the perspective that reading is an almost instinctive, natural process. They believe that explicit instruction in phoneme awareness, phonics, structural analysis, and reading comprehension strategies is unnecessary because oral language skills provide the reader with a meaning-based structure for the decoding and recognition of unfamiliar words. . . . (p. 16)

Further, quoting researcher Keith Stanovich, he impugned the scholarly integrity of meaning-centered researchers: "The idea that learning to read is just like learning to speak is accepted by no responsible linguist, psychologist, or cognitive scientist in the research community" (p. 16).

The kindest interpretation of Lyon's (1998) resort to Stanovich's gratuitous opinion is that he holds descriptive, nonexperimental research to be insufficiently "trustworthy," so that those who advocate such untrustworthy research must not be "responsible." But even the advocacy of untrustworthy research should warrant nothing more than a critique of the empirical and research claims. A willingness to jab at the integrity of meaning-centered reading researchers must be a reflection of something more than the scientific issues.

For example, it may reflect a defensiveness against the potent threat that meaning-centered research poses to the experimentalist's paradigm and the associated political agenda of neophonics. It may represent a comment intended to intimidate those teachers who find themselves sympathetic to meaning-centered reading theory and practice. Indeed, when one considers neophonics as a legally mandated paradigm, that is, as a *political program,* then opponents must be cleared from the scene in order to minimize political obstacles that stand in its way. The tactics used to clear away political opponents are, unfortunately, not the same as those used to debate mere scientific adversaries.

The essential correctness of this way of understanding Stanovich's and Lyon's (1998) charge of irresponsibility against meaning-centered reading researchers can be appreciated by considering that meaning-centered reading enjoys vast support among classroom teachers. In Chapter 1, for example, it was pointed out that the 70,000-member National Council of Teachers of English has taken a position in its favor, and against the position of the NICHD, regarding letter-sound decoding as holding no privileged position in either the theory or practice of reading.

The notion of natural reading development is a real and potent threat to advocates of neophonics, because it strongly suggests that, instead of overwhelming our classrooms with direct instruction of phonics, and perhaps wasting billions of dollars on irrelevant phonics materials, we focus on creating social conditions that help promote this natural development. But this, in turn, demands a reconsideration of our nation's political and economic priorities, because it will certainly include the view that poverty itself, in the setting of extreme discrepancies between the rich and the poor, is the *primary* crisis from which illiteracy and other social ills follow. Confronting illiteracy will mean confronting the causes of poverty, and more equitably distributing society's wealth.

Apart from these political considerations, though, Lyon and Stanovich (Lyon, 1998) appear to not understand the meaning-centered view of learning to read. There is, in principle, no necessary conflict between a naturalistic understanding of learning to read and a role for some type of direct instruction. For example, just as there may be a neurologically based "critical stage" for learning to speak (Lenneberg, 1967), past which learning perhaps becomes unnatural and difficult, so too might there be a critical stage for learning to read naturally, past which some type of instruction may be necessary. But this is an empirical issue, not yet on the NICHD's reading research agenda.

Indeed, the NICHD hints at a recognition of the comparability between learning to speak and learning to read, in terms of there being such a critical stage. The NICHD has repeatedly emphasized that children who fail to learn how to read past the age of 9 are destined to remain nonreaders. "We have also learned that if we delay intervention until nine years of age (the time that most children with reading difficulties receive services), approximately 75% of the children will continue to have difficulties learning to read throughout high school," testified Lyon (*Testimony of G. Reid Lyon,* 1998, par. 30). "Failure to develop basic reading skills by age nine predicts a lifetime of illiteracy," he testified later (*Testimony of G. Reid Lyon,* 2001, par. 10). This has become a matter of such urgency to the NICHD, that a focus of high priority is on identifying "children at risk" at as young an age as possible, in order to not lose any precious years when they could be enrolled in the proper phonological processing program. This urgency has been communicated to an accommodating and invertebrate popular press, which has been doing its part to promote the NICHD agenda. Thus, we have *The Balti-*

more Sun's and *The Los Angeles Times*' regularly appearing section entitled "Reading by Nine."

But observe that the NICHD, on this view, is putting the cart way before the horse. The notion that learning to read qualitatively changes by age 9 should immediately ring a bell that we may very well be dealing with a neurologically based critical stage phenomenon. Indeed, the NICHD has no other explanation for the age-9 phenomenon. Yet, if this is truly what we are dealing with, then programs that promote natural reading development should be put in place as early as possible, with direct instruction being considered for older children, not the other way around. The early measures would include maximizing real reading time in the classroom, enriching the classroom environment with authentic print, and immersing children in written language activities that are functional and meaningful.

Proponents of explicit phonics instruction typically argue that, because written alphabets are artificial technologies, not natural systems like oral language, they must be explicitly taught. But again there is no compelling basis for this logic. Flat surfaces such as wooden floors and paved sidewalks are unnatural. Does that mean that children must be taught how to walk on such surfaces, whereas they will learn to walk naturally if placed on pristine, rocky fields? The absurdity of this position becomes apparent with the observation that the artificial technology of flat surfaces probably makes learning to walk easier. Perhaps alphabetic writing systems are the flat surfaces of language, rendering the development of linguistic competence potentially simpler. Lack of timely exposure, not the technology itself, may be the culprit in certain types of reading problems, but this too is an empirical, not a purely logical, problem. Much of this, of course, remains speculative, but clearly points to the need to study the matter further.

There is also no contradiction between claiming that learning to read is natural and acknowledging the existence of nonliterate cultures and illiterate individuals in literate cultures. Certainly, no one disputes the notion that learning spoken language is natural, but this naturalness does not mean that learning will occur in the absence of the proper environmental exposure. When a biologically normal child is prevented from being exposed to, and interacting with, spoken language, the latter will simply not develop naturally, as unfortunate cases like Genie amply demonstrate (Curtiss, 1977). Physical growth occurs naturally, as long as it is exposed to the proper nutritional media. French is learned naturally, as long as you are exposed to it at the proper age.

Likewise, no advocate of natural reading development has ever claimed that learning to read will arise spontaneously without proper environmental exposure. The phenomenon of illiteracy within a literate culture simply means that some children in that culture lack adequate access to environmental print and written language. The argument that a naturalistic view of reading entails the view that all cultures should have a written language is simply absurd. The only claim made by advocates of naturalistic learning is that *if* a written language has been developed by the culture, and *if* an individual has the proper exposure to it, then reading will be learned naturally.

And, finally, no advocate of meaning-centered reading and its naturalistic corollaries have ever claimed that there is no role for phonics in the theory and practice of reading. As the NCTE position paper (February, 1999) eloquently stated, letter-sound relationships are one of a number of resources available to readers in their interaction with written text as they attempt to construct meaning. When prompted by the reader's own negotiation of the text, a question regarding a letter-sound connection may be an entirely appropriate, and individualized, opportunity for instruction.

The neophonics panoply of illogic and confusion regarding the psychology and pedagogy of phonics is unfortunately not compensated for by any great insight about the system of phonics itself, other than to declare, without discussion, that it is a system, or that it is "elegant." In fact, some of the research reports used in the NRP meta-analysis show just how poorly thought through their notion of phonics actually is. By not investigating and studying their own subject matter, they mix together heterogeneous notions of phonics, and wind up comparing apples and oranges.

For example, in two of the research articles included in the NRP meta-analysis, Foorman and her coauthors (Foorman et al., 1991; Haskel et al., 1992) used a set of 60 stimulus words to test the effectiveness of letter-sound instruction on children's oral reading accuracy. The words were described as having either "regular" or "exceptional" spellings, but these notions were nowhere defined in the articles.

In trying to make sense of these terms, I asked why Foorman (Foorman et al., 1991; Haskel et al., 1992) characterized the 60 words the way she did (Strauss, 2003). For example, the word *phase* was listed as an exception. It cannot be on the basis of the voiced [z] pronunciation of the letter *s*, because *hose*, with the same [z] pronunciation, is labeled as regular. It cannot be on the basis of having a silent *e*, since *rate* and *fate* are regular. It can only be because of the initial *ph*. But what is the problem with this? I conjectured that the phonics rule turning *ph* into [f] is one in which the resulting sound derives from neither of the two letters in the digraph, because *p* generally becomes [p] and *h* generally becomes [h]. But Foorman listed *share* as regular, and *sh* exhibits this exact formal behavior, in which the pronunciation is neither [s] nor [h].

In response to this critique, Foorman et al. (2003) replied as follows:

> The exceptional words represent inconsistencies in sound/spelling mapping rather than the letter/sound correspondences to which Strauss refers. For example, Strauss correctly points to the regularity of the *ph* to /f/ correspon-

dence. However, the /f/ to *ph* mapping is less predictable because of the more frequent representation of /f/ by *f.* (p. 719)

But this immediately undermines the entire NRP meta-analysis project for phonics, because we now learn that the NRP was aware of the existence of different types of correspondences, yet we never find out whether the pooled studies were assessed along this parameter. Did all of the studies interrogate children with a sound-letter corpus of test stimuli, or did some use a letter-sound corpus? If the collection was heterogeneous, then there is a serious problem with pooling them together for a meta-analysis, because what counts as regular in a sound-letter system may not be regular in a letter-sound system, and likewise for exception words. In other words, they are *qualitatively* distinct types of correspondence systems, so the findings on studies of one do not automatically carry over to the other.

Here is how the difference shows itself. The word *comb* is exceptional in Foorman's (Foorman et al., 1991; Haskel et al., 1992) sound-letter system, presumably because *mb* is not the usual way to spell the sound [m]. But final *mb* is *always* pronounced [m]—there are no exceptions to this (*bomb, dumb, lamb, limb*)—so it is thoroughly regular from a letter-sound perspective.

The word *hose* is regular in Foorman's (Foorman et al., 1991; Haskel et al., 1992) system. But is *s* the "more frequent" spelling of the sound [z], rather than *z* itself? It certainly is not more frequent in word-initial position, as is obvious with examples like *zany, zip,* and *zoo.* So suppose we allow the frequency issue to apply to more restrictive alphabetic contexts. Then we can say that *s* is (perhaps) more frequent between vowels in single-syllable words with a final, silent *e,* as in *chose, rose, muse,* and *ruse.* But there are also words such as *base, close* (adverb), *dose,* and *house.*

Or consider a word such as *wind* (a stormy wind). This must be regular on Foorman's (Foorman et al., 1991; Haskel et al., 1992) spelling-sound account, because the more frequent spelling of the short [I] sound is with the letter *i.* But this word is actually an exception in the system of letter-sound rules, because the letter *i* in single-syllable words ending in *ind* is more frequently pronounced [ay]: *bind, find, grind, hind, kind, mind, rind,* and *wind* (wind a wristwatch). Therefore, *wind* (a stormy wind) is regular in a sound-letter system and exceptional in a letter-sound system.

Taken together, this means that the sound-letter system and the letter-sound system for English are not the same. They have distinct classes of regular and exception words. Therefore, studies such as Foorman's (Foorman et al., 1991; Haskel et al., 1992) that use the sound-letter system represent a *specific type* of phonics study, and cannot be legitimately regarded as a *generalizable type* of phonics study without further research into the matter. As far as I know, this has not been done. Clearly, this is one of the major theoretical flaws of the NRP meta-analysis.

Indeed, the entire NRP meta-analysis should be scrutinized for just what conception of correspondence systems was used in each of the pooled studies. If they were a heterogeneous gemisch of incomparable conceptions, letter-sound in one, sound-letter in another, mixed letter-sound and sound-letter in another, and perhaps even something altogether different in still another, then the NRP meta-analysis is scientifically meaningless. We simply do not know what it is about, no matter how loudly its sponsors might yell that it is a meta-analysis of phonics.

So, a rather remarkable aspect of neophonics is that, despite its self-described trustworthiness, it fails to be convincing in every important way—in epistemology, psychology, and pedagogy. There is, indeed, not even a scientific investigation of the alphabetic principle itself, its "nonnegotiable" law. Rather, the alphabetic principle is merely an article of faith, and stands as the subject matter of no empirical investigation whatsoever, neither in terms of what the letter-sound relationships actually are, nor in the logical organization of these relationships. Traditionally accepted correspondences are merely assumed, as if simplifications made for purposes of easing classroom instruction and writing phonics textbooks represent some type of scientific hypothesis. This is pseudoscience, not science, and pseudophonics, not scientific phonics.

The mere assertion of being "systematic" begs every single important question about phonics. Is the system that relates letters and sounds profoundly simple, profoundly complex, or somewhere in between? Is it learnable by known mechanisms of knowledge acquisition and development? Is it teachable in its unsimplified form, or must we distort it, perhaps beyond recognition, in order to make it classroom friendly? What principles characterize its systematicity?

These questions are crucial and need to be addressed, because strong claims are being made about the role the system plays in becoming a reader. What if we discover a level of complexity that challenges teachability? What if we discover aspects of letter-sound connections that are mediated by something other than the alphabetic principle, such as the logographic principle?

Thus, the necessary empirical investigation of letter-sound relationships, when performed with an eye toward understanding the system that underlies them, takes neophonics seriously on its own terms, in an area that is central ("nonnegotiable") to its own work, but which it has utterly ignored. Taking on this empirical task, in which letter-sound relationships are investigated independently of their potential role in learning and teaching, *in order to understand what it is that may need to be learned or taught,* is tantamount to reclaiming the science of phonics from its neophonics obfuscation.

An empirical analysis of letter-sound relationships is a theoretical prerequisite to any claims about its role in reading. Simply stated, we should know what it is we are talking about when we make bold claims that phonics must be taught, or that phonics is a nonnegotiable aspect of reading, or that phonics is better learned if the reader has a minimal level of phonemic awareness. Phonics, like validity and reliability, is a technical term.

Phonics, unlike religious dogma, is a phenomenon that requires ongoing, continual empirical investigation. The fact that it is steeped in classroom tradition does not protect it from this requirement. Likewise, traditional notions of grammar, the staple of many classroom language arts lessons, bear little resemblance to the results of modern empirical investigations of sentence structure that are universally recognized as landmark in how they have advanced our understanding not only of language, but also of the human mind itself.

Imagine if experimental studies in reading used categories of syntax that were traditional in the classroom, but utterly outmoded and irrelevant in scientific linguistics. We might then see studies about nouns that sought to determine whether a reader could recognize people, places, and things. Or, we might see studies about verbs that depended on a reader being able to recognize "action" words. Given what we have learned from empirical research on the structure and semantics of nouns and verbs, such studies would be nothing more than laughable.

Phonics could be a serious scientific subject, indeed a very interesting one, if the lessons of modern linguistics were applied to it, and deeper aspects of the rules were investigated, such as their formal properties and the nature of their mutual interactions. We would then even have a basis for carrying out legitimate phonics experiments, because we would at least know what the studies were about.

In this regard, the work of Richard Venezky (1999) stands alone in its importance and instructiveness. Venezky (p. 7) identified two formal properties of phonics rules that relate spellings to sounds. Some phonics rules turn a letter directly into a sound, such as the rules that turn *b* and *t* into the sounds [b] and [t], respectively, in the word *bit.* He refers to these rules as expressing a "relational" function: A rule *relates* a letter to a sound.

Other rules, however, do not turn letters into sounds, but rather "mark" one letter in the word as acquiring a new relational value under the influence of a second letter. Thus, silent *e* marks the preceding vowel as long, as in the word *bite.* Or, the letter *u* immediately following a *g* marks that *g* as hard, as in *guild* and *plague,* whereas it may be soft otherwise, as in *gin* and *page.*

Venezky's (1999) work expresses one aspect of the formal heterogeneity of phonics rules, and is based on an empirical observation about word spellings and corresponding sounds. Someone interested in the psychology of phonics could devise experiments that tested the sensitivity of subjects to the relational-marking distinction. We could further ask whether such a distinction played a role in reading. Empirically, we could investigate whether words dense with marking functions (e.g., *plague*) were more difficult to identify than words that were not (*bit*). Even from a descriptive standpoint, we could ask whether readers were more likely to produce miscues on words that were dense with marking functions. The answers, though, are not given in advance. These are empirical questions that require empirical investigations. And it would be no less empirically interesting to discover that, whereas relational and marking functions played a role in the phonics system, they played no distinctive role in reading.

As neophonics advocates have asserted that the alphabetic principle expresses a systematic relationship between letters and sounds, we can evaluate this notion by asking empirically based questions that directly address the properties of the presumed system. For example, Venezky's (1999) relational and marking functions operate at the level of the system, even though they are properties of individual rules, because they represent two general categories, one of which any particular phonics rule must fall into. And their empirical character is demonstrated in the observation that they do not exhaust the logically possible types of phonics rules. For example, we can imagine rules that identify the function of one letter as marking a second letter to mark a third letter, though such rules have been neither identified nor proposed. Or, we can imagine phonics rules that operate not on letters, but on the sounds that have been created from letters by previously applied rules.

Another approach to understanding phonics as a system is to look for evidence that bears on questions about how phonics rules interact. Do the rules apply simultaneously or in a sequence? Does the application of one rule block the application of another? Do the rules start at the beginning of the word and work their way east, or perhaps at the end of the word and work their way west? In investigating such questions, we may discover interesting, general principles. The principles would represent properties of the phonics system, not of the individual rules themselves.

As we shall see, the system of letter-sound correspondences in English is a collection of heterogeneous rule types, interacting in accordance with principles of broad generality. Curiously, there are nonphonics rules that also relate letters and sounds in the system. And, the behavior of letters in many words is such that it expresses information about the word's morphosyntactic functioning, not merely its pronunciation. Thus, phonics rules constitute part of a complex system. They are not alone in expressing letter-sound relationships, nor is that all they do. It is the whole system that converts letters to sounds, though this is not the specific function of a number of the system's rules or components. Based on such findings, the questions that can be asked regarding how phonics relates to the theory and practice of reading are legion.

Chapter 9

The Principle for Competing Phonics Rules

Artificial notions of what phonics rules are supposed to look like lead inevitably to the formulation of empirically inadequate rules. We have already observed, for example, that some phonics rules connect letters to sounds on the basis of the word's grammatical category, which means that the reader must first identify the word in order to set the phonics rules in motion. The notion that phonics rules are supposed to lead to word identification is, at least in those examples, thoroughly undermined. The only way an advocate of phonics as a tool for word identification can express the relevant letter-sound connection is to excise the grammatical information from the rule, thereby distorting it, and leaving it empirically compromised.

Although one might wish to argue that phonics rules must be simplified in order to make them classroom-friendly, it cannot be denied that such simplification is, in actual fact, a distortion and falsification of the rules. No real scientific insight into the nature of phonics as a system can be achieved if the system is constrained, at an abstract level, by such utilitarian principles. Stated differently, in order to understand how letters relate to sounds, these relationships must be studied independently of how they are utilized. Indeed, we will be on much firmer ground in understanding just how phonics rules are actually utilized if we first develop an undistorted, empirically based model of what the rules are and how they interact.

The examples that Bloomfield (1942/1961) cited in summarizing his position on phonics are a good place to begin, because they implicitly express certain aspects of phonics as a system. Bloomfield's examples included the words *pin, nip, pit, tip, tin, nit, dip, din, dim,* and *mid,* and the pronounceable nonwords *pid, nin, pim, mip, nid, nim,* and *mim.* The phonics rules that underlie the letter-sound connections in these words and nonwords are:

The letter *d* is pronounced [d].
The letter *p* is pronounced [p].
The letter *m* is pronounced [m].
The letter *n* is pronounced [n].
The letter *t* is pronounced [t].
The letter *i* is pronounced [I].

The systematicity of Bloomfield's (1942/1961) phonics lies in the observation that the pronunciation of any word or nonword is derived entirely from the pronunciation of each component letter, with variations occurring only according to the permutations of the letters themselves. Another way of stating this is that the phonics rules do not refer to specific words, nor to strings of letters, but rather to single letters, no matter what word or nonword they appear in, and no matter where in the word they appear. Thus, *p* is pronounced [p] and *n* is pronounced [n] whether the letter begins or ends a word, as in *pin* and *nip*. In addition, the rules permit no exceptions. Thus, *p* is always and only pronounced [p], and *n* is always and only pronounced [n].

The phonics rules that underlie Bloomfield's (1942/1961) examples are, with one important exception to be discussed later, maximally simple. Indeed, it is not possible to imagine a simpler system. It might even appear as if the notion of a maximally simple system of independent phonics rules, each one applying exceptionlessly to a single letter to produce a single sound, is empirically rooted in the data of actual letter-sound conversions, such as we see in Bloomfield's examples. But this simple system is, in some sense, only an ideal, as previously noted.

It appears more accurate to say that Bloomfield (1942/1961) had a preconceived idea of what an ideal phonics system should look like, and then found examples to support this. The ideal system has rules of the simplest form possible, namely, one letter becoming one sound, with no rule interaction, no exceptions, and no other constraints.

This historically was also the view of 18th- and 19th-century British spelling reformers, who did more than carefully select out examples from real English that would portray a maximally simple system. In seriously proposing new symbols altogether, or new conventional spellings, the goal was to transform the system from an irrational complexity to a more rational, natural, teachable, and learnable simplicity.

The mindset of the spelling reformers was both accurately and humorously portrayed by the linguist Geoffrey Sampson (1985). Sampson (p. 194) noted:

> [English orthography] falls very far short of the ideal. English, together with French, are remarkable among European languages for the extent to which their spelling-systems depart from the principle of one-to-one correspondence between the sequence of segment-types that occur in a spoken utterance and the sequence of graphemes which appear in its written equivalent.

Because of this departure from the ideal, the spelling reformers, according to Sampson (p. 194), believe that "our spelling is simply chaotic," and that "this is a thoroughly bad thing." They would prefer that:

> if it were possible by a wave of a magic wand to equip every adult English-speaker with competence in a new, phonemic system of spelling, and to replace the millions of books and papers in our libraries and filing-cabinets by copies written in the new system, then to do so would confer a great boon on future generations of English-speakers. (p. 194)

The loss of the "beauty" of traditional spelling would be made up for by its new "rationality," thus justifying changing the spellings of *conquer* and *passionate,* for example, to *konker* and *pashunut.*

But everyone knows that real written English simply does not work according to the reformer's ideal of one-letter-one-sound and one-sound-one-letter correspondences. So, from an inquisitive and scientific standpoint, we should ask why English spelling-sound relationships are not maximally simple and, more crucially, whether this means that departures from the maximally simple system represent real, significant aberrations, flaws in an otherwise perfect system. Viewed scientifically, the answer to this question can only be determined by first empirically investigating patterns of English letter-sound correspondences and the phonics rules needed to adequately describe them.

With this in mind, it can be noted that, although the consonant letters in Bloomfield's (1942/1961) examples express a true formal simplicity, in which a single letter is converted to a single sound no matter where in the word the letter appears, this is not as clearly true for the vowel letter *i.* Thus, when a consonant letter is written alone, with no neighboring letters, though perhaps not technically pronounceable, the associated sound is apparent. The singly written *s* is pronounced [s], *p* is pronounced [p], and so on. But when the letter *i* appears alone, as in the pronoun *I,* it is pronounced [ay], not [I].

Similarly, each vowel letter written singly is pronounced with its long letter name: *a, e, i, o, u.* Of course, the word *a* is pronounced either as long [ey] or reduced schwa [ə], depending on accent and stress. The singly written *e, o,* and *u* are not actual words, but when not followed by a consonant letter, are pronounced with a long vowel sound. For letter *e* we have *be, the, me, she,* and *we.* For *o* we have *go, ho, no,* and *so.* For *u* we have only rare cases, such as *gnu,* but this reflects a widespread prohibition in English spelling against words ending in the letter *u* or *v,* even though words can end in the sounds [uw] and [v], as in *threw* and *save* (Venezky, 1999, p. 7).

In general, the only time a short vowel pronunciation appears is when it is followed by a consonant letter, as in Bloomfield's (1942/1961) *pin, nip,* and so on. Exceptions to this include words spelled with the letter *a* immediately preceded by a consonant letter, as in *fa, la, ma,* and *pa.* This vowel pronunciation is, interestingly, that which ordinarily occurs for the letter *o,* as in *fog, lot, mop,* and *pop,* not the short pronunciation of the letter *a* itself, as the contrasting vowel sounds of *hat, lap,* and *mat* make clear. In other words, to the extent that actual English words constitute empirical evidence that bears on the matter, a vowel letter devoid of neighboring letters, and thus standing alone, is pronounced long, though a short pronunciation may be induced under certain, more restrictive and complex, spelling contexts.

Therefore, Bloomfield's examples do not really represent the ideal he seemed intent on promoting. In the word *pin,* for example, while the phonics rules for *p* and *n* are the formally simple "letter *p* is pronounced [p]" and "letter *n* is pronounced [n]," the behavior of the vowel letter is different. Standing alone, the rule for letter *i* is "letter *i* is pronounced [ay]." But this would produce the incorrect pronunciations [payn], [nayp], and so on.

Instead, the rule for the vowel letter *i* in Bloomfield's (1942/1961) examples must be "letter *i* is pronounced [I] when immediately followed by a word-final consonant letter." More accurately, the rule also stipulates that "a vowel letter is pronounced short if it is immediately followed by two consonant letters," as in *milk, mint,* and *mist.*

As a consequence, words such as *pin, nip, tip,* and *pit* are hybrids, in terms of rule complexity. The phonics rules for the consonant letters are of maximally simple form. The rule for the vowel letter *i* is not, as it specifies a more complex alphabetic context in which the short pronunciation is produced.

With respect to an ideal, formal simplicity, two types of rules exist, each empirically based. The first is the simplest rule type possible, "letter *x* is pronounced [y]," as in "letter *p* is pronounced [p]," "letter *n* is pronounced [n]," and "letter *i* is pronounced [ay]." These can be referred to as the basic, or "default," rules for the individual letters specified.

The second type of rule departs from ideal simplicity, because it specifies additional letters that must be present in order for the rule to apply, as in "letter *i* is pronounced [I] if immediately followed by a word-final consonant letter." These can be referred to as nonbasic, nondefault, or complex rules.

From this perspective, Bloomfield (1942/1961) might have done better to select examples such as *be, he, me, we, I, hi, pi, go, no,* and *so,* because these are sounded out only by default rules. Thus, *be* undergoes "letter *b* is pronounced [b]" and "letter *e* is pronounced [iy]."

Conjecturing about Bloomfield's (1942/1961) choice of words, it seems that examples like *pin* and *nip* may have been selected over *be, he,* and *me* in order to convey the notion that consonant letters receive their default pronunciations no matter where in the word they appear, including both initial and final position. In addition, Bloomfield's examples convey a sense of limitless permutability—*pin-nip, pit-tip, dim-mid*—thus indirectly demonstrating the productivity of his phonics principles. Finally, *pin, tin, nip, dim,* and so on are all content words, which is an open, productive class of words, with no limit, in principle, to the number of words in the class, again demonstrating the productivity and generality of the associated phonics rules. Words such as *he, me, we,* and *I* are grammatically functioning words that belong to a closed, unproductive, essentially small and finite class of words, thus possibly suggesting that the associated phonics rules are also narrow, applicable only to this class.

There is an obvious difference, however, between an unproductive grammatical class of words, such as personal pronouns, and the phonics rules that sound them out. Certainly, the consonant letters in *he, me,* and *we,* as well as in *be, hi, no,* and *so,* are pronounced with the productive, default sounds. In principle the vowels need function no differently.

A number of exceptions have already appeared, and their phonics behavior needs to be analyzed. Consider the behavior of the letter *a* in *ma* and *pa.* This is the idiosyncratic [a] sound. The rule needed to correctly sound out the words in which it appears is "the letter *a* is pronounced [a] when final in the word and preceded by a consonant letter."

Or consider the words *do* and *to.* These are also pronounced with an idiosyncratic vowel sound, namely [uw]. But, unlike *ma* and *pa,* these are unrepresentative of similarly spelled words in which the letter *o* does receive its default pronunciation, such as *Bo, go, lo, no,* and *so.* In fact, the existence of the word *do,* as in *do, re, mi,* shows that the phonics rule for the verb *do* applies to the word itself, rather than the letter sequence *d-o.* Therefore, we need to have rules that idiosyncratically apply to the full letter sequence: "in the word *do,* the vowel letter *o* is pronounced [u]," "in the word *to,* the vowel letter *o* is pronounced [uw]."

A simple *w* or *y* immediately after the vowel letter can also produce nondefault pronunciations, as in the following examples:

1. Final *ay*: *bay, day, gay, hay, jay, lay, may, nay, pay, ray, say, way.*
2. Final *ew*: *dew, few, Jew, mew, new, pew.*
3. Final *ey*: *grey, hey, whey.*
4. Final *oy*: *boy, coy, joy, Roy, toy.*
5. Final *ow*: *low, mow, row, tow.*
6. Final *uy*: *buy, guy.*

The first group of examples may in fact be regular, if we simply exclude the letter *y* from the set of consonantal letters, as seems phonetically appropriate. Then the vowel letter *a* is sounded out with its default value, long [ey], because it is not followed by a consonant letter. In order to prevent it from undergoing the rule converting letter *a* to short [a], as in *ma* and *pa*, this [a] rule must specify that letter *a* is not only preceded by a consonant letter, but also that it is the final letter of the word.

The second group of examples exhibits a nondefault [uw] sound, therefore requiring a phonics rule that states, "letter *e* immediately followed by letter *w* is pronounced [uw]." An idiosyncratic subset of these words also palatalizes the initial consonant, that is, a [y] sound is inserted between the consonant and the [uw] vowel sound. There is dialect variation with this, sometimes palatalizing the *n* in *new*, and sometimes not. There must be a rule, therefore, that specifies that in the palatalized words *few* [fyuw] and *pew* [pyuw], for example, the initial consonant letter is pronounced palatalized. The word *sew* is entirely unique in its letter-sound relationship, and needs its own rule: "In the word *sew*, the vowel letter *e* is pronounced [ow]."

The third group is unusual in that the long vowel sound is not the expected default vowel. Thus, even if letter *y* is not counted as a consonant letter, there still would be a need for a special phonics rule just for this group. The rule is: "letter *e* followed by *y* is pronounced [ey]."

The fourth group requires a phonics rule that produces a phonetically lower vowel sound than the mid level default sound for the letter *o*. The rule is: "letter *o* followed immediately by letter *y* is pronounced [ɔ]."

The fifth group appears to require no special rule, as the pronunciation of the vowel letter *o* is just its default sound [ow]. This pronunciation can be obtained by characterizing final *w* as a nonconsonant letter. Then letter *o* becomes sound [ow] in virtue of the rule that applies to vowel letters when no consonant letter follows, as discussed previously.

However, there are a number of words that exhibit a different pronunciation of the vowel letter, including *how, now, brown,* and *cow*. This pronunciation is the short vowel sound [æ]. It should be noted that the vowel sound in *how, now, brown,* and *cow* is not the short vowel ordinarily associated with the letter *o*, namely [a], as in *hot, not,* and *rot*. Rather, the vowel sound of *how, now, brown,* and *cow* is phonetically more anterior in the mouth than the vowel [a]. Thus, this is an idiosyncratic vowel for this letter, unpredictable on the basis of known patterns. Therefore, the words that exhibit this letter-sound correspondence need their own special rule: "letter *o* before *w* is pronounced [æ]."

But now there are two rules for spellings with final *ow*. And there are indeed some words that undergo both rules, such as *bow* and *sow*. Therefore, words in final *ow* either undergo the short-vowel rule (*how, now*), the long vowel rule (*low, mow*), or both (*bow, sow*). There is no obvious alphabetic basis for this distinction, so letter strings are simply categorized according to which pattern they follow.

Finally, the sixth group, consisting of *buy* and *guy*, requires a rule that produces neither the long default value of letter *u*, namely, sound [uw], nor its usual short value [ʌ], as in *but* and *gut*. The necessary rule is: "letter *u* before final *y* is pronounced [a]."

One immediately obvious result of this attempt to identify the phonics rules that describe patterns of English letter-sound relationships is the rapid proliferation that occurs even when the domain of interest consists of nothing more complicated than single-syllable words. It seems that almost any new type of spelling pattern provides a potential basis for a new rule, and, indeed, there is no obvious reason why this cannot be the case.

The rules that describe the previous exception groups depart from the simple, default rules in obvious ways. Instead of turning a single letter into a sound no matter where in the word the letter appears, the exception groups are characterized by rules that apply to letters that find themselves huddled with specific alphabetic neighbors. It is only when these neighbors are present that the rule for that group can apply.

But there is a simple, logical problem that exists when the system contains both default rules and nondefault rules, that is, two types of rules that, in principle, apply to the same letter, as in "letter *i* is pronounced [ay]" and "letter *i* immediately followed by a word-final consonant letter is pronounced [I]." Notice that in a word such as *big*, the stated conditions that allow each of these rules to apply is satisfied. The nondefault rule can apply, because there is a word-final consonant letter immediately following the vowel letter. But the default rule can also apply, because the word contains the letter *i*. Yet only the nondefault rule applies in this example.

Therefore, the phonics system must have a mechanism of some sort that correctly selects from a set of competing phonics rules the one that actually does apply. Such a mechanism readily suggests itself. In general, a nondefault rule takes precedence over, and preempts, a default rule that applies to the same letter. The system immediately recognizes a nondefault rule because it specifies the alphabetic context in which a letter-sound conversion is made. It immediately recognizes a default rule because there is no alphabetic context for the letter-sound conversion.

Consider the way this principle works in the various exceptions discussed earlier. In words such as *ma* and *pa*, the two competing phonics rules are "letter *a* is pronounced [ey]" and "letter *a* preceded by a consonant letter and final in the word is pronounced [a]." The words *ma* and *pa* contain the letter *a*, which means that, in principle, nothing yet prevents the default rule from applying. But this would produce the incorrect pronunciations [mey] and [pey]. However, according to the proposed principle, the nondefault rule takes precedence, and blocks the application of the default rule, thereby producing the desired pronunciations [ma] and [pa].

The words *do* and *to* receive their correct pronunciations because the rules "in the word *do,* letter *o* is pronounced [uw]" and "in the word *to,* letter *o* is pronounced [uw]" take precedence over, and block, "letter *o* is pronounced [ow]," thereby preventing pronounciations [dow] and [tow].

Similarly, the correct pronunciation of *new* is produced because "letter *e* followed by letter *w* is pronounced [uw]" takes precedence over, and blocks, "letter *e* is pronounced [iy]." The correct pronunciation of *grey* is produced because "letter *e* followed by letter *y* is pronounced [ey]" takes precedence over, and blocks, "letter *e* is pronounced [iy]." The correct pronunciation of *boy* is produced because "letter *o* followed by letter *y* is pronounced [ɔ]" takes precedence over, and blocks "letter *o* is pronounced [ow]." And the correct pronunciation of *buy* is produced *since* "letter *u* followed by letter *y* is pronounced [a]" takes precedence over, and blocks, "letter *u* is pronounced [uw]."

Words such as *how, now, brown,* and *cow* pose a problem. If the proposed principle holds, then "letter *o* followed by letter *w* is pronounced [æ]" should take precedence over, and block, "letter *o* is pronounced [ow]." This would prevent the correct phonic conversions in words like *row* and *tow.* They would be pronounced [ræw] and [tæw], not [row] and [tow].

Clearly, this nondefault rule must be declared optional in the system. That is to say, it may or may not apply, meaning that in either case the result is an acceptable pronunciation of the spelled word. For the word *how,* the nondefault rule applies, thereby blocking the application of the default rule, and producing the desired [hæw]. For the word *row,* the nondefault rule does not apply, leaving the default rule free to apply, producing the desired pronunciation [row].

There is now an immediate explanation for the existence of pairs such as *bow* [bæw]-[bow] and *sow* [sæw]-[sow]. In the first member of the pair the optional nondefault rule applies, whereas in the latter, the nondefault rule does not apply.

An interesting empirical prediction follows from this analysis. Because the nondefault rule is optional, in principle, it may or may not apply. If the rule specifies a certain letter sequence, such as *ow,* rather than individual words, such as the words *how, now, brown,* and *cow,* then it is also optional for these words. This means that the system permits a phonics conversion in which the nondefault rule does not apply to these cases. But then the default rule will apply, and the pronunciations [how], [now], [brown], and [kow] will be produced. These are not *actual* words, at least not with spellings utilizing *ow.* Therefore, they must be regarded as *possible* words of the language. Similarly, because the nondefault rule is optional, it may apply to spellings such as *row* and *tow,* producing the pronunciations [ræw] and [tæw], which must again be considered possible words of the language. Certainly no one would be surprised to read in a story about a character named Lowery that his friends refer to him with the nickname Low, pronounced [læw], or that another character is named Zow, and that readers vary in pronouncing this name as [zæw] or [zow].

The principle that selects the nondefault rule over the default rule can be called the Principle for Competing Phonics Rules (PCPR). Because this principle does not specify any particular rules, but simply makes a distinction between two types of rules and characterizes their mutual relationship, it can be thought of as a property of the whole system. It is a principle that organizes the application of phonics rules, by settling a dispute, as it were, between two rules, both of which find the letters they want to sound out in a word, but where only one rule may apply.

Additional examples provide empirical evidence that the PCPR needs to be revised and generalized. Consider the words *dint, hint, lint, mint,* and *tint.* These are pronounced with the expected nondefault pronunciation [I], because two consonant letters immediately follow the vowel letter. But a single exception to this pattern exists, namely, the word *pint,* which is pronounced with the default pronunciation [paynt].

The words *dint, hint,* and so on do not undergo the default rule for letter *i* because the PCPR blocks that rule from applying. But *pint* unexpectedly does undergo the default rule. Therefore, it must be blocked from undergoing the nondefault rule. However, there is nothing yet in the system that can accomplish this feat.

In order to exempt *pint* from the nondefault rule, it can simply be assigned the status of exception to the nondefault rule. This, in turn, can be accomplished with a rule of the form "the word *pint* is an exception to the rule 'a vowel letter immediately followed by two consonant letters is pronounced short.' " Then, when the nondefault rule should otherwise apply to *pint,* it will be unable to do so (* denotes exception to rule):

p i n t	
*	The word *pint* is an exception to the short-vowel rule.
Blocked	A vowel letter immediately followed by two consonant letters is pronounced short (short-vowel rule).
[ay]	Letter *i* is pronounced [ay].

Because the nondefault short-vowel rule is blocked from applying, it cannot itself block the default rule, thus leading to the desired pronunciation. But there is still no principle that will make the exception-assigning rule take precedence over the short-vowel rule, which is necessary if the phonic conversion is to produce the desired result.

A simple generalization of the PCPR, however, will accomplish this goal. The PCPR balances a nondefault rule that applies to a certain letter with a default rule that applies to the same letter, tipping in favor of the nondefault rule. From a formal standpoint, it can be observed that the nondefault rule specifies a sequence of letters, one of which is the letter undergoing the phonic conversion, and the others of which represent the necessary alphabetic context. A default rule contains only the single letter undergoing the phonic conversion. This means that, instead of characterizing the PCPR as selecting a nondefault rule over a default rule that converts the same letter to a sound, the PCPR can be characterized as selecting the rule that applies to a string of letters containing the target letter over the rule that applies to the single target letter by itself. Then, the reason "letter *i* immediately followed by two consonants is pronounced [I]" takes precedence over, and blocks, "letter *i* is pronounced [ay]" is not simply that the former is a nondefault rule and the latter is a default rule. Rather, it is that the former applies to a letter sequence that is more highly specified than the latter.

More generally, therefore, the PCPR can be formulated as follows:

> Principle for Competing Phonics Rules: If phonics rule R applies to a sequence of letters, and phonics rule R′ applies to a letter or letter sequence contained entirely within the sequence of letters for rule R, then rule R takes precedence over, and blocks, the application of rule R′.

Because letter *i* is contained entirely within the letter sequence *int*, the rule for the latter takes precedence over, and blocks, the application of the rule for *i* alone. Because letter sequence *int* is contained entirely within letter sequence *pint*, the rule for *pint* (the exception rule) takes precedence over the rule for *int*.

Likewise, the word *ma* is converted to [ma], not [mey], because letter string *a* lies entirely within letter string *ma*. The word *new* is pronounced [nuw], not [niy], because the letter string *e* is contained entirely within the letter string *ew*. Similar behavior follows from the fact that letter string *e* is contained entirely within letter string *ey*, *o* is contained entirely within *oy*, *o* is contained entirely within *ow*, and *u* is contained entirely within *uy*.

The revised, generalized PCPR expresses the observation that rules can compete for application to a word even when both are nondefault rules. From this perspective, default rules simply represent the lower limit on phonics rules, applying to a single letter independent of its alphabetic context. Nondefault rules are, in a sense, exceptions to the default rules. But nondefault rules may themselves describe a fairly productive pattern, in which case there can be exceptions to the nondefault rules. This is precisely the case for *pint* compared to *pin* compared to *pi*. Whereas *pi* undergoes only default rules, *pin* undergoes default rules for its consonant letters, but a nondefault rule for its vowel letter. And *pint* undergoes a still narrower

pi	*pin*	*pint*	
---	---	*	*Pint* is an exception to the short-vowel rule.
---	[I]	blocked	Letter *i* immediately followed by a word-final consonant letter or by two consonant letters is pronounced short (short-vowel rule).
[ay]	---	[ay]	Letter *i* is pronounced [ay].

FIG. 9.1. Phonics rules for *pi, pin, pint.*

nondefault rule, which makes it an exception to the more general non-default rule, thereby allowing the default pronunciation to appear, as shown in Fig. 9.1. Even though both *pi* and *pint* are pronounced with the same vowel letter, the formal structure of the sequence of rules that assigns this vowel to each word is different. That is to say, their phonic structures are distinct.

The generalized PCPR has widespread applicability. Consider digraphs such as *ch, ph, sh,* and *th.* Again, words containing these digraphs are, in principle, susceptible to both of the default rules for the consonants, as well as the nondefault rules, namely "*ch* is pronounced [č]," "*ph* is pronounced [f]," "*sh* is pronounced [š]," and "*th* is pronounced [θ]." But *c* and *h* each lie entirely within *ch, p* and *h* entirely within *ph, s* and *h* entirely within *sh,* and *t* and *h* entirely within *th.* Therefore, *ch* must become [č], *ph* must become [f], *sh* must become [š], and *th* must become [θ].

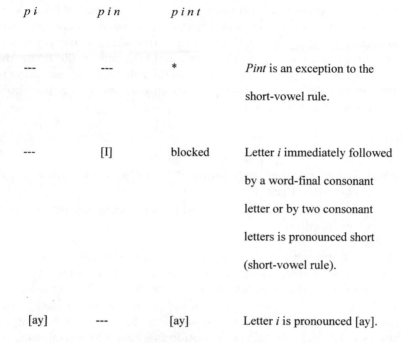

Words with final *ind* are pronounced with the long vowel [ay], as in *bind, find, hind, grind, kind,* and *mind.* But *wind* is pronounced either short (a stormy wind) or long (wind a wristwatch). The short pronunciation is the expected one, because the vowel letter is immediately followed by two consonants. This means that words in *ind* must undergo a phonics rule that makes them exceptions to the short-vowel rule: "Letter *i* immediately followed by *nd* is an exception to the short-vowel rule." By the PCPR, this exception rule will block the short-vowel rule, because *ind* is a more restrictive version of *i*CC (C = consonant). But *wind* (a stormy wind) is an exception to this exception rule, and is therefore governed by a rule of the form "the word *wind* (a stormy wind) is an exception to the rule '*ind* is an exception to the short-vowel rule.' " As an exception to an exception rule, the short-vowel pronunciation will appear:

wind	
*	*Wind* is an exception to the *ind* rule.
blocked	Letter *i* immediately followed by *nd* is an exception to the short-vowel rule.
[I]	Letter *i* immediately followed by two consonant letters is pronounced [I].

So, again, even though *wind* is pronounced with the same vowel sound as *hint* or *mint*, its logical structure in the phonics system is distinct from the logical structure for these, which are not exceptions to the *ind* rule.

The PCPR is simply an expression of the phenomenon of exceptions, and draws on traditional approaches to this phenomenon in formal linguistics (Kiparsky, 1973). It formalizes the notion that exceptions apply to more specific classes of letter strings than nonexceptions. But there are degrees of exceptions, and embeddings of exceptions, as we have seen. In a serious sense, therefore, once we leave the territory of default rules, everything is an exception. This is inherent in the nature of the phonics system for English, one in which there is a systematic departure from the one-letter-one-sound ideal. But to call this departure less than ideal in no way compromises the fact that it is indeed elegantly organized. The PCPR emerges organically from the way language is organized.

Furthermore, the phonics system, as we have seen, can describe the pronunciations of both actual and possible words. However, in general it does not specify which words are actual and which ones are possible. Both actual *low* [low] and possible [læw] can occur. It is only knowledge of the language, and more specifically, its lexicon, that permits a reader to make this distinction. Therefore, the phonics system itself will not permit a reader to decide between an actual word and a possible word. It is only when a reader assumes that a word on the page is a real word of the language, a reasonable assumption when one is reading for meaning, that the appropriate pronunciation can be selected.

The one exception to this lies in the existence of phonics rules that apply to specific, individual words, such as the word *wind* (a stormy wind) being an exception to the *ind* rule, or the word *do* undergoing its own rule for the vowel letter, or other traditional sight words undergoing their own idiosyncratic rules, like *said* undergoing a rule assigning [E] to the letters *ai*. But what is truly interesting and significant about these examples is that the idiosyncratic rules can only apply to actual words, not possible words. Thus, it makes no sense to say that there is a special rule that applies idiosyncratically to the possible word *fleg* that converts the vowel letter to the sound [o]. How could such a rule enter the language if the form to which it applies is not an actual word? Therefore, an ideal system of phonics rules applies ideally to possible words only. But once we are dealing with actual words, that is to say, with real human language, the potential now exists for such words to take on a life of their own within the phonics system, and for their own idiosyncratic peculiarities within the system to add to their identity.

Bloomfield (1942/1961) and the spelling reformers both avoided the complicating factors of exceptions and competing rules. Bloomfield avoided them by simply not discussing them in his illustrative examples. The spelling reformers avoided them by creating new spellings. The end result is a system that is advertised as both psychologically and pedagogically more accessible to children.

Where does neophonics stand on this issue? Nowhere is the matter explicitly discussed, but we certainly can infer its stance from several pertinent observations. The literature of neophonics mainly addresses the teaching and learning of phonics. Thus, its interest appears to lie at the levels of psychology and pedagogy. But it defines the alphabetic principle in abstract terms, independently of psychology and pedagogy, as the systematic relationship between written spellings and spoken words. The alphabetic principle is "elegant," a term typically applied to mathematical proofs. There is, therefore, a deep chasm between what neophonics proposes conceptually, and what it proposes practically. The disappointing omission of any serious study of its "nonnegotiable" alphabetic principle leaves too many questions open. All we can say at present is that by not studying the core of its own subject matter, which is the very system of letter-sound correspondences itself, it is as if physicists decided not to pursue their study of the material universe beyond some superficially simple patterns, because in so doing they would be uncovering phenomena that were just too difficult to teach to children anyway. Fortunately, physicists have chosen not to adopt this thoroughly antiscientific posture.

Chapter **10**

Theoretical Implications of *r*-Controlled Vowels

Many commercial phonics programs devote some space to teaching children about *r*-controlled vowels. In words that exhibit this phenomenon, the pronunciation of a vowel letter is altered by a neighboring letter *r*. Thus, we find distinct pronunciations of the vowel letters in *bad* and *bard*, and in *sit* and *sir*.

At first glance, the patterns appear simple enough. But a deeper investigation shows that there are very interesting theoretical implications of the rules that affect the pronunciation of a vowel letter in the presence of a neighboring letter *r*.

First, in order for the rules describing these pronunciations to work right, they must interact with other rules in accordance with more general principles of the phonic system. That is, they don't just automatically work right on their own.

Second, although phonics rules are traditionally taught as correspondences between letters and sounds, the rules needed to describe *r*-controlled vowels include some of an entirely different character. Specifically, these new rules convert sounds into other sounds.

And third, where we encounter exceptions to the rules, it can be observed that the unexpected pronunciation indirectly conveys a message about the word itself, thereby contributing to its connotation. The phonics system is flexible enough that there are linguistic advantages to breaking the rules.

Overall, an investigation of the interesting class of *r*-controlled vowels leads to the important conclusion that the phonics system, once empirically elucidated, is intricate and complex, and thoroughly distinct in character from the traditional notions. Let us therefore turn to a discussion of these theoretically significant words.

Our starting point is with the notion of the *beat* of a syllable. The beat derives from the vowel nucleus of the word. Thus, *hen, fit,* and *bun* are spoken with a single beat consisting of the vowels [ɛ], [I], and [ʌ], respectively, along with the surrounding consonants.

Some English words, however, are pronounced with the interesting phonological property of having a beat formed around a vowel-like pronunciation of the sound [R]. This vocalic [R] constitutes the beat in words such as *her, fir,* and *burn.* The phonics literature refers to the vowels in these pronunciations as "*r*-controlled vowels." Notice that the orthographic vowel does not show up in the word's pronunciation. The words *her, fir,* and *burn* are not pronounced [hɛr], [fIr], and [bʌrn], with distinct vowels. Rather, the vocalic *r*s are identically pronounced, leading to homonymous pairs like *her* and *Hur, fir* and *fur, tern* and *turn.*

Words with *r*-controlled vowels, and their interesting exceptions, display patterns of letter-sound correspondence that provide evidence for two principles of the phonics system that can be added to the Principle for Competing Phonics Rules (PCPR). The first is a principle that describes the interaction of phonics rules that do not compete with each other, and which shall be called the Principle for Noncompeting Phonics Rules. The second is a principle that identifies the types of elements that can undergo phonics rules, and includes among these not only letters of the alphabet, but sounds themselves.

The conversion of *er, ir,* and *ur* to syllabic [R] is subsumed under the PCPR. The rules that create syllabic [R] are "letter sequence *er* is pronounced [R]," "letter sequence *ir* is pronounced [R]," and "letter sequence *ur* is pronounced [R]." Letters *e* and *r* are each contained entirely within *er, i* and *r* are each contained entirely within *ir,* and *u* and *r* are each entirely contained within *ur.* This means that the rules creating syllabic [R] will take precedence over, and prevent the application of, the rules applying to the individual letters of the inputs.

Thus, in the conversion of *her* to [hR], the rule for *er* applies, and, even though letters *e* and *r* are present, the default rules for these letters cannot apply. They are blocked by the nondefault rule "letter sequence *er* is pronounced [R]" because both *e* and *r* lie entirely within the string *er.* The word also undergoes the default rule for letter *h,* producing the sound [h], and the final pronunciation [hR].

The following question can therefore be posed: What is the relationship between the rule converting letter *h* to [h] and the rule converting the string of letters *er* to [R]? Does one apply before the other, for example, must words be sounded out starting at the beginning or at the end? Or do they apply simultaneously to the input spelling *her*?

Either solution will yield the desired pronunciations. The following phonic conversions show this:

1. *h* is sounded out first: *her* is pronounced [h]*er*, which is then pronounced [h][R].
2. *er* is sounded out first: *her* is pronounced *h*[R], which is then pronounced [h][R].
3. *h* and *er* are sounded out simultaneously: *her* is pronounced [h][R].

The reason all three options work is that the rule for letter *h* and the rule for letter string *er* are entirely independent of each other. They do not influence each other in any way. It is as if the two parts of the word, *h* and *er*, are blind to each other's phonic destiny.

Approaching the matter scientifically amounts to asking whether there is any empirical evidence for one or another of these solutions. Empirical evidence is not the same as logical possibility. Logically, all three solutions produce the desired results. Empirically, we want to know if there are any letter-sound patterns that necessitate one or more of the solutions being thrown out.

Indeed, there is an interesting phonic pattern in English that has some bearing on this question. Consider words that begin with an initial letter *c*. These will undergo a phonics rule that turns the *c* into an [s] when it is immediately followed by an *e* or an *i*, but into a [k] otherwise. We thus have *cell, cent, city*, and *cite*, but *car, cop*, and *cut*. Now compare *cert* with *curt*. These require the phonics conversions "*c* before *e* is pronounced [s]," and "*c* before *u* is pronounced [k]." But the proper application of these phonics rules requires that *er* and *ur* have not already been turned into [R], because then we will lose the alphabetic context needed to properly decode the letter *c*, as shown in Fig. 10.1. In these applications, the rule for the letter *c* will no longer see a following *e* or *u* if the syllabic *r* rule applies first. The system will not be able to create the correct consonant sound. This conclusion can be generalized by stating that phonics rules do not apply antidromically, that is, beginning at the end of the word and working their way toward the beginning.

c e r t	c u r t	
[R]	[R]	syllabic *r* rule
?	?	*c* is pronounced [s] or [k]

FIG. 10.1. Incorrect application of the rules.

The two remaining options are: (a) phonics rules start at the beginning of the word, and work their way orthodromically through the word, and (b) phonics rules apply whenever their alphabetic requirements are satisfied. In the absence of empirical evidence one way or another, we can say that this is an open question in the scientific study of phonics.

Despite the still unsettled nature of this empirical matter, there is a certain naturalness and plausibility to the principle that rules apply whenever their alphabetic or other requirements are satisfied, unless prevented from doing so by the PCPR. Although the evidence from *cert* and *curt* shows that phonics rules cannot apply antidromically, beginning at the end of the word and working their way toward the beginning, we can generalize this to the claim that the rules cannot apply directionally at all. Thus, they also do not apply orthodromically (beginning at the beginning), or start in the middle and work their way toward both ends.

On these grounds, the phonics rules that sound out *cert* and *curt* apply all at once to the words, as in Fig. 10.2. Notice that the PCPR blocks the application of the rules "letter *e* is pronounced [iy]," "letter *u* is pronounced [uw]," and "letter *r* is pronounced [r]," because *e*, *u*, and *r* are each contained entirely within the letter strings *er* or *ur*.

It is precisely the overlapping nature of the strings undergoing the rules for letter *c* and the rules for *er* and *ir* that allows empirical evidence to be uncovered that helps to better characterize the phonics system. Specifically, the rule for letter *c* applies to the strings *ce* and *cu*, in our examples, while the rule for syllabic *r* applies to the strings *er* and *ur*, as in Fig. 10.3. Despite the overlapping of strings, the rules affect distinct letters, namely *c* and *er* or *ur*. In this important sense they are noncompetitive, because the letter *c* is not contained entirely within *er* or *ur*, and the letter strings *er* and *ur* are not

c e r t   *c u r t*

[s] [R] [t]   [k] [R] [t]

Rules: Letter *c* is pronounced [s] before letters *e* or *i*.

Letter *c* is pronounced [k] before letters *a*, *o*, or *u*.

Letter *t* is pronounced [t].

Letter strings *er*, *ir*, and *ur* are pronounced [R].

FIG. 10.2. Phonics rules applied to *cert* and *curt*.

FIG. 10.3. Letter *c* rule and syllabic *r* rule applied to *cert* and *curt.*

contained entirely within the strings *ce* or *cu.* Thus, the PCPR does not block the application of one or the other of these. Both will apply.

The principle that governs the application of these rules, and that applies more generally in the phonics system, is the *Principle for Noncompeting Phonics Rules*:

> Principle for Noncompeting Phonics Rules: Phonics rules apply as soon as their alphabetic (and other) requirements are satisfied, unless prevented from doing so by the Principle for Competing Phonics Rules.

This principle governs the application of rules that overlap, such as the letter *c* rule and the syllabic *r* rule, and rules that do not overlap, such as the letter *c* rule and the letter *t* rule.

The theoretical implications of *r*-controlled phonics rules go a step further. Consider words spelled with a consonant letter other than *r* following the letter *a.* The pronunciation of the letter *a* is [æ], a vowel made low and anterior in the mouth. The following examples exhibit this pronunciation:

bat, cat, fat, hat, mat, pat, rat, sat, vat
ban, can, fan, man, pan, ran, tan, van
bad, dad, fad, lad, mad, pad, sad, tad

Words with *r* following the letter *a* are pronounced with a vowel sound [ɑ] which is retracted still further in the mouth, closer to the [a] of *cot, hot,* and *lot*: *bar, car, far, jar, par.* Indeed, there is a noticeable difference between the actual pronunciations [bɑr], [kɑr], and [fɑr], compared to [bar], [kar], and [far]. As with *r* following other vowel letters, words with *r* following *a* are not pronounced with the sound that appears before other consonant letters. Instead, they are *r*-controlled, though not with syllabic [R]. This means that we need a special rule to describe the pronunciation of the letter *a* immediately before *r*: "The vowel letter *a* immediately followed by the letter *r* is pronounced [ɑ]."

Now, *ar* undergoes further *r*-coloring when the letter immediately preceding the *a* is *w.* Thus, compare the pronunciations of *war, warm, wart, dwarf, swarm,* and *thwart* to *bar, harm, Bart, scarf,* and *thar* (thar she blows).

The vowel with preceding *w* and following *r* is phonetically rounded, and the rule we need to describe this can be called "the war rule": "letter *a* immediately preceded by the letter *w* and immediately followed by the letter *r* is pronounced [ɔ]."

A theoretically challenging situation obtains with words such as *wharf.* Here, the letter immediately preceding the letter *a* is *h,* not *w.* Nevertheless, the vowel letter *a* is pronounced as rounded [ɔ], not unrounded [a]. The *war* rule seems to apply, as if it somehow ignores the intervening *h.* Certainly, a reasonable hypothesis as to why the letter *h* is ignored is that its phonic value is ø (zero), that is, it is silent, a pattern regularly seen in words with *wh: wheel, what, why, whine, which, whistle,* and so on, though not *who, whom, whole,* and *whore.*

We might therefore wish to set up the system so that the *war* rule applies only after the *h* has been silenced. The phonic conversion would proceed as follows:

w h a r f	
[ø]	Letter *h* immediately preceded by letter *w* is not pronounced.
[ɔ]	In the letter string *war,* the vowel letter *a* is pronounced [ɔ].

In this phonics conversion, the *war* rule is actually not able to apply to the word *wharf,* because its alphabetic requirement is the string *war.* But, if we interpret the silencing of a letter, such as *h,* as abstractly changing the spelling, as if to say that the letter is now invisible, then the *war* rule can apply once the silencing rule has applied.

Apart from the fact that there is as yet no independent empirical evidence for the existence of invisible letters (but see the discussion later of silent *e*), the two phonics principles so far developed will require that *wharf* become [w] [ø] [ɑ] [r] [f], all accomplished simultaneously, by the Principle for Noncompeting Phonics Rules, with the vowel sound [ɑ], not [æ], by the PCPR. Unfortunately, [wɑrf] is not the desired result.

Notice, however, that we can maintain the two general principles, and correctly convert the written *wharf* to the sound [wɔrf] if we reconfigure the *war* rule so that it applies not to the *letters w-a-r,* but to the *sounds* [wɑr]. The rule will have the form "[wɑr] is (re)pronounced [wɔr]," converting one sequence of phonemes into another, as follows:

w h a r f	
w [ø] [ɑ] r [f]	Letter *h* in *wh* is pronounced [ø]. Letter *a* in *ar* is pronounced [ɑ]. Letter *f* is pronounced [f].
[w] [r]	Letter *w* is pronounced [w]. Letter *r* is pronounced [r].
[ɔ]	Sound sequence [wɑr] is changed to [wɔr].

In this phonics conversion, the phonics rules apply in groups at three stages. First, letters *h*, *a*, and *f* undergo the indicated rules, with the PCPR preventing letter *w* from being sounded out, as it is entirely contained in *wh*, as well as preventing letter *r* from being sounded out, as it is entirely contained in *ar*.

At this point, therefore, the rules have created an intermediate string consisting of letters and sounds, namely, *w*[ø] [ɑ] *r*[f]. Because there are still two letters in this expression, the word has not yet been fully sounded out. The default rules for letters *w* and *r* apply simultaneously, in virtue of the Principle for Noncompeting Phonics Rules, producing [wøɑrf], which, phonemically, is equivalent to [wɑrf].

But this pronunciation is subject to a further change, namely, "[wɑr] is repronounced [wɔr]." The rule, of course, can only apply at this point, because phonemic [wɑr] did not exist at a prior stage.

This phonics characterization of the word *wharf* maintains the PCPR and the Principle for Noncompeting Phonics Rules, by supplementing the phonics conversion with a new type of rule, one that converts not a letter to a sound, but rather, one sound into another sound, specifically, [ɑ] into [ɔ].

There is, in fact, interesting independent empirical evidence for the rule that converts phonemic string [wɑr] into phonemic string [wɔr]. Notice that the essence of this rule is that the conversion of [ɑ] to [ɔ] is based on the presence of an immediately preceding [w] sound, and an immediately following [r] sound, not an immediately preceding *w* letter and immediately following *r* letter. We have already observed that words spelled with *wh* and words spelled with *w* alone undergo the rule, and that the phonic value of *h* in these words is [ø]. Thus, what they also have in common is that the phonic value of both *wh* and *w* is [w].

But the phoneme [w] is the result of other letter-sound conversions as well, in words that also undergo conversion of the orthographic *a* to phonemic [ɔ]. Consider the words *quart* and *quartz*. Despite not having the letter *w*, or the letter sequence *wh*, these words also convert the letter *a* to phonemic [ɔ]. And it is clearly no coincidence that the phonic value of *qu* is phonemic [kw], in which phoneme [w] makes its appearance. Thus, what words in *war*, *whar*, and *quar* all have in common is the sound [w], not the letter *w*, so that the conditioning of the [ɑ]-to-[ɔ] conversion must be accomplished by that phoneme, and not by the letter.

The words *war*, *wharf*, and *quart* will undergo the phonic conversions in Fig. 10.4. The first line of conversions is constrained by the PCPR, which delays the conversion of letters *r* in *war*, *w* and *r* in *wharf*, and *q* and *r* in *quart*, because these letters lie entirely within the respective nondefault rules that apply to them, namely, "*a* in *ar* is pronounced [ɑ]," "*h* in *wh* is pronounced

w a r	w h a r f	q u a r t
[w][ɑ] r	w [ø][ɑ]r [f]	q [w][ɑ] r [t]
[r]	[w] [r]	[k] [r]
[ɔ]	[ɔ]	[ɔ]
[w ɔ r]	[w ɔ r f]	[k w ɔ r t]

FIG. 10.4. Phonic conversions for *war, wharf,* and *quart.*

[ø]," and "*u* in *qu* is pronounced [w]." By the Principle for Noncompeting Phonics Rules, letters *f* and *t* are sounded out in the first line.

The second line sounds out the letters that were blocked from undergoing a phonic conversion in the first line. At this point, all the words have been sounded out. But because they now contain the sound sequence [wɑr], the additional rule that changes [wɑr] to [wɔr] will apply.

What is striking in the sounding out of these three words is that the sound [w] is manufactured in three distinct ways: (a) by conversion of *w* to [w] in *war*; (b) by conversion of *wh* to [w][ø], equivalently to [w], in *wharf*; and (c) by conversion of *qu* to *q*[w] in *quart.* But by whichever conversion the phoneme [w] is produced, it will then condition the subsequent conversion of [ɑ] to [ɔ].

This analysis captures the significant generalization that the re-sounding out of [wɑr] as [wɔr] is determined not by the presence of certain arbitrarily related letters, but rather by the presence of letters that have in common the interesting property that they will all eventually turn into the phonemic sequence [wɑr], and by different routes. It is therefore entirely appropriate, in fact desirable, to create [ɔ] by means of a rule that turns one phonemic string into another, because such a rule expresses this empirically observed generalization. The initial analysis does not express this, and any analysis that creates [ɔ] directly from letter strings *war, whar,* and *quar* does not express what *war, whar,* and *quar* all have in common. Except for their common conversion to [wɑr], the input strings *war, whar,* and *quar* are as arbitrarily related as are the input strings *war, shar,* and *car,* and the presence of [ɔ] should be expected no more from the former than it is from the latter.

The theoretical significance of this analysis is that it highlights an interesting feature of the phonics system, which is that there are not only rules that apply to letters, but also rules that apply to sounds. The latter can be referred to as phonemically based phonics rules.

Another instance of a phonemically based phonics rule occurs in a slightly different alphabetic environment. Consider words in *wa, wha,* and

TABLE 10.1
Phonetically Retracted Versus Anterior Pronunciation of Letter *a*

Retracted [a]	*Anterior [æ]*
wad	*bad*
what	*bat*
quad	*gad*
squat	*sat*
squad	*sad*
swamp	*sap*
swat	*hat*

qua, but without a following *r.* These are pronounced with a more retracted low vowel than the vowel that appears in similar words without a preceding *w, wh,* or *qu,* as the examples in Table 10.1 demonstrate.

We again have a situation in which the words with the retracted [a] sound all share the property that the phoneme immediately preceding this vowel is [w], no matter how that [w] is created. This means that an empirically adequate conversion of letters to sounds will make use of the rule "[wæ] is changed to [wa]," assuming a prior conversion of letter *a* to sound [æ], as shown in Fig. 10.5.

In the first line, the short-vowel rule for letter *a* applies, along with certain nondefault and default rules for consonant letters. In *what,* the *w* is blocked from turning into [w], because it lies entirely within the letter string *wh,* which undergoes the rule that silences *h.* But, still being available, and now with no competing rule, *w* will turn into [w] in the next round of rules, along with "*q* is pronounced [k]." Finally, as shown in the third line, [æ] is repronounced [a], because it is in the sound string [wæ].

The lone exception to the phonemic [wær] rule is *quark,* and the lone exception to the phonemic [wæ] rule is *quack.* The words are pronounced [kwɑrk] and [kwæk], not [kwɔrk] and [kwak]. They must be treated as ex-

w h a t   q u a d   s q u a t   s w a t

w [ø] [æ][t]   q[w][æ][d]   [s]q[w][æ][t]   [s][w][æ][t]

[w]   [k]------------   --[k]----------   ---------------

[a]   [a]   [a]   [a]

FIG. 10.5. Phonic conversions for *what, quad, squat,* and *swat.*

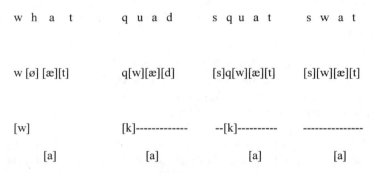

ceptions to the [wɑr] and [wæ] rules, respectively. They are sounded out as follows:

q u a r k	
*	*Quark* is an exception to the *war* rule.
q [w] [ɑ] r [k]	Letter *u* in *qu* is pronounced [w].
	Letter *a* in *ar* is pronounced [ɑ].
	Letter *k* is pronounced [k].
[k] [w] [ɑ] [r] [k]	Letter *q* is pronounced [k]
	Letter *r* is pronounced [r]
blocked by *	Sound string [wɑr] is repronounced [wɔr].
[kwɑrk]	Final pronunciation
q u a c k	
*	*Quack* is an exception to the [wæ] rule.
q [w] [æ] [k]	Letter *u* in *qu* is pronounced [w].
	Letter *a* is pronounced [æ].
	Letter sequence *ck* is pronounced [k].
[k]	Letter *q* is pronounced [k].
blocked by *	Sound string [wæ] is repronounced [wa].
[kwæk]	Final pronunciation

The phonic conversion of *quack* makes use of the rule "letter string *ck* is pronounced [k]." For both *quark* and *quack*, the exception rule assigns a property to the word that subsequently prevents application of the designated rule.

On this account, again, it is important to appreciate that the exception rules do not necessarily suggest some inherent flaw in the system. They simply represent a formal mechanism that allows certain written words to depart from their expected pronunciations. Any model of phonics must somehow express this phenomenon. In the present case, there may even be some advantage. The vowel of the word *quark* is pronounced as it would be in German, perhaps thereby preying upon a popular stereotype to convey its scientific sense. The word *quack* displays a vowel sound that, especially in its contrastive behavior with the expected sound, promotes the onomatopoeic timbre of the word, a vocal representation of a duck sound.

Indeed, Nobel physicist Murray Gell-Mann (1978), who coined the term *quark*, actually intended it to be pronounced as *quork*. He explained:

> I employed the sound 'quork' for several weeks in 1963 before noticing 'quark' in *Finnegans Wake*, which I had perused from time to time since it appeared in 1939 . . . The allusion to three quarks seemed perfect . . . I needed

an excuse for retaining the pronunciation 'quork' despite the occurrence of *Mark, bark, mark,* and so forth in *Finnegans Wake.* I found that excuse by supposing that one ingredient of the line "Three quarks for Muster Mark" was a cry of "Three quarts for Mister . . ." heard in H. C. Earwicker's pub.

Thus, despite the best of intellectual intentions, Gell-Mann's desired pronunciation of *quark* could not overcome the one society would find more satisfying.

Now the systematic relationship between letters and sounds includes three types of phonics rules: (a) rules that convert letters to sounds, (b) rules that assign exception status to strings, and (c) rules that convert sounds to other sounds. It should be clear that it is not individual phonics rules that convert letters to sounds, but rather the phonics system as a whole, a part of which is indeed a set of traditional letter-sound rules.

Chapter **11**

The Phonics of Silent *e*

Can anyone's imagination conjure up a phonics classroom without the famous silent *e*? That magical little grapheme sits alone at word's end, curled up like a cat, sometimes nestled behind a taller consonant. Facing east, it points its wand westward at an otherwise unsuspecting vowel, transforming it from short and stubby to long and proud. It utters not a whisper in the process. Truly, it is the strong, silent hero, an awesome icon of classroom culture that, like a character in an animated cartoon, survives every bomb, dagger, poison, and insult. Who dares call into question its gloriousness?

Through decades of unofficial dogma, and now by way of official dogma, our children will continue to learn that a short vowel in a word will become long if a silent *e* follows it. But dare we question this? Is there another explanation to the pattern of short and long vowels?

How can we even demonstrate that another pattern exists? The answer, as always in a scientific investigation, is to look at the empirical data. And when we do that in words with a silent *e* this is what we find: there is no silent *e* rule that creates long stem vowels out of short ones. Rather, these vowels start out long, and stay long. Silent *e* exhibits an entirely different function from what is traditionally taught. It protects stem vowels from undergoing rules that would otherwise make them short. It is therefore high time for silent *e* to speak out about its true role in the English alphabetic system.

The functions of the famous silent letter *e* are actually multiple, so its phonics is correspondingly complex. Part of the complexity is due to the fact that silent *e* not only plays a role in the determination of the quality of the preceding vowel, but also figures as a silent placeholder for words that, without it, would violate spelling rules. Indeed, it becomes apparent from an investigation of the phonics of silent *e* that the phonics system as a whole interacts intimately with the spelling system.

Traditionally, silent *e* is the final vowel letter of a word that also contains a preceding vowel letter. Silent *e* receives no pronunciation. The preceding vowel letter is pronounced long. Thus, even from a traditional standpoint, two phonics rules are needed to describe the behavior of silent *e*:

Rule *e*1: Silent *e* is pronounced [ø].

Rule *e*2: The vowel letter preceding silent *e* in the word is pronounced long.

So, a word such as *make* undergoes both of these rules: Letter *a* is pronounced [ey], and letter *e* is pronounced [ø]. Along with the ordinary rules for letters *m* and *k*, the word is ultimately sounded out [meyk].

However, the default value of a vowel letter is already long, and the presence of silent *e* simply assures that the stem vowel will be pronounced with its default sound. In saying that the stem vowel is pronounced long because of a special rule like Rule *e*2, there is an unnecessary redundancy in the system. The long vowel can be produced either by the usual default rule for the vowel letter, or by Rule *e*2.

Indeed, this is an undesirable state of affairs, because it is only by accident that Rule *e*2 produces the same sounds as the default rules for the vowel letters. Rule *e*2 could just as easily stipulate a short vowel, an *r*-controlled vowel, or some other nondefault vowel sound.

A more desirable state of affairs is one in which silent *e* does not directly turn the stem vowel letter into a long vowel sound, but rather, sets up a situation in which the default rule is permitted to apply. Then it is no accident that the vowel sound before silent *e* happens to be just the set of default sounds.

There is independent evidence that this is the empirically correct approach. By way of the spelling system, words typically lose their silent *e* letter when certain suffixes are attached. Thus, we have *shade* and *shady*, *race* and *racist*, *ride* and *riding*. Indeed, from the observation that silent *e* is absent before a suffix that begins with a vowel letter or the letter *y* (or that does not begin with a consonant, cf. *base-baseless*, *whole-wholesome*, *safe-safely*), we can infer that it is the silent *e* that is missing when *e*-initial suffixes are added to a stem. Thus, we have *write-writer*, *rude-ruder*, *rude-rudest*, *shave-shaven*. If silent *e* directly determined the preceding long stem vowel, then there would be no explanation for the long stem vowel in all of these suffixed forms, because they do not contain the silent *e*. As a consequence, the long-vowel rule before silent *e* would have to be expanded manyfold to produce a long vowel also before suffixes *y*, *ist*, *ing*, *er* (agent), *er* (comparative), *est* and *en*:

A stem vowel is pronounced long before silent *e*.
A stem vowel is pronounced long before suffix *y*.
A stem vowel is pronounced long before suffix *ist*.
A stem vowel is pronounced long before suffix *ing*.
A stem vowel is pronounced long before suffix *er* (agent).
A stem vowel is pronounced long before suffix *er* (comparative).
A stem vowel is pronounced long before suffix *est*.
A stem vowel is pronounced long before suffix *en*.

Again, the simplest solution is to allow the default rule for vowels to apply in these cases.

It should be observed that a stem vowel is pronounced long before the various suffixes, provided it is also pronounced long when the suffixes are not present. Thus, in comparison to *line* and *lining*, there is also *win* and *winning*. And compared to *safe* and *safest*, there is also *odd* and *oddest*. This pattern suggests that, if there were a silent *e* rule that rendered the preceding stem vowel letter long in pronunciation, there would have to be some way to express the connection that silent *e* has to these suffixes. For example, the rule for a stem vowel could be that it is long when followed by (certain) suffixes, and that silent *e* was actually an abstract suffix. Or, there could be a rule that undid the spelling change that was responsible for eliminating silent *e* from words with suffixes. Then, silent *e* would reappear, abstractly that is, and the pattern of having a long vowel before both silent *e* and the various suffixes could be expressed.

Of course, there is no independent evidence for either of these solutions. Silent *e* conveys no independent part of speech or semantics that could justify a special suffix status. It appears in nouns (*grape, spice*), verbs (*shine, whine*), and adjectives (*sane, wise*). And reconstructing an abstract silent *e* before suffixes, in order to group the two together, is entirely *ad hoc*.

Thus, describing an interesting letter-sound pattern of English is rendered overly complex if the description is in terms of a direct effect of silent *e* on stem vowels. It is rendered simpler, and more in keeping with other letter-sound patterns, such as the default status of the long-vowel pronunciation, if there is no special silent *e* effect on the stem vowel letter.

Of course, the default rule will apply, and will create the desired vowels, as long as no nondefault rules apply. The nondefault rule of particular concern is the one that produces short vowels. In the previous discussion of Bloomfield's (1942/1961) examples, it was noted that, in general, a short vowel appears when followed by a word-final consonant letter (*pin*) or by two consonant letters. This means that, in the presence of silent *e* and of all the other suffixes, the short-vowel rule will be unable to apply, because silent *e* and the suffixes constitute a violation of this alphabetic requirement of the short-vowel rule.

Compare again *pi, pin,* and *pine.* In *pin,* only a word-final consonant letter follows the stem vowel letter *i,* so it undergoes the short-vowel rule and is pronounced [pIn]. In *pi,* no consonant letters follow the stem vowel. In *pine,* the silent *e* immediately after the consonant letter *n* keeps that *n* from being word final. Therefore, the short-vowel rule does not apply to either of these words. The default rule turns the vowel letter into the sound [ay].

In this way, it can be appreciated that there actually is no silent *e* rule, other than the one that silences the *e* to [ø]. The pedagogical tradition of teaching that a stem vowel is long before silent *e* is just a colloquial shorthand for stating that the short-vowel rule does not apply before silent *e,* and that the vowel therefore acquires its long, default value.

Consider an inflected form of the word *pin,* namely, *pinning,* which retains its short vowel. Clearly, the doubling of the letter *n* creates a short vowel environment, preventing *pinning* from undergoing the default rule for the stem vowel.

The appearance of a short vowel before a pair of identical consonants is a well-known pattern of English spelling and pronounciation. It shows up in words like *putt, watt, fill,* and *fizz.* It determines the pronunciation of acronyms, such as *GATT.* It is responsible for the existence of a geminate (double) consonant cluster in nonword stems that contain short vowels, such as *happy* and *silly,* as opposed to *lazy* and *zany,* with long-vowel pronunciations. It is responsible for the spelling rule that requires the addition of a geminate consonant when adding vowel-initial suffixes such as *win-winning* and *bat-batter.*

Of course, the extra consonant must itself undergo a silencing rule. Because the extra consonant is provided, at least in the suffixed cases, by the spelling requirements of English, it can be appreciated that the function of this spelling change is not to insert a consonant letter that will exhibit its own pronunciation, but rather to ensure the proper pronunciation of other letters in the word, in particular, the stem vowel.

The two-consonant conditioning of the short-vowel rule immediately explains the existence of words in English that contain silent *e,* but where the stem vowel is pronounced short. This occurs in words such as *dance, trance, prance, barge, large, Marge, hence, pence, whence, tense, prince, wince, binge, cringe,* and *hinge.*

Why do these words contain a silent *e,* even though the stem vowel is pronounced short? Consider how they would be spelled and sounded out if the silent *e* were not present. The words *dance, trance, prance, hence, pence, thence, prince,* and *wince* would not only violate a spelling rule of English that prohibits final *nc,* but, on analogy with nonnative loanwords such as *banc,* or abbreviations such as *inc.*, would be pronounced with a final [k], not [s]. Hence, the function of silent *e* is not to produce a long stem vowel in these words, but rather to soften the final consonant *c*, which has the alternative phonic values [k] and [s].

Likewise, silent *e* in a word such as *tense* constrains the phonic value of the preceding *s*. Without silent *e*, the letter *s* would be pronounced as voiced [z], as in the word *tens*. The function of silent *e* is, again, not to determine the pronunciation of the stem vowel letter, but rather the pronunciation of the immediately preceding consonant *s*.

In words with final *rge* or *nge*, silent *e* serves to prevent a hard pronunciation of the letter *g*. Thus, compare *bing* with *binge*. Again, its function is not to produce a long stem vowel.

In words such as *badge*, *ledge*, and *ridge*, the silent *e* once again does not produce a long stem vowel. Its presence this time serves to avoid a violation of the spelling rules of English, which disallow a final *dg*, even though the sound it represents, namely [ĵ], can end a word's pronunciation. Indeed, [ĵ] is the final sound of *badge*, *ledge*, and *ridge*. The more general spelling rule for *dg* is that it can neither begin nor end a word. If a word begins with the sound [ĵ], it must be spelled either with the letter *g* or the letter *j*, as in *gem* and *jet*, not *dgem* or *dget*. If it ends with the sound [ĵ], this sound must be spelled *dg* if the preceding vowel is short, or *ge* if the preceding vowel is long, as in *page* and *rage*. There are some nonnative loanwords with final *j*, such as *Raj* and *Haj*.

Summarizing thus far, it is clear that silent *e* has a number of functions, only one of which is to influence the quality of the stem vowel. In fact, it performs this function indirectly, by setting up the alphabetic conditions that prevent the short-vowel rule from applying, because the rule applies to a stem vowel that is followed either by two consonants or by a single consonant that ends the word. The presence of silent *e* following a stem vowel and a single consonant prevents that consonant from terminating the word, thereby blocking the application of the short-vowel rule. The vowel then undergoes its long, default conversion.

Other functions of silent *e*, as observed, are to prevent *nc* from terminating a word, to prevent *dg* from terminating a word, to soften a preceding *c* in words with *nc*, to soften a preceding *g* in words with *ng*, and to render an immediately preceding letter *s* voiceless in pronunciation when it appears in the cluster *ns*.

Certain patterns of exceptions exist. For example, words such as *range* and *strange*, and *haste* and *baste* exhibit a long vowel in the presence of silent *e* even though there are two consonant letters. For *range* and *strange*, silent *e* functions to produce a soft *g* sound (compare *rang* and *range*). But the long vowel means that words spelled with *ange* are exceptions to the short-vowel rule that should apply before two consonants.

In *haste* and *baste*, silent *e* serves no obvious function for the preceding consonants. They are pronounced exactly the same in the pseudowords *hast* and *bast*. Words in *aste* are also exceptions to the short-vowel rule.

A final class of exceptions consists of words such as *dove* (bird), *give, have, live* (verb), *love,* and *shove.* Clearly, the silent *e* functions here to prevent a word-final letter *v*. These words, though, are pronounced with a short vowel, where a long one is expected. However, there is no mechanism in the system thus far developed that could produce this short vowel. For example, simply stating that the words are exceptions to the ordinary default rule for vowels still does not trigger any particular short-vowel rule. The words cannot be spelled *dovv, givv,* and *havv,* because this would violate the idiosyncratic spelling rule of English that prohibits geminate *v* (Venezky, 1999, p. 13). These words must undergo a special, nondefault rule that gives the stem vowel of words ending in *ve* a short pronunciation. Then, words like *dive, dove* (verb), *live* (adjective), *shave,* and so on, are exceptions to this rule.

Therefore, the rules that apply to stem vowels in words spelled with *ve* may in fact be the only phonics rules in English where there is a direct influence of silent *e* on the stem vowel. But the rule creates a short vowel, not a long one, contrary to classroom tradition. This empirical finding should be kept in mind the next time a teacher is forced to teach a profit-friendly silent *e* rule, or a child is made to suffer through it.

Chapter 12

The Naturalness of Exceptions to Phonics Rules

The complexity of the phonics rules proposed previously may seem somewhat strange. What does it mean to say that one phonics rule assigns an exceptional status to a string or word with respect to another phonics rule? Why should phonics rules behave according to a Principle for Competing Phonics Rules (PCPR)?

But reflecting on the panoply of phonics rules, and on the global principles governing their interaction, makes it clear that there is a fundamental naturalness to their formulation. Consider the simple rules for digraphs, such as "*ph* is pronounced [f]" or "*ch* is pronounced [č]." To say, for example, that "*ph* is pronounced [f]" applies to an input string like *Phil*, and that "*p* is pronounced [p]" and "*h* is pronounced [h]" do not, is simply another way of saying that *Phil* is an exception to the latter rules.

Thus, the PCPR simply describes the conditions under which an input string is an exception to a rule, and undergoes another rule instead. From this perspective, it is entirely natural to expect the phonics system to also include rules that simply assign exception status to certain strings. In this manner, the system allows words that are exceptions to the exceptions. Thus, *pint* is an exception to the short-vowel rule, which itself is an exception to the default rule "*i* is pronounced [ay]."

The existence of exceptions to exceptions can be seen whenever there are three groups of words with respect to a rule: (a) *pi* and *hi* undergo only default rules, yielding [pay] and [hay]; (b) *pin, sin, hint* undergo the "*i* is pronounced [I]" rule, which is an exception to the default rule "*i* is pronounced [ay]," and because no other nondefault rules apply to these words, they can be called *first-order exceptions*; (c) *bind, find,* and *grind* are *sec-*

ond-order exceptions, with pronunciations determined by the rule "*ind* is an exception to the short-vowel rule for letter *i*," which itself is an exception to the default rule for vowel letter *i*; (d) *wind* (a stormy wind) is a *third-order exception,* because it is an exception to the *ind* rule, which itself is an exception to the short-vowel rule, which itself is an exception to the default rule for the vowel letter *i*.

The full phonics system is replete with these layered exceptions. Thus, *ma* and *pa* are first-order exceptions to the default rule for the letter *a*. Words ending in *ild* and *old,* such as *child, mild, wild, cold, gold, hold, mold, sold,* and *told,* are first-order exceptions to the short rule for vowel letters *i* and *o*. The word *have* is an exception to the default rule for the vowel letters *a* and *e,* thus making it a double first-order exception. Clearly, the status of a form as a first or higher order exception does not mean that its pronunciation pattern is unusual, nor that its spelling pattern is all that strange. The theoretical significance of the order of an exception is still unstudied, but an interesting empirical question is whether these exception parameters play a role in some aspect of literacy development, such as invented spellings, the pronunciation of unfamiliar words, and so on.

The reasons for the existence of layered exceptions are several. First, we can immediately observe that there is a mismatch between the number of alphabetic letters in the system (26) and the number of phonemes in the spoken language (about 45). There can only be 26 default rules. Some sounds of the language therefore do not have their own, private letters. Of necessity, therefore, some letters will be used to represent more than one sound, creating conditions for both default and nondefault rules.

First and higher order exceptions can also arise from the existence of quite natural phonemic alternations in the spoken language. Because inflectional suffixes spelled with the letter *s* are pronounced with a voiceless [s] sound when immediately following a voiceless consonant sound, as in *tops, pots,* and *pocks,* but with a [z] sound otherwise, then an invariant spelling of the suffix must undergo nondefault rules to produce its range of pronunciations. As previously noted, the invariant spelling of a morpheme that has variant pronunciations serves the useful purpose of conveying the identity of the suffix. Therefore, the exception rules of phonics follow necessarily from this advantageous function.

First and higher order exceptions will make their appearance when phonics patterns come face to face with other requirements of the system. Some of the most unforgiving requirements come from the spelling rules. For example, there are only rare exceptions to the prohibition against final *v* and *u,* such as colloquial *gov,* nickname *Bev,* or loanword *gnu.* The written language needs one or more mechanisms to render words legal with respect to the spelling rules. In English, this often takes the form of a placeholder silent *e*. But then the spellings thus created to satisfy the spelling requirements, such as *have* and *give,* will of necessity complicate the phonics patterns.

Historically, many spelling patterns have absolutely nothing to do with pronunciation. In his wonderful *Encyclopedia of the English Language,* Crystal (1995) pointed out a number of these. Early printers, for example, would simply add letters to a word in order to make a sequence of words fit neatly into a line, so that "line justification was often achieved by shortening or lengthening words rather than by varying the word spaces. Variarion in the final *e* of a word was a common result" (p. 274). In this way, some words actually acquired several spellings, such as *dog, dogg, dogge.*

Crystal (1995) also noted that "16th-century scholars tried to indicate something of the history of a word in its spelling. The *b* in *debt,* for example, was added by people who felt it was important for everyone to know that the word comes from *debitum* in Latin" (p. 275). Other words that changed their spellings accordingly are *doubt, reign,* and *island.* The practice, according to Crystal (p. 275), overextended to words such as *delight* and *tight.*

Crystal (p. 67) discussed the well-known example of 16th century schoolmaster Richard Mulcaster, who was influential in achieving some regularization of English spelling, but who did not equate regularization with phoneticization. Mulcaster advocated "increased use of a . . . silent *e*" to mark a preceding long vowel (p. 67). As with words with silent *gh,* however, it is generally felt that Mulcaster's idea was applied a little too liberally, so that short vowels and silent *e* now cooccur in *some, gone, done, give, love,* and *have.*

In the end, English spelling "is an amalgam of several traditions" (Crystal, p. 275). But the traditions themselves are hardly potent enough to prevent the natural history of language from producing mismatches between spellings and pronunciations. Over time, an unavoidable discrepancy between spellings and pronunciations results simply from the *physical* difference between visual matter and auditory matter. Oral language is quick to produce, and dissipates almost immediately once uttered. Visual language is slower to produce, but persists. It is in virtue of this difference that spoken language works best in immediate space and time, whereas visual language works best over prolonged space and time.

The flip side of this, of course, is that the pace of oral language change is significantly different from that of visual language. It is the material character of oral language that frees it up to undergo change at a much more rapid pace than that of visual language. So, an earlier version of a spoken language will, after a period of decades or centuries, turn into a variety of distinct languages and dialects. But the visual representation of that language remains relatively fixed and stable.

It is this differential rate of change, ultimately due to the different properties of the physical media, that leads to a separation over time between spellings and their pronunciations. Even if they start out perfectly transparent, with each letter of a word's spelling corresponding unambiguously to a phoneme of the spoken language, there will be a historical divergence, with spellings more transparently representing older pronunciations of the word. Conversely, such spellings less transparently represent contemporary pronunciations.

This is indeed borne out by countless examples. Consider the *l* that appears in the spelling of words such as *would* and *should*. This *l* is silent in modern English pronunciations. So why is it part of the spelling of these words? Clearly, it is because the spelling represents an earlier stage of the word, corresponding to an oral language in which it was pronounced. Indeed, Old English spellings reflected the contemporary pronunciations of *wolde* and *scyld*, which included the sound [l].

This diametrical opposition between the physics of a visual medium and the physics of an auditory medium takes form in the phonics system, where spellings and pronunciations stand in relation to one another. Though we can rationally unravel the uneven oral and visual changes over time, and understand why a particular spelling is opaque with respect to its pronunciation, the formal phonics system has no privileged access to its own history. Thus, changes that may have taken centuries to materialize are forced to confront each other in the moment. This confrontation must lead to a disturbance in the system, because simple, general, default rules are no longer capable of expressing all the spelling-sound relationships.

Clearly, a rule does not have to be specifically characterized as an exception rule for it to function as such. Even a rule like "*ph* is pronounced [f]," which looks rather benign, and applies virtually across the board, expresses the exceptional status of *ph* words with respect to the rules "*p* is pronounced [p]" and "*h* is pronounced [h]." Exceptional patterns may still be quite regular.

In an important sense, therefore, any phonic pattern governed by a rule other than a default rule is an exception pattern, but it is really only for expository purposes that the term *exception rule* has been used in the more limited sense of referring to rules that actually assign an exception status, marked with an asterisk, to a string. And, strings can acquire or develop multiple exception patterns. The embedding of exceptions occurs on input strings of ever-increasing size. The limiting string in such a sequence is a particular, individual word

Thus, "*ea* is pronounced [iy]," as in *beak, beat, feat, freak, heat, leak, neat, peak, peat, seat,* and *wheat,* expresses the observation that words with *ea* are exceptions to "*a* is pronounced [ey]." Nothing more than *ea* needs to be specified in the rule's input. In particular, we do not need to encode in the rule the specific words that undergo it. These will be found simply by a scanning of the input string for the substring *ea*.

But *steak*, idiosyncratically pronounced [steyk], and not the expected [stiyk], needs its own rule: "*steak* is pronounced *st*[ey]*k*." A similar idiosyncratic rule applies to *great*. Such rules have an entire word as input, expressing the observation that it is the word itself that is the exception, not simply the string of letters that constitutes the word's spelling. They are whole-word exceptions, and undergo whole-word phonics rules, which is the theoretical significance of the phenomenon of sight words.

Similiarly, we can say that "*said* is pronounced *s*[E]*d*" expresses the observation that the word *said* is an exception to "*ai* is pronounced [ey]," "*plaid* is pronounced *pl*[æ]*d*" expresses a similar observation; "*one* is pronounced [wʌ]*n*" expresses the observation that the word *one* is idiosyncratically pronounced with an initial [w] and an unexpected vowel; "*gone* is pronounced *g*[a]*n*" expresses the observation that the word *gone* is an exception to the default rule for vowel letter *o*; and "*son* is pronounced *s*[ʌ]*n*" expresses the observation that the word *son* is an exception to "*o* is pronounced [a]."

Yet how can we be certain that it is not the letter strings *said, plaid, one, gone,* and *son* that are exceptions, rather than the words themselves? The answer, as always in a scientific investigation, depends on what is revealed by an examination of the empirical evidence.

Consider simple examples like *tone* and *lone*. These undergo the usual rules that convert them to [town] and [lown]. In fact, these rules are phonically general, applying to most input strings with an initial consonant and stem vowel *o* in the setting of a silent *e*.

Now consider the pronunciation of the word *one*. If the rule that converted *one* into a phonemic string with an initial [w] applied to the letter string *one*, and not to the word *one*, then it should also apply to *tone* and *lone*, indeed, to any string containing the letter string *one*. But this is clearly not the case. Words with a consonant letter before *one*, that is, C*one*, are not pronounced [Cwʌn].

Therefore, to maintain the hypothesis that "*one* is pronounced [wʌ]n" applies to the letter string *one*, and not to the word *one*, we would have to say that *tone* and *lone*, in fact, all words spelled with a consonant letter followed by *one*, are exceptions to the rule for *one*. This rule would be "C*one* is an exception to the rule '*one* is pronounced [wʌ]n.' " But this is an entirely *ad hoc* solution, forced on us solely by the assumption that "*one* is pronounced [wʌ]*n*" applies to the letter string *one*, not the word *one*. It turns a whole class of regularly behaving words into an otherwise unnecessary exception class, because this exception status is entirely avoidable with the more natural assumption that "*one* is pronounced [wʌ]*n*" applies to the word *one*. As such, *tone* and *lone* are not pronounced with a [w] sound for the very simple reason that they do not contain the *word one*, but only the *letter string one*.

Phonics rules can apply to successively larger domains, approaching the level of the word. Thus, what I have called a default rule applies to a single letter, without regard for neighboring letters. Some rules apply to a small string of letters, such as *ph* or *sh*. Others apply to a single letter, but only in the setting of certain other letters, such as letter *i* becoming long [ay] when followed by word-final *nd*. And still others apply to single or multiple letters, but only when they occur in specific words, such as *ai* becoming [E] in *said*, *ea* becoming [ey] in *break*, *great*, and *steak* (but not in *bread*, *grease*, and *stealth*).

Not all words can, even in principle, undergo word-level phonics rules. Such rules can apply only to an already existing word. They cannot apply to possible but nonexistent words, such as those used in experimental studies of decoding. It makes no sense to say that a phonics rule exists that applies to the possible though nonexistent word *glig*. What peculiarity of English could possibly prompt such a rule? On what basis would someone even know that it existed, having no prior experience with *glig*?

Word-based phonics rules do not arise in a vacuum. There can be no such rule that applies to the nonexistent *glig* in anticipation of its coinage some time in the future. Instead, word-based phonics rules arise in the course of the actual history of the language, which affects written and oral forms differently, engendering a divergence of path for the two, and leading, in some cases, to letter-sound relationships that are so opaque as to apply only to one particular word.

When experimental scientists use possible but nonexistent words as a way to test phonological processing and knowledge of phonics, they are only getting at a portion of the rules that actually exist, and certainly not the ones that reflect the real-life linguistic and nonlinguistic forces that operate on the lexicon, and that push individual words to their own, unique phonic identities. Possible but nonexistent words have no history, so their phonic structure will be ahistorical and pure. This is a position hardly distinguishable from that of the spelling reformers, and reflects a misguided notion of how human language is supposed to work. It is a view that sets up an unattainable and sanitized version of language that is supposed to provide simple minds with the key to learning.

The fundamental difference, therefore, between possible written words and actual written words is that only actual words tolerate, indeed are defined by, a capacity for idiosyncratic uniqueness in phonic behavior, which itself is the result of accumulated forks in the road that develop historically between visual and auditory media. But this phonic chasm between possible and actual words just highlights how misleading it is to study the phonological processing of possible words as a means of understanding the phonological processing of actual words. In the same way that there is a qualitative difference between reading for sound and reading for meaning, so that the study of the former does not carry over to the study of the latter, so too does the qualitative difference between the phonic behavior of possible words and that of actual words render the study of the former nontransferable to the latter.

It should be abundantly clear, as already pointed out, that individual phonics rules do not necessarily convert letters to sounds. Rather, it is the system as a whole that does this. The complex system of phonics—a system that relates a set of alphabetic letters to a larger set of phonemes, that interacts with a set of spelling rules, that turns strings of letters into exceptions to rules, that converts some derived sounds into others, that obeys principles that evaluate whether one string is contained within another—was not molded by history to be classroom friendly, or to be a lesson-plan entry for a reading curriculum. History could not care less about such matters.

Contrary to Foorman and colleagues (Foorman et al., 1997), even if some aspects of the system were "intentionally" and "conventionally" constructed, once in the system they evolve and take on a life of their own, moving way beyond any alleged initial intention or convention. The model of phonics explicated earlier was developed simply to explain the empirical facts of this evolved letter-sound system, and its logical organization. It is only by studying the system of interest that we can assess whether, and to what extent, it needs to be known in order for someone to be a competent reader.

The psychology and pedagogy of phonics are separate, though related matters. They deal with whether and how letter-sound relationships are learned, and whether and how letter-sound relationships are to be taught in order for them to be learned. But even if we agree that the system must be known, and must be learned in order to be known, and must be taught in order to be learned, no classroom teacher would believe that directly teaching the full complex formal system is the way to accomplish this. Clearly, the millions of proficient readers who have never been taught phonics as such constitute crucial evidence in favor of the view that the full system is not "nonnegotiable."

Still, one could argue that, as with virtually every other classroom subject, the material must be simplified in order to make it teachable and learnable, not to mention fun, attention grabbing, and meaningful, a "valuable gift" rather than "hard work" for the students. The various commercial phonics programs, which of course bear little resemblance to phonics as an abstract system and which are more accurately called *pseudophonics*, may be thought of as pedagogical material that allows a beginning reader to enter the system. It is a key that unlocks the door to further development of the phonics knowledge base needed to become a proficient reader.

This is the most generous interpretation one can make of commercial phonics programs, given that the actual system of phonics is profoundly more complex than what these programs express in their materials. But we must then ask: What will the developing reader have gained by entering this system?

One empirically supportable answer to this question has already been provided by Richard Venezky (1999), who stated the following:

> Phonics is a means to an end, not an end itself. Its functions are somewhat speculative, but most scholars agree that at least three are crucial to the acquisition of competent reading habits. One is to provide a process for approximating the sound of a word known from listening but not recognized quickly by sight. For this to work, decoding patterns need not generate perfect representations of speech. Instead they need to get the reader close enough that, with context, the correct identification can be made. (p. 231)

Venezky's important point is based, in part, on the observation that phonics rules converting letters into sounds cannot by themselves guarantee a single pronunciation for any given word spelling. Sometimes more than one pronunciation is available for a single spelling. Sometimes information other than letter-sound correspondences is needed in order to identify a written word's pronunciation. Thus, in more than one way, even if the alphabetic principle were a necessary condition for pronunication of a written word, it is far from a sufficient condition.

There are numerous examples that demonstrate this, some of which have already been discussed. A stem vowel immediately followed by a consonant letter *v* and final, silent *e* can be pronounced either short or long, as in *give* and *hive.* The short-vowel forms are whole-word exceptions to the rule that assigns a long vowel in the setting of silent *e.*

Words with an interdental fricative [ð], such as *gather, rather, tether,* and *slither,* have a short stem-vowel pronunciation, on the basis of the word being monomorphemic. An exceptional short-vowel pattern appears in single morpheme forms with vowel letter *o,* such as *brother, mother, other,* and *smother,* thus requiring that *bother* be singled out as a whole-word exception, which thereby allows it to undergo the usual short-vowel rule.

When the final *er* is a suffix, the stem vowel can be long, provided it is long in the unsuffixed form. This can be seen in pairs such as *bathe-bather* and *teethe-teether.* The possibility therefore exists for dual pronunciations, as in *lather* (soap) and *lather* (lathe operator), corresponding to the morphological status of these words as either monomorphemic or bimorphemic.

Simple words ending in *ow* can also have more than one pronunciation, but in this case there is no internal morphological information that can supplement the phonics rules to make the correct identification. Alongside *how, now,* and *cow,* as well as *know, low,* and *mow,* all of which have a single pronunciation, we also have the dually pronounced *bow* and *sow.*

Monomorphemic words like *water* and *river* contrast with *fiber* and *Rover.* A stem-vowel pronunciation is retained in the affixed form: *grow-grower* and *slow-slower.* These complexities again create the possibility of dual pronunciations, as in *shower* (take a shower) and *shower* (shower of dogs), or *tower* (tower of Babel) and *tower* (tower of cars).

Words with the vowel digraph *ea* can be pronounced either as short [E] (*bread, sweat*) or long (*bead, seat*). Dual forms exist, as in *read* (past and present tense) and *lead* (a lead pipe, lead a band). The stem vowel is retained in suffixed forms, as in *breaded, sweating, beaded,* and *seated.*

The only written word types whose pronunciations are both unambiguous and completely determined by the letters in the word's spelling are those that undergo rules that essentially have no exceptions. This can be seen in examples like *pin, pit, tip,* and *tin,* each of which has only one pronunciation, completely unconnected to the word's morphological or syntactic status. It is no wonder that Bloomfield (1942/1961) chose such words to elucidate his conception of an ideal phonics system. And it is no wonder that fundamentalist phonics primers grind out unnatural language about *fat cats* and *mats.* Yet even in these cases, pronunciation alone will not suffice to narrow down a word's identification, given the abundance of homonyms and productive metaphorical extensions in the language. To identify *bat* (rodent) versus *bat* (baseball tool) versus *bat* (to hit a ball) versus *bat* (flicker an eyelash), or *pit* (fruit component) versus *pit* (mining site) versus *pit* (confront), and so on and so on, a reader who only used letter-sound conversions would be entirely unsuccessful.

Therefore, it is perfectly clear that the pronunciation of written words depends on more than just alphabetic information, and that the alphabetic principle is insufficient to explain letter-sound conversions. Perhaps most damaging to phonics fanatics is that *pronunciation, no matter how it is derived, still does not guarantee word identification.* Thus, the raison d'être of pedagogical phonics, that it is needed so that a reader can identify a word, is undermined by an empirical elucidation of the phonics system.

Strangely, Lyon (cited in Clowes, 1999, par. 7) insisted that context does not aid in identifying a word:

> Surprisingly, and in contrast to what conventional wisdom has suggested in the past, expert readers do *not* use the surrounding context to figure out a word they've never seen before. The strategy of choice for expert readers is to actually fixate on that word and decode it to sound using phonics. (par. 10, emphasis original)

But it is absolutely necessary for him to hold this completely untenable position in order to be a consistent advocate of intensive phonics instruction, because if one acknowledged that context *could* in fact aid in identifying a word, then one should also advocate research to see whether context is actually *indispensable* in identifying a word. If it is, then a pedagogy of isolated, intensive phonics would be irretrievably undermined.

Even Venezky's (1999) study, probably the most rigorous work on the rules of letter-sound relationships, concluded that context is an indispensable element in a reading instruction program that uses phonics. Indeed, there is so much empirical evidence that supports the role of nonphonics contextual information in reading (Goodman, 1965, 1973, 1976, 1994; Smith, 1994), even in mere word identification, that the only way to make sense of Lyon's assertion (Clowes, 1999) is to acknowledge that he is at least being consistent in advocating a view that is forced on him solely by the logic of his paradigm.

The empirical evidence against Lyon's view (Clowes, 1999) is so potent that it cuts in two ways: context aids in word identification, and reliance only on phonics cannot lead to word-identification. At best, therefore, even if we agree that the goal of instruction should be to teach children word identification strategies, phonics can only take the learner so far. Pounding phonics into the minds of little children will not magically narrow things down any more, even if we believe in magical thinking.

Chapter 13

Applications of Scientific Phonics

A scientific theory demonstrates its explanatory power when it sheds light on phenomena not originally considered in the development of the theory itself. In this chapter, I discuss some simple examples that suggest the potential power of a scientific theory of phonics. Hopefully, they will prompt further investigations. But before proceeding to these examples, and in order to clarify certain concepts, I first restate some of the important problems that distinguish scientific phonics from pseudophonics.

A scientific study of phonics is rooted in two important notions. First, it is based on an empirical investigation of the patterns of letter-sound connection *as they actually exist in the language*, not as they exist in unscientific, pragmatically inspired commercial primers. Second, it recognizes the relevance to the study of letter-sound relationships of the logically distinct, yet empirically interrelated, notions of epistemology, psychology, and pedagogy.

Pseudoscientific phonics, on the other hand, prides itself on experimental studies that use traditional patterns, themselves the stock of phonics primers, as if there were some scientific basis for their existence. In fact, they merely represent simplistic formulations of letter-sound relationships that, at best, only approximate the empirical truth. Pseudoscientific phonics inappropriately conflates the categories of epistemology, psychology, and pedagogy, leading to the baseless conclusion that a teachable and classroom-friendly, yet nonscientific, letter-sound pattern is one that a developing reader needs to learn in order to become a reader, and needs to know in order to be a reader.

Thus, although the neophonics community blows its horns for "research-based" instructional practices in reading, and for science that is "trustworthy" because it is "valid" and "reliable," it has not even undertaken to demonstrate the validity of its own notion of phonics, a notion that underlies the instructional practices and assessment materials it uses in its experiments. Calling a letter-sound connection "phonics" does not make it so, just as teaching children to recognize a common noun if it refers to a person, place, or thing is only a pretense of scientific syntax.

With this understanding, consider how an advocate of neophonics might respond to the following hypothetical study. A group of children undergoes intensive training on certain phonics patterns, over a reasonably long period of time. However, pre- and posttraining assessments reveal no improvement in their decoding skills. Upon careful scrutiny of the study, everyone agrees that the experimental design was pristine, the sample size more than adequate, and the statistical analysis flawless. So, why didn't the children benefit from the instruction?

Suppose we are able to rule out any question about possible learning disabilities on the part of the children, and teaching disabilities on the part of the teachers. What remains at this point as the most likely culprit is the actual instructional material itself.

Perusing these materials, we discover something curious. It seems that the researchers employed an instructional phonics pattern for vowel digraphs, in which the children were taught to pronounce the digraph by sounding out only the first letter of the pair, and ignoring the second. To demonstrate the pattern, the children were given lessons on the spellings and pronunciations of words like *Mae, maid, gauge, team, teen, tie, goat, hoe, true,* and *juice.* The pattern was readily committed to memory, as it was contained in the catchy jingle: "When two vowels go walking, the first one does the talking." In fact, the children could repeat this jingle so quickly and accurately, it was obvious that it had become automatic.

Of course, the clever children noticed that the fabled Aesop, author of the tales that their teacher had been reading to them during recess, had a name that disobeyed the jingle. Prompted by this delightful finding, the children quickly found other exceptions: *plaid, said, gauze, bread, head, lead, been, heir, tier, trio, broad, blood, food, good, should,* and *duo.* The teacher could not keep their hands down. Indeed, they found more words that were jinglephobic than jinglephilic. Fortunately, having learned from past experience, they set aside ample space on the blackboard for such recalcitrants.

But now we have found a hypothesis that may explain why the children's decoding skills did not improve: They were taught an incorrect phonics pattern. They should have been taught that the jingle probably holds for most words in *ai, ee,* and *oa,* but after that, it's up for grabs, with words in *au, ei,* and *oo* virtually never following the pattern.

But is this a plausible hypothesis for a neophonics researcher? The answer is a decisive "no." Indeed, on what grounds could a neophonics researcher claim that *any* pattern is correct or incorrect? The neophonics researcher has no independent theory of letter-sound connections on which to base such a claim. The only claim that can be made is that some phonics lessons impart good decoding skills when taught, whereas others do not. This may be trustworthy pragmatics, but it is hardly trustworthy science.

Thus, in principle, an advocate of intensive phonics instruction who pushes "research-based" instructional practices undermines the very claim to scientific trustworthiness when there is no independent theory of letter-sound relationships. Without such a theory, we simply do not know if what is being taught is a real phonics pattern, only an approximation of a phonics pattern, or no phonics pattern at all, that is, a bogus pattern. This is *not* to argue that only scientific phonics should be taught in the classroom, and that there is no place for simplified approximations. That is another matter altogether. Rather, the issue is that neophonics, in the end, is grounded in pragmatism and not, as it claims, in valid and reliable science.

Even less satisfying for those eager to develop a scientific understanding of the forms and functions of written language is that neophonics, in lacking an empirically based theory of letter-sound relationships that is independent of the teaching and learning of decoding, has nothing to say about various other written-language phenomena that also exhibit letter-sound connections. These include children's invented spellings, dialect or nonstandard spellings, and spellings from historically earlier forms of the language. But because scientific phonics sets the abstract system of letter-sound relationships apart from how it is learned or taught, it can easily ask whether the laws of the system that are derived from conventional contemporary written English are applicable elsewhere.

Children's invented spellings constitute one class of written words that may be profitably evaluated against the backdrop of general laws of letter-sound connection. The letters used in these spellings are not motivated by a desire to be classroom friendly, or to conform to traditional patterns, at least at the earliest stages. Rather, the sizable and interesting literature on invented spellings has shown that the unconventional spellings used by young, developing writers are based on their tacit knowledge of phonetic categories, and on strategies that manipulate letter names (Read, 1975).

Typically, for example, a child at a very early stage of writing development will represent long vowel sounds with letters whose names are pronounced with those sounds. The letter *a*, for example, spells the sound [ey], and letter *e* spells the sound [iy]. The same letters are used to represent the phonetically lax, short counterparts of these long and tense sounds, such as letter *a* spelling the sound [ɛ], and letter *e* spelling the sound [I].

Can scientific phonics, with its notion of an abstract letter-sound system that contains rules of a certain form, add to our understanding of invented spellings? Consider one first grader's writing samples with "translation" by Temple et al. (1982, p. 60). This child wrote *I GOT BET BAY MSKEDAS AN ET HRT*, translated as *I got bit by mosquitos and it hurt*, and *I EM GONE TO FRJEYE AN I HAV A HEDAC*, translated as *I am going to Virginia and I have a headache.*

Notice, first of all, that this writer's invented spellings exhibit well-documented characteristics. The letter *J* is used to spell the sound that begins its name, that is, [ĵ] (*FRJEYE* "Virginia"). A short-vowel sound is spelled with the vowel letter whose long-vowel pronunciation is the phonetically tense variant of that short vowel. Thus, the letter *E* is used to spell the sound [I] (*BET* "bit"; *ET* "it"), the short, phonetically nontense variant of long, tense [iy].

But Temple et al. (1982) made an additional interesting and important observation about these invented spellings. They pointed out that "every letter in the sample stands for a sound, and no letters are supplied unnecessarily" (p. 60). That is, there are no silent letters. Thus, in *FRJEYE, F* stands for [f], *R* stands for [R], *J* stands for [ĵ], and so on.

Some sounds are not supplied with a letter. There is no letter for the [n] sound of *Virginia.* And the [d] of *and* lacks a letter, though perhaps this is also missing in the child's ordinary pronunciation of the word.

In this system, therefore, each letter has a corresponding sound, but not every sound has a corresponding letter. This principle manifests itself in a number of additional ways. There are no consonant digraphs to be found in the spellings of *HEDAC* "headache," and *GONE* "going." There is no vowel digraph or silent *e* in the spelling *HEDAC* "headache." The syllabic *R* of *HRT* "hurt" and *FRJEYE* "Virginia" is spelled with a single letter *R*, not with a vowel-*R* combination. Silent *e* is absent in *HAV* "have."

For this child, an otherwise expected vowel letter is absent not only when the vowel sound is syllabic *R*, or the [ø] of silent *e*, or derived from a conventionally written digraph, but in the first syllable of the word *MSKEDAS* "mosquitos" as well. In this word, instead of a vowel letter appearing in the first syllable, the letter *S* seems to take on this syllabic function. Indeed, from an articulatory standpoint, there is an almost immediate transition from [m] to [s], and the [s] can be elongated in its oral rendering, analogous to any vowel sound.

Given this observation , all of the invented spellings in this simple corpus can be seen to obey the principle that, within words, letters representing consonant and vowel sounds must alternate with one another, as shown in Fig. 13.1. Notice that, in order to maintain this template, letter *Y* must be regarded as a consonant letter only, not as a vowel letter, so that it not only spells the sound [y] in *FRJEYE*, but, in addition, it requires the intrusion of an otherwise unconventional vowel letter in the spelling *BAY* "by." The word for "and" keeps its *N*, but therefore does not permit its *D*, because that

V CVC CVC CVC CVCVCVC VC VC CVC

I GOT BET BAY MSKEDAS AN ET HRT.

V VC CVCV CV CVCVCV VC V CVC V CVCVC

I EM GONE TO FRJEYE AN I HAV A HEDAC

FIG. 13.1. Structure of invented spellings.

would create two consonant letters in succession. The word for "going" is spelled *GONE*, because the otherwise expected *GOEN*, in containing two successive vowels, would violate the template.

Clearly, the template is a feature of the spelling system alone, and not of the pronunciations of the words, because not all of the spelled words match the template phonetically, insofar as they do not all have alternating consonant-vowel pronunciations, as in *mo*[sk]*uitos*, *Virgi*[ny]*a*, and *a*[nd].

The template immediately expresses the notion that for this child, a word's spelling only approximates its pronunciation, a finding consistent with Venezky's (1999, p. 231) notion of the role of letter-sound connections in word identification. In addition, the requirement that each letter have a corresponding sound, in conjunction with the general absence of consonantal digraphs, vocalic digraphs, double letters to represent syllabic *R*, and so on, strongly suggests that the individual letter-sound correspondences that describe the corpus are all of the simplest form: A phoneme is represented by a single letter, without reference to any other letter in the word's spelling. The phonics rules for the first sentence of this corpus can be expressed as in Table 13.1.

TABLE 13.1
Phonics Rules for Invented Spellings

I GOT BET BAY MSKEDAS AN ET HRT.		
I is pronounced [ay].	*A* is pronounced [a].	*A* is pronounced [æ].
G is pronounced [g].	*Y* is pronounced [y].	*S* is pronounced [z].
O is pronounced [a].	*M* is pronounced [m].	*A* is pronounced [ə].
T is pronounced [t].	*S* is pronounced [s].	*N* is pronounced [n].
B is pronounced [b].	*K* is pronounced [k].	*H* is pronounced [h].
E is pronounced [I].	*E* is pronounced [iy].	*R* is pronounced [R].
T is pronounced [t].	*D* is pronounced [d].	

Clearly, all of the rules in Table 13.1 have a default form, where a single letter becomes a sound without influence from any neighboring letters. But on closer inspection, we see that certain letters can represent more than one sound. Thus, letter *A* can spell the sounds [a], [ə], and [æ]. Letter *E* can spell the sounds [I] and [iy]. Thus, whereas the individual rules exhibit a default form, the system as a whole does not exhibit a strict default function, in which each letter has one, and only one, default phoneme.

Of course, the previous examples can be described by nondefault rules that turn letters into sounds in virtue of their appearing in a specified alphabetic context. Thus, the letter *E* is pronounced [I] when followed by a word-final consonant letter, as in *BET*.

However, there is little independent evidence for the use of nondefault spellings by this young writer. For example, even though the word *I* is spelled with the letter *I*, which appears to be a conventional spelling, this could just as easily follow from the letter being used in a default fashion. The spelling *HEDAC*, however, uses *E* in a conventional way, to spell short [ɛ], whereas the typical invented patterns use *E* for the sounds [iy] and [I]. This conventional short-vowel usage does suggest a nondefault correspondence.

The strategy of using a simple alternating consonant-vowel template in conjunction with rules that, for the most part, hold to a simple, default form, is a hypothesis about this stage of this particular child's writing development. It is obviously preliminary. The analysis is motivated solely by the desire to demonstrate the possibility of using constructs from a scientific theory of phonics to understand certain aspects of literacy.

It should be acknowledged that an abstract model of letter-sound relationships is also missing from meaning-centered approaches to reading. But then, its adherents have not claimed that the alphabetic principle is the "nonnegotiable" element of reading. What it has claimed, that attention to meaning is central and paramount, it has also studied, so that we now have a much better understanding of the cognitive resources that thinking beings use in this task.

A scientific understanding of phonics distinguishes the abstract letter-sound system from how it is learned, and whether it needs to be taught. Meaning-centered advocates have addressed this issue as well. There is abundant evidence that a child who appears weak with a certain letter-sound pattern in some situations may nevertheless exhibit little difficulty in other situations. This immediately poses the question of whether the pattern needs to be explicitly taught, or if we just need to alter the reading situation so as to better elicit what the reader already knows.

For example, Goodman and Marek (1996) described a young reader named Amy, whose teacher wanted to know if she was correctly learning the *ea* digraph. The teacher prepared a word list containing *ea* words, with instructions for Amy to identify whether the word was pronounced with the vowel sound of *each*, *head*, or *great*. (A fourth sound for *ea* occurs in the pronunciation of the word *bear*, which is distinct from the vowel sound of *dear*, *fear*, and so on.) The teacher also composed a short story filled with *ea* words, and had Amy read the story aloud. On the word-list assignment, Amy missed 15 of the first 31 words (she did not complete the task), identifying *sweat* and *pheasant*, for example, as pronounced with the vowel sound of the word *each*. She missed 1 word out of 19 in the short passage, and had no difficulty with the words *sweat* and *pheasant*.

Amy was thus quite erratic in decoding *ea* on her worksheet, but she pronounced nearly every *ea* word in her text reading exactly as expected. Thus, for Amy, there was slightly better-than-chance performance on word identification in isolation, in which the demand is greater on using letter-sound knowledge, and near-perfect performance on words in the context of a story, where grammatical and extragrammatical cuing sources are available.

Does Amy need extra instruction in decoding *ea*? Anyone who believes that her accurate rendition of the text words is due to successful decoding must acknowledge that she already knows the pattern. This is especially true if context is not utilized, as Lyon (Clowes, 1999) has claimed. Therefore, giving her lessons on decoding *ea* will not teach her anything she does not already know.

But if context is not utilized, including syntactic and textual features, how else can the discrepancy in Amy's oral readings be explained? Clearly, neophonics offers no solution to this problem. The *ea* pattern is no different for a word in isolation versus the same word in a text. But if a neophonics advocate acquiesces to the utility of contextual information, as this case strongly argues for, then the alphabetic principle suddenly becomes very negotiable.

How might an advocate of meaning-centered reading explain Amy's performance? Of course, it is perfectly clear that utilizing syntactic and textual cues must be playing a role, because these are what distinguish the text-reading setting from the individual-word-reading setting. These cuing systems enhance Amy's oral reading performance.

Conversely, depriving Amy of opportunities to use these cuing systems impairs her oral reading performance, and can also lead to the erroneous conclusion that her problem lies in decoding. Removing ordinary cuing systems imposes a performance obstacle on Amy, such that we may underestimate her actual reading proficiency.

In this example, evidence from text reading indicates that Amy does know the *ea* patterns. However, when assessments deprive readers of ordinary linguistic cuing mechanisms, what they know may not be appreciated. Then, if teaching is thought of as something needed to fill in knowledge gaps, it may be deemed necessary in such mistakenly diagnosed readers.

But scientific phonics, unlike pseudophonics, understands that spellings can, at best, only approximate a word's pronunciation, and that pronunciation is, in any case, an insufficient means to word identification. To the extent that word identification plays a role in reading, and this may not be all that great, contextual information must be utilized.

But we have seen that contextually rich assessment materials, which encourage a reader to recruit a broad range of cuing systems, can also reveal the reader's proficiency with the more narrow cuing systems, such as letter-sound relationships, a proficiency that may be missed if assessment materials are overly narrow. Now, mistakes can be avoided regarding which aspects of reading need to be taught, or focused on, in reading classrooms.

The use of assessments in deciding aspects of a reader's proficiency, and in formulating an appropriate teaching plan, also finds its niche in certain special populations, such as stroke patients with language impairments. In these neurological settings, assessments are also called *diagnostic tests,* and teaching and learning for the purpose of recovering lost language function is called *rehabilitation.* Despite the medical terminology, the concepts involved are virtually identical to those in a more traditional educational setting.

Consider the case of a 58-year-old man whom I will call "Phil" (discussed in Strauss, 1999). Phil suffered a stroke in the posterior region of the left hemisphere. As a result of this stroke, he developed severe difficulty understanding language, a condition known as receptive aphasia. His speech was fluent, exhibiting normal intonation and phoneme articulation, but was characterized by numerous nonsense words, or jargon, and was mostly incomprehensible. Presumably, this feature followed from the problem with self-monitoring that accompanies difficulty with comprehending.

In one task, I gave Phil various written materials to read aloud, which he did following some practice sessions. These materials included passages from stories, magazine advertisements, and other "authentic" texts. In a separate session, Phil read aloud individual words, selected as every 10th word from the text passages, but now appearing in isolated fashion on index cards. Text readings and individual-word readings alternated.

In reading an isolated word on an index card, Phil would typically point sequentially from left to right to the individual letters of the word and produce an oral expression, sometimes a full syllable in length, corresponding to each letter. Table 13.2 shows some examples of this fingerpointing reading. Virtually every word that Phil read from an index card was read in this fingerpointing fashion. However, in striking contrast to these oral renditions, Phil's production of fingerpointing reading was practically nonexistent when reading connected, authentic text. In texts consisting of 171, 114, 82, and 61 words, he read with fingerpointing on 3, 1, 0, and 4 words, respectively. Generally, Phil read these texts with normal prosody and seg-

TABLE 13.2
Phil's Fingerpoint Reading (Strauss, 1999)

Printed Word	*Phil's Fingerpointing Oral Reading*
other	5–*h*–*a*–2–3
and	*prach*–*a*–*a*
were	*space*–*h*–*a*–3
entangling	*p*–*h*–*o*–*o*–*o*–*o*–*o*–*1*–*1*–*1*

mental articulation, though, as with his spontaneous speech, it was mostly incomprehensible.

How do we account for this remarkable disparity? Consider that, in reading the individual words, Phil breaks them down into their component letters, a mental phenomenon that is overtly reflected in his fingerpointing behavior. Indeed, each fingerpointing vocalization corresponds to a single letter in the word, and each letter is rendered with fingerpointing. Phil, almost literally, wears his mental behavior on the end of his sleeve.

Now, this complex psychomotor behavior is strikingly parallel to that of a reader who breaks down individual written words into their component letters and attempts to sound each of them out. We can say that Phil exhibits an aphasic variant of phonics.

But why is this a substantially unpreferred reading behavior when the written material consists of whole, connected text? A plausible hypothesis is that connected text provides Phil, as it does any reader, far more linguistic resources than individual words in isolation, and that the oral readings reflect these differences. Connected, written text achieves its visual appearance not simply on the basis of containing lots of individual words, but, quite obviously, also on the basis of these words having a syntactic and textual organization. None of this is available to individual words on a flash card. Reading connected text with normal prosody shows that Phil is sensitive to the syntactic and textual features of the written material. With these cuing systems unavailable for isolated words, Phil is left only with a string of letters to mentally process. Unless he readily recognizes the printed word as a whole, which is already problematic because of his aphasia, he will recruit the only available cuing systems and use them accordingly. Phil's reading behavior shows that phonics, or a quasiphonics componential recognition strategy, is utilized when it is virtually the only cuing system available. But, when other cuing systems are available, it is relegated to a marginal and subordinate role.

Phil's oral reading behavior is not an isolated case. First of all, a "letter-naming" strategy among aphasic readers for words read in isolation has been discussed in the aphasia literature, and is the subject of a lively debate among researchers interested in single-word processing (cf., e.g., Bub et al., 1980;

Warrington & Langdon, 1990; Warrington & Shallice, 1980). I documented other individuals with receptive aphasia besides Phil in whom there is a near disappearance of this behavior when the reading material is authentic, connected text (Strauss, 1999). Consider the oral readings of "Betty," a 61-year-old woman who had a stroke in the left frontoparietal lobe of the brain. Standardized testing using the Western Aphasia Battery (WAB, Kertesz, 1982) showed some halting, expressive difficulties, in addition to her difficulties with understanding speech. When asked to read individual words from the WAB, she exhibited the same fingerpointing behavior seen with Phil. She pointed sequentially from left to right to each individual letter and read aloud a syllable of varying complexity for each of the letters. Table 13.3 shows some of these oral readings. But on connected-text reading, she exhibited the fingerpointing behavior on only 4 of 428 words.

Like Phil, Betty exhibited the same pattern of fingerpointing oral reading, in which a componential, quasiphonics behavior is exhibited prominently for words in isolation, but far less prominently for words in context. Phonics is a strategy of last resort. It is used when other cuing systems are inadequate by themselves, or simply unavailable.

An interesting type of oral reading miscue, often seen in poor readers, shines a light on what happens when a reader not only shuns text-based cuing systems, but is also not saved by relying primarily on the letter-sound system. Abundant evidence exists that poor readers often overuse graphophonic information at the expense of other cuing systems, such as morphology, syntax, and semantics. Weaver (2002) provided numerous examples of this, such as one young reader who produced "The girls of the vengil" where the text showed "The girls of the village," and another who produced "School was not as imprentice" where the text showed "School was not as important" (p. 66). Another poor reader rendered "Well, we heard the farmer's wife screaming" as "Well, we heard the fam wif scring" (p. 135) and still another rendered "was in real trouble" as "was in ruh duhroo" (p. 138).

A curious occurrence in the oral readings of some readers is a tendency to either repeat or abandon an otherwise correct response. Weaver (2002,

TABLE 13.3
Betty's Fingerpoint Reading From the Western Aphasia Battery Test (Strauss, 1999)

Target Word	*Betty's Fingerpointing Oral Reading*
comb	eet-oh-eet-oh
pencil	o-e-e-o-e-o
matches	eet-r-e-e-r-e
screwdriver	eet-r-e-e-e-e-r-e-e-r-e

p. 218) reported a poor reader who read "my head bowed" as "my head bl-, bow, bow," at which point the teacher interrupted to tell the child that the reading was correct.

But why should such a phenomenon occur? Why would a reader repeat a word that is already correctly sounded out? Most certainly, there are numerous factors, but one may be this: A developing reader who is taught that print needs to be sounded out, in order for words on the page to be identified, does not necessarily read with the belief that words can be recognized using other cuing systems. Because the epiphany of word recognition is expected to follow automatically once the correct pronunciation is produced, the reader's sole obligation is to produce the correct sounds.

A reader who repeats an acceptably produced word may therefore not have experienced that purported automatic next step. Though the reader has turned the print into sound, sound, by itself, has not yet been turned into word recognition. But what more can the reader do? All the letters have been decoded, accurately in fact, and context is not regarded as an available resource. So the only option is to say the word again, and again and again if necessary, to see if that will spark recognition.

In terms of teaching, and if context is *verboten*, what more can an advocate of intensive phonics offer at this point, except more phonics? And if that still fails . . . ?

Part IV

DEFENDING SCIENCE AND DEMOCRACY AGAINST NEOPHONICS

In order to obtain a definite result, one must want to obtain namely that result; if you want to obtain a definite result, you will obtain it. . . . I need only those people who obtain what I need.

—Lysenko (cited in Sheehan, 1993, p. 223)

Chapter 14

The Neophonics Counterrevolution in Science

I began the preface of this book with a characterization of the current scene in reading education, and education in general, as a frontal assault by the government against teachers, students, and parents. This assault is being undertaken on behalf of the government's corporate clients, who, in fact, represent only a small minority of the population. Under attack are not only quality public education, but science and democracy as well. Unless this attack is repudiated, the complex social fabric that interweaves education, science, and democracy is doomed to unravel. At risk are the victories and gains of past struggles that have won the rights to public education, academic freedom, and freedom of speech and thought.

The first step in defending against this attack is to understand where it is coming from, as well as the nature of the weaponry being used. Then we can face the problem head on, and disarm the attackers with appropriate arguments. Without playing their game, the sallies of the resistance will be far more effective and convincing if they are based on quality education, trustworthy science, and democratic decision making.

For every single policy program, two fundamental questions need to be posed: Who benefits from this program? Who loses from it? I have tried to provide preliminary answers to both of these questions. As I have argued, the government's program is a scheme to remake the U.S. labor force. It is the domestic side of the neoliberal program of globalization, or "free trade" among nonequals, with corporate America occupying the position of first among nonequals, and doing what it feels it needs to do to maintain that status.

It is a plan conceived and drafted in back rooms, with no democratic discussion or input from those most affected, despite public claims to be for their benefit. As with all coercive policy, it threatens high-stakes punishments against those who don't measure up. In this, the plan lays bare its cynical contempt for democracy.

It also lays claim to public schools and public moneys, that is, to public capital, for the private use of corporate America. In this, it is a new welfare entitlement for the super rich, in which the contents of the public coffers, the accumulated labor of working people, are channeled into what amounts to an extreme makeover for public schools. Where previously stood a school, there now stands a factory, whose product is corporate America's 21st-century employee. This handout of public resources is defended on the grounds that corporate America is the principle buyer of a commodity it calls "a high-school graduate."

But the plan is in fact destroying the quality of public education by sterilizing the curriculum, abandoning the arts, and pitting students and teachers against each other. It should be challenged by all those who believe in freedom and democracy, including democracy in education.

As if adding insult to injury, the government's new digital literacy is nothing more than a form of literacy whose highest genre is the technical manual and handbook. And, as if adding insult to insult, the weapon it is using to invade classrooms in the name of confronting an alleged literacy crisis is a pseudoscientific slop it calls phonics. This weapon of mass delusion has to be force-fed to people with a generous helping of law, because there is no doubt that its odious flavor would be widely rejected as unpalatable in a more democratically run educational system.

Thus, the neophonics attack on science goes hand in hand with the attack on democracy. Indeed, it is also an attack on the democratic practice of science. In this instance, to defend science is to defend democracy. And defending both is a defense of quality education.

The alternative to resistance is to watch a doomed freefall of science, education, and democracy that will also take children's mental health down along with it, a phenomenon that has unfortunately already begun. Government bureaucrats may try to pass off all of this as the regrettable, but unavoidable, collateral damage of an otherwise necessary public policy. However, to the extent that we can predict the untoward consequences, there should be a serious public debate to decide whether we are willing, as a society, to accept the risk.

The National Council of Teachers of English (NCTE) has issued a public demand that addresses this problem head on. According to the NCTE (1998, par. 4) "neither Congress nor any other federal agency should establish a single definition of reading or restrict the type of research used in funding criteria for preservice or inservice teacher education and professional development programs." This eminently reasonable demand, one that supports the professionalism of teachers and the needs of individual students, should be generalized to encompass any attempt by the government to prescribe a single definition of science, or scientific method. Unfortunately, the government's single definition of reading presupposes a single, acceptable scientific method, namely, experimental design.

The consequences of a state definition of science, or of acceptable scientific method, has played itself out already in an unfortunate chapter of Soviet history. The parallels between that chapter of history and the current U.S. government stance on reading not only shows us the tragedy that lies before us if no resistance is launched, but also teaches a lesson about the possibility of turning things around and emerging victorious in the defense of freedom from abusive and illegitimate government intervention.

That the U.S. government program is an actual attack cannot be in doubt. Its four-star science Generals issue bellicose words that reflect thoughts of similar posture. Recall the remark of Reid Lyon (2002, p. 84): "If there was any piece of legislation that I could pass it would be to blow up colleges of education." With this single elitist salvo, Lyon revealed his impatience with science, academia, and the democratic process.

Compulsive students of Soviet history will immediately recall one V. K. Milovanov, who, in a parallel paroxysm of bureaucratic bluster, declared, "Until the present time departments of genetics have continued to exist: we should have liquidated them long ago" (quoted in Graham, 1974, p. 217). Behind both Lyon's (2002) and Milovanov's remarks lies the phenomenon of Lysenkoism.

Though the term *Lysenkoism* is frequently used as a synonym for pseudoscience, it is far more complex than that. It is pseudoscience that has roots in specific historical conditions. The parallel between those historical conditions that gave rise to Lysenkoism in the Soviet Union and the ones that are producing neophonics today in the United States teaches an invaluable lesson about the profound importance of democracy, and the need to remain vigilant against those forces in society that, while giving it swollen lip service, have no lasting commitment to it when their own material interests are at stake.

The young Soviet Union, following civil war, imperialist attack from more than a dozen countries, and international isolation, was faced with a famine of exorbitant proportions. At the same time, crop yields needed to be dramatically increased, not only to feed the mostly peasant population, but also to generate a surplus that could support the growing, nonagrarian industrial centers.

At the time, western biology revolved around Mendelian genetics, whose agricultural applications, though certainly promising, could only proceed at their own pace, and could offer no guarantees or promises about when the agricultural crisis would be resolved. Lysenko, an agronomist of peasant origin, proposed a radically different solution to the problem, called "vernalization," which won the ears of the Ukrainian Commissar of Agriculture, and eventually those of Stalin himself. By employing vernalization techniques, Lysenko insisted, a more rapid increase in crop yields could be achieved than anything the Mendelian geneticists could promise. "Vernalization Means Millions of Pounds of Additional Harvest" was the title of a speech delivered by Lysenko at the Second All-Union Congress of Collective Farmers and Shock-Workers, and Stalin, who was in attendance, shouted "Bravo, Comrade Lysenko, bravo!" (quoted in Graham, 1974, p. 214).

Whereas genetics emphasized the biologically given determinants of crop characteristics, such as their size, shape, color, and nutritional value, as well as their potential yield and time to harvest, vernalization emphasized the role of the environment, and claimed that a proper engineering of the environment could overcome inherent and undesirable biological limitations. For example, it could overcome a time to harvest that was too slow to feed the population.

Lysenko was not the originator of the idea of vernalization. It had been discussed and investigated previously, but was abandoned by most of its adherents in the face of the dramatic scientific achievements of Mendelian genetics. Undeterred, Lysenko believed it was ideal for the complex Soviet agricultural scene, with its vast expanses of land and variations in local climate. He insisted, for example, that winter grains could be grown in the springtime by pretreating seeds in a winterized environment, that is, with submersion into cold water.

In time, vernalization actually became Soviet state policy. Genetics was removed from school textbooks, and prohibited as a topic of discussion at scientific conferences. Supporters of genetics were forced to recant their views. Some geneticists were arrested on charges of being "Trotskyites" and "agents of international fascism." The internationally respected Soviet geneticist, N. I. Vavilov, founder in 1919 of the Laboratory of Applied Botany in Petrograd, and the first president of the Academy of Agricultural Sciences, was arrested in 1940 and sentenced to death. He died in prison from heart disease. Add to all of this the policy of forced collectivization of the farms, and it is not hard to imagine the Stalinists naming their policy "No Farm Left Behind."

Lysenko and vernalization were eventually rejected by even the most sycophantic Stalinist hacks following years of abysmal crop yields. Despite earlier support, Khrushchev denounced the pseudoscience that Lysenkoism had been all along. Scientists who had charged Lysenko with carrying out sloppy experiments, and even falsifying data, not to mention squandering countless rubles, were vindicated.

How could such a sinister social phenomenon arise? And how does all of this relate to neophonics?

In asking these questions, we immediately project the idea that Lysenkoism is far broader in scope than its signature scientific theory. Its essence goes beyond the single individual who is its leading exponent. It represents the pinnacle, or perhaps trough, of politically corrupted science.

Lysenkoism arises from a constellation of several mutually interacting social factors. First, a social crisis deemed urgent, and requiring immediate attention and a scientific solution, is identified by the nation's ruling elements. Second, a scientific solution to the social crisis is proposed, from within the ranks of the scientific community itself. Third, the ruling elements accept and adopt the proposed scientific solution, and provide its proponents with the political and economic means to carry it through, and to subdue any opposition along the way. Fourth, advocates of alternative or opposing scientific positions are treated as *political* enemies, so the methods for countering them, though including some ordinary scientific discourse (mostly for show), are increasingly those typically used in the political suppression of dissent. Fifth, this treatment of alternative scientific views as a political opposition leads to the suppression, retardation, and ultimate derailing of science itself.

But all these characteristics are still insufficient to explain Lysenkoism, because we do not as yet have a *pseudoscientific* approach to the crisis. The state authorities that solicit, adopt, promote, and finally protect the plan for solving the crisis could, if cool, calm, and collected, consider positions that are more scientifically defensible. But it is precisely the extreme sense of urgency, and the concomitant loss of disinterested, sober, rational reflection, that increases the likelihood of a snake-oil solution rising to the top. Hawkers of such tonic have always promised results faster than the speed of science itself.

Furthermore, it is precisely the corrupt character of the state decision-making apparatus that eliminates what would otherwise be the most important corrective measure and quality control against flawed proposals: democracy. Democratic, unfettered exchange of ideas is the optimal mechanism to increase the likelihood of a realistic, scientifically sound solution to a social problem.

In the end, of course, there is no guarantee that the best solution will be selected, even in a truly democratic system. But real freedom of thought and of exchange of ideas has the utilitarian virtue of allowing society as a whole to maximize its chances for success in both identifying urgent social problems and finding the right path to their solutions. The best possible science needs democracy.

The urgency of Lysenkoist thinking has been noted by a number of writers. The renowned Soviet-era scholar Zhores Medvedev observed the following:

> Besides demanding that the ten to twelve years required to develop cereal varieties for different regions be reduced to four years (by using hothouses), the decree posed the problem of renewal of the composition of varieties throughout the whole country with all essential characteristics in nearly all crops. . . . The resolution was published in the name of the Central Control Commission of the party and the U.S.S.R. Commissariat of Worker-Peasant Inspectorate. (p. 18)

He continued:

> Along all lines the resolution was contrary to Vavilov's position and to realistic possibilities, not only of Soviet but of worldwide plant breeding. But it served as a base for subsequent criticisms of AIPB (All Union Institute of Plant Breeding, of which Vavilov was a prominent member, SLS), and of Vavilov as being incapable of solving the problems. The resolution served this purpose well, although the three- to four-year program it put forth was not fulfilled even in thirty years. Vavilov viewed the accelerated goals for renewal of seed very skeptically, while Lysenko immediately published a solemn pledge to develop new varieties with preplanned characteristics in two and one-half years. (p. 19)

And, as noted by Loren Graham (1974, p. 222), "Lysenko's impatience—linked with the impatience of the government in its hopes for rapid economic expansion—drove him to the hope for short cuts." Indeed, only an urgent social crisis, fueled by desperation, could account for the rapid rise of Lysenko through the ranks of the Soviet science bureaucracy.

Besides the more visceral appeal that derived from a sense of urgency, vernalization was also promoted as ideologically superior to genetics. The Stalinist bureaucrats, appealing to the sympathies of the masses from whom they usurped power, promoted vernalization as consistent with "Marxist dialectics," and dismissed genetics as inherently fascistic. In this they were able to score some points with the public by explaining that genetics was being used to buttress both the American school of eugenics and Hitlerian racial superiority theories. Marxist geneticists, for their part, explained that these were just grotesque aberrations of an otherwise legitimate science.

Eventually, in the face of the undeniable agricultural misery, Mendelian genetics and a relative increase in academic freedom returned. Dissident Soviet scientists played a key role in this thaw, and the struggle against Lysenkoist pseudoscience was simultaneously a struggle for democracy in science, for academic freedom, and for general freedom of speech, all of which had been dragged down.

Serious problems in education and schooling notwithstanding, the current scene in reading and education satisfies all the necessary criteria to characterize it as a new Lysenkoism. And even though it may still be in a relatively early stage, the damaging social consequences are already being felt.

The pivotal public issue in Lysenkoism is the identification of a social crisis requiring an urgent solution. Mass famine qualifies without question. It can be qualified even further as a *humanitarian emergency*, because the very lives of millions of people are at stake.

The social urgency in the new Lysenkoism is the literacy crisis. But this is a crisis that lies in political economy, and in the acutely felt needs of a single social class, corporate America, regarding its fate vis à vis corporate Europe and corporate Asia. It is not the same type of social crisis as a famine, which affects large masses of people, which no child could fail to identify, and which should most definitely arouse the public to action.

Still, it is the identified crisis. The scientific solution to this new Lysenkoist crisis, we are told, is intensive phonics, that is to say, lots and lots of phonics. Like vernalization, phonics was around long before Lyon (*Testimony of G. Reid Lyon,* 1998) and the Business Roundtable (Augustine et al., 1996) identified a literacy crisis. Like vernalization, phonics was surpassed by a superior scientific theory, specifically, by meaning-centered reading and reading instruction, which views letter-sound correspondences as only one of a number of linguistic resources available to a reader to construct meaning. Like vernalization, phonics has its share of supporters within the scientific community, but, also like vernalization, its chief argument is ideological superiority. The former is better Marxist dialectics, and the latter is better science, though in both cases, recalcitrant facts are simply ignored.

The state sponsorship of phonics finds expression in the Reading Excellence Act (1998), and in No Child Left Behind (2001). Its enforcement proceeds in tandem with the What Works Clearinghouse, the new phonics police force. And the media has participated in the vilification of whole-language teachers and educators, trying them in the press, and finding them guilty of contributing to the illiteracy of minors. For example, according to the Ponnuru (1999, p. 36), "a large increase in the proportion of high-school graduates who are illiterate or barely literate has coincided with the eclipse of phonics in this century; more than 40 million Americans are illiterate today." As Ponnuru's article explained, the malefactor of this defilement of reading's heavenly body has been whole language.

The pseudoscientific nucleus of Lysenkoism, at least in the case of neophonics, represents a true step backwards in the course of intellectual events. Whereas paradigms in science exhibit progressive, revolutionary change, as Thomas Kuhn explained in his famous book *The Structure of Scientific Revolutions* (1996), the new Lysenkoism of neophonics represents the antithesis of this, a scientific *counterrevolution* against meaning-centered theory, teaching, and learning.

Scientific revolutions occur when a crisis within a scientific paradigm is resolved by the adoption, within the scientific community, of new, empirically supported principles that redefine what counts as a theoretically significant problem, and the way that problem is solved. The crisis itself is characterized by recurrent and accumulating cases of unsolvable problems. The new principles provide solutions to these problematic cases. Ideally, the scientists should be under no coercion to believe in any particular point of view, and should rely, ultimately, on their own sense of logic, reason, and argumentation.

A scientific counterrevolution, such as we are presently witnessing with neophonics, is the forced return to a previous paradigm, with the crucial feature that this return is aided and abetted by the state, because the previous paradigm was abandoned as a result of its having been scientifically discredited, and no new scientific evidence exists to vindicate it. The necessarily weak scientific arguments inevitably advanced for returning to the discredited paradigm covers for a new political agenda. Together, they produce an argument that the older scientific paradigm is indispensable in solving a certain *social* crisis.

That a retrogressive change such as neophonics or vernalization is possible in science is due to the fact that scientific practice, as Kuhn (1996) explained, is actually a social enterprise. Research must be funded, findings must be published and disseminated, and new practitioners must be recruited. For better or worse, the social forces that influence funding, publishing, and training may include scientists, but also nonscientists with their own agendas. If the agenda with the most powerful social backing demands the suppression or elimination of one paradigm in favor of a previous one, a counterrevolution can occur.

Neophonics is a scientific counterrevolution in that its scientific predecessor, a meaning-centered paradigm for understanding reading, one that enlightened us more about the reading process and reading assessment than phonics ever did, was attacked, vilified, and ultimately legislated out of the classroom, only to be replaced with a paradigm that historically was the darling of behaviorist linguists and psychologists, and offered no more to our understanding of reading than stimulus-response behaviorism offered to our understanding of language.

Indeed, the phonics part of neophonics is just a leftover relic of a previous, behaviorist linguistic paradigm, a survivor of the Chomskyan revolution that happened to not suffer the same fate as the taxonomic models of grammar that were its congeners and contemporaries. But then, all revolutionary changes have been uneven in their results. Even the American Revolution, despite proclaiming democracy, did not do away with chattel slavery, or grant women the right to vote. And just as a return to chattel slavery would be called a counterrevolutionary event by most anyone's criteria, the principle is not fundamentally different in the case of neophonics.

On a scientific level, the enemy in the neophonics crosshairs is a model of reading in which the reader's unwavering focus on meaning, and not on the sounding out of letters or the identification of individual words, is the primary purpose of the reading act. This model explains proficient reading as an interaction between a reader and an author, mediated via the author's text, in which the reader constructs meaning by means of mental projections of tentative meaning hypotheses. These hypotheses are continually tested against both the reader's background knowledge and beliefs, and the author's incoming text elements. Letter-sound relationships are not ignored. Rather, they represent just one of a number of cognitive resources used in the task of constructing meaning. Compared to other resources, though, such as knowledge of syntax, semantics, and text genre, it is relatively inefficient in leading the reader to meaning.

The meaning-centered paradigm received support from two revolutionary, Kuhnian (Kuhn, 1996) insights about language. The first of these insights was due to Noam Chomsky (1965, 1972), whose linguistic studies sounded the death knell for the behaviorist's stimulus-based understanding of language use. The second was due to Kenneth Goodman (1967, 1970), who recognized the centrality of real-time meaning construction in reading, and that this is fashioned from nonautomatic linguistic and extralinguistic raw material that the reader brings to the page.

Chomsky (1972) emphasized the "creative" aspect of language use as fundamentally "stimulus-free," and observed that "it is because of this freedom from stimulus control that language can serve as an instrument of thought and self-expression, as it does not only for the exceptionally gifted and talented, but also, in fact, for every normal human" (p. 12).

The model of language that Chomsky (1972) developed emphasized the fundamental role of "grammar," understood as an abstract, formal representation of the knowledge possessed by a language user of the rules governing the relationship between linguistic form and linguistic meaning. Such knowledge, according to Chomsky, is employed in the actual use of language, such as in allowing one "to speak in a way that is innovative, free from stimulus control, and also appropriate and coherent" (p. 13).

A speaker's freedom from stimulus control can be understood as grounded in his or her subjective, communicative intention, which, in turn, is influenced by characteristics of the speaker's mental state. These characteristics are independent of external stimuli. According to Levelt (1991, p. 3), "in planning an utterance, there is an initial phase in which the speaker decides on a purpose for his next move. This decision will depend on a variety of factors, and not in the last place on the speaker's needs, beliefs, and obligations." It is such "planning," "purpose," as well as "needs, beliefs, and obligations" that render speaking free from an otherwise stimulus-controlled automaticity.

But it is not only productive language, such as speaking, that is free from stimulus control. Receptive language, like listening, is as well. The listener's interpretation of the speaker's communicative intention is no less a function of "needs, beliefs, and obligations." The listener also has a "purpose" for listening. Thus, listening itself is not simply an automatic response to the speaker's physically rendered stimuli, such as speech sounds and gestures, but rather the nonautomatic construction of meaning every bit as stimulus free and subjectively guided as the speaker's.

To even talk about "needs, beliefs, and obligations" implies a conception of mental structure and mental life that leaves little room for stimulus-based behaviorist explanations. Contemporary studies of linguistic communication utilize many other mentalist categories, including intension, presupposition, and speaker meaning versus literal meaning. These categories are equally applicable to an analysis of reading, provided we understand reading as another instance of human linguistic communication.

Of course, to raise such a perspective presupposes a particular philosophical point of view. Under Leonard Bloomfield's (1933/1994) pre-Chomskyan behaviorist model of language, meanings were, ultimately, purely physical, and so could be transferred through a physical medium. Bloomfield regarded the meaning of a linguistic utterance as the sum total of all the observable physical stimuli that triggered that utterance, and all the observable physical responses that the utterance then triggered in turn.

In Chomsky's generative grammar, however, literal meanings are the "senses of sentences" (Katz, 1972), and sentences are abstract, formal structures, not defined along physical dimensions. Literal meanings of sentences are related to "intended meanings" via rules of reasoning shared by the interlocutors. Like other "mental" aspects of language, meanings are "causally connected with, but not identical to, states of the nervous system" (Jackendoff, 1983, p. 24). The riddle of communication, as discussed in chapter 2, is to understand how meanings, as abstract entities, are transferred through physical media from one brain to another. As I pointed out, the riddle is solved by appreciating that the physical elements of language do not contain meaning *per se*, but rather are *clues* to meaning, and are used as such by interlocutors in constructing meaning.

The second Kuhnian (Kuhn, 1996) insight about language, due to educator and reading researcher Kenneth Goodman, fundamentally altered the way reading is understood. Adopting Chomsky's understanding of language use as a stimulus-free phenomenon, and noting that such stimulus-free behavior applies equally to both productive speech and receptive listening, Goodman advanced the revolutionary notion that these principles are equally applicable to written language. As a corollary, Goodman emphasized that receptive language, whether listening or reading, is as much a mentally active language event as speaking or writing, guided all along by the listener's or reader's purposeful intention to construct meaning.

Rather than passively and automatically responding to the stimuli of letters, the reader brings his or her "needs, beliefs, and obligations" to the task of meaning construction, using them to process material on the printed page. Such processing of linguistic material is navigated by the purposeful, nonautomatic, stimulus-free goal of constructing meaning. Sounds do not act on a mentally passive listener, nor do alphabetic letters on a mentally passive reader. According to Goodman, the facts of interpretation are better explained by adopting a paradigm that views the listener and reader instead as acting on these external stimuli. In the specific case of written language, it is the alphabetic letters that are under the control of the reader, and not the reader who is under the control of the letters.

Goodman's (1967, 1970) insights derived from the observations and descriptive analyses of hundreds of readers. His most potent method of analysis, called "miscue analysis," involved comparing the graphophonic (letter-sound), morphological, syntactic, and semantic properties of an individual's oral reading of a text to those same properties of the text itself.

In essence, Goodman (1965, 1973, 1976) proposed comparing the linguistic properties of the reader's oral text to the linguistic properties of the writer's written text. He discovered that readers who understand what they are reading utilize letter-sound relationships as one of a number of linguistic resources, or cuing systems, along with other cuing systems, as they construct meaning. One important piece of evidence for this, in Goodman's research, was the recurrent phenomenon of semantically acceptable miscues, in which a reader produces a different word or phrase when reading aloud than what is actually on the page, but where this new construction is semantically coherent with the rest of the text, despite being phonically distinct. We see this, for example, when a reader says *yard* for *garden,* or *toad* for *frog.* Such a reader utilizes lexical and syntactic information, along with letter-sound information, in the construction of meaning.

On the other hand, a poor reader, someone who fails to demonstrate understanding, often produces oral linguistic constructions that are phonically close to the printed language, but that may be semantically nonsensical, perhaps even nonlinguistic. Such a reader, for example, might render the printed *farmer* as *fam, real* as *ruh,* or *village* as *vengil.*

Goodman (1967, 1970, 1994) also discovered that good readers routinely make decisions about rejecting or accepting meanings. They may return to an earlier portion of the text to correct what they have read, and are more likely to do this if their current interpretation is problematic, perhaps containing mutually contradictory ideas. The good reader's purpose in reading is, clearly, the construction of coherent, plausible meaning.

The poor reader, on the other hand, is more likely to accept nonsensical meaning. Such a reader may say *fam* for *farmer*, or *scring* for *screaming*, and leave it uncorrected. Insofar as such readers also exhibit greater attentiveness to phonic accuracy, we can say that their purpose in reading is not the construction of coherent and plausible meaning, but rather the accurate conversion of letters to sounds. The poor reader's oral productions demonstrate an overreliance on phonic information, and an underutilization of other cuing systems.

Goodman's (1967, 1970, 1994) theory of reading relies on categories of mental activity that reflect the paradigm-changing advances of Chomsky's (1957, 1965) theory of grammar and language. The reader's construction of meaning is a purposeful, goal-driven search-and-discover enterprise, subject to willful changes in strategic thinking about why the author's language is what it is. Such mental activity operates at a level that is independent of the letters on the page, despite being tied to them. That is to say, proficient reading is a stimulus-free mental activity, whereas phonically dense poor reading is tied more closely to the alphabetic stimuli.

Chomsky (1972) remarked that the stimulus-free character of speaking "is a serious problem that the psychologist and biologist must ultimately face and that cannot be talked out of existence by invoking 'habit' or 'conditioning' or 'natural selection' " (p. 13). Yet it is precisely such invocation that characterizes the historical roots of phonics.

In his primer on phonics, Leonard Bloomfield (1942/1961) wrote:

> In order to read alphabetic writing one must have an ingrained habit of producing the phonemes of one's language when one sees the written marks which conventionally represent those phonemes. A well-trained reader, of course, for the most part reads silently, but we shall do better for the present to ignore this fact, as we know that the child learns first to read aloud. . . . It is this habit which we must set up in the child who is to acquire the art of reading. If we pursue any other course, we are merely delaying him until he acquires this habit in spite of our bad guidance. (p. 26)

Bloomfield (1942/1961) added that "alphabetic writing merely directs the reader to produce certain speech sounds. A person who cannot produce these sounds cannot get the message of a piece of alphabetic writing. If a child has not learned to utter the speech sounds of our language, the only sensible course is to postpone reading until he has learned to speak" (p. 27).

But the mental processes that underlie proficient reading, as discovered by Goodman (1967, 1970), "cannot be talked out of existence" by such behaviorist dogma. Put differently, the behaviorist paradigm is simply incapable of explaining the fundamental characteristics of proficient reading. This is the reason why Goodman's model of reading has been so convincing for so many years to so many teachers, educators, and researchers. Goodman and his cothinkers provided ample evidence for the view that reading is an example of receptive language, and that receptive language is an active and fundamentally stimulus-free, purposeful act of meaning construction. This understanding resulted in a shift of paradigms away from the previously dominant behaviorist paradigm of stimulus-response explanation, in which letter stimuli trigger vocal responses. Yet the contemporary neophonics enterprise, in which meaning depends first on letter stimuli turning into sounds, then sound stimuli becoming meanings, is ultimately dependent on these very same behaviorist assumptions, no matter how much it may be cloaked in the the verbiage of cognitive psychology.

Thomas Kuhn (1996, p. x) characterized a scientific "paradigm" as "universally recognized scientific achievements that for a time provide model problems and solutions to a community of practitioners." He called a historical change of paradigms a "revolution," examples of which include those associated with Copernicus, Newton, Lavoisier, and Einstein.

But "revolution" in science, as elsewhere, suggests a net forward or progressive change. Though not the only argument in support of changing paradigms, "probably the single most prevalent claim advanced by the proponents of a new paradigm is that they can solve the problems that have led the old one to a crisis" (Kuhn, 1996, p. 153). In the history of science, this is generally what we see, with later paradigms being regarded as better able to explain phenomena than earlier ones.

Goodman's (1967, 1970) model of reading claims to have solved at least one "crisis" found in prior models, and specifically in models that viewed letter-sound conversion as the fundamental psychological operation. The crisis is the sheer number of English words whose spellings either violate, or render excessively complex, the supposed rules of letter-sound relationships. The crisis, in other words, is that letter-sound regularity may not be a typical feature of English alphabetic writing, in which case its purported significance and centrality in reading may be no more than wishful thinking on the part of its adherents.

Indeed, Chomskyans pointed out that the letters of English spellings convey more than just sounds (C. Chomsky, 1970; Chomsky & Halle, 1968). Letters convey information about the identity of morphemes and words, as discussed earlier, for example, in the case of inflectional suffixes. A victory for the spelling reformers would have liquidated this feature of English spelling.

In some situations, also noted earlier, the phonic problem is entirely unsolvable without the higher level information that the phonic letter-sound relationship is supposed to lead us to in the first place, as with initial *th* and final *s*. The higher level information is therefore needed to obtain the correct phonic relationships, not the other way around.

Examples such as these are fundamentally unsolvable within the currently recycled paradigm that views phonics as a mechanism for arriving at the correct identification of a word. These examples behave in a manner that is, in fact, directly counterposed to efficient word recognition. In order to know how to sound them out, they must first be recognized, and their morphological and syntactic properties determined. Only then can they be correctly "decoded." In order to know that the initial *th* of *that* is voiced, we must first be able to recognize that it is the word *that*. Then we would be able to say, "Oh, because it is the word *that*, its initial *th* is pronounced voiced." Clearly, once the word has already been identified, determining its pronunciation yields virtually no additional useful information.

Supporters of the neophonics counterrevolution will, of course, never present it as such. Its science will be marketed instead as a positive experience. A nostalgic "back to basics" will be the catchphrase, though the key term here is *back*, meaning a step backwards. Unfortunately for the neophonics camp, the need to solve a social crisis does not by itself vindicate a discredited scientific paradigm. And, as we have already seen, the social crisis may not appear equally urgent in the eyes of everyone concerned.

Because vacuum-packed sciences are hard to come by, and independent, isolated academic departments are not synonymous with independent fields of science, there is every reason to expect that the retrogressive move that constitutes a scientific counterrevolution will bring down other scientific theories with which it interacts. Consider, for example, Reid Lyon's (*Testimony of G. Reid Lyon*, 2001) remarks on the scope and seriousness of the literacy crisis as it relates to rising out of poverty:

> We have learned our most vulnerable children are those born into poverty. Thankfully poverty rates appear to be declining [sic]. However children from poor families are still much more likely to enter school with limited vocabularies, meager early literacy and other pre-academic concepts, and a motivation to learn that is already on the wane.
>
> What makes this such a frustrating issue is that it does not have to be this way. Poverty begets poverty, and the major perpetuating factor is school failure, which, in turn, is typically the result of reading failure in school. The cycle goes on! (pars. 7–8)

Lyon also pointed to the association between reading failure, on the one hand, and drug abuse and crime on the other. In general, he noted that inability to read is part of a cycle of social failure, which includes loss of self-esteem.

Lyon's (*Testimony of G. Reid Lyon*, 2001) remarks must prompt an immediate double take. At the same time that he demanded "the most trustworthy science" when it comes to reading theory and reading instruction, he adopted the scientifically discredited, elitist-inspired thesis of poverty-associated "cultural deprivation," replete with "limited vocabularies" and waning "motivation to learn," in order to advance the argument that the poor would have the opportunity to rise like a phoenix from the flames of poverty, as long as society provides them with a properly engineered remedy. For Lyon, poverty is assumed. But learning to read can be the ticket to school success, and the latter the passport to the middle class and beyond.

Lyon's (*Testimony of G. Reid Lyon*, 2001) remarks recall the cultural-deprivation thesis, which became infamous in the late 60s, when Arthur Jensen (1969) extended its logic to draw conclusions about the supposed genetic inferiority of African Americans. Jensen argued that compensatory educational interventions failed to improve school achievement among Black students. The compensatory interventions themselves were intended to treat problems that arose as a result of the culturally deprived, "illogical" language and inadequate vocabularies of these students. Jensen explained the failure of compensatory education to help these students on the basis of their having genetically predetermined inferior intellectual capabilities. The linguistic premise of Jensen's argument, namely the claim of inferior language, was roundly refuted in the important work at the time of the linguist William Labov (1969).

With this as historical backdrop, it is alarming to see an agency of the federal government base its recommendations for reading research and practice in part on the baseless linguistics of cultural deprivation. Insofar as the NICHD has defended its work on reading on the grounds that it is rooted in "the most trustworthy" science, one is entitled to ask whether the NICHD regards the cultural-deprivation view of the language of poor children as also scientifically trustworthy, and of impeccable scientific quality. If not, then Lyon's (*Testimony of G. Reid Lyon*, 2001) comments need urgent clarification, because the real social crisis may be the massive, government-sponsored promotion of a social engineering policy that has built-in elitist assumptions.

But if the NICHD regards linguistic deprivation as based on "the most trustworthy" science, then one is further entitled to ask what Lyon (*Testimony of G. Reid Lyon*, 1998) meant when he said that "children who have a difficulty understanding that spoken words are composed of discreet individual sounds that can be linked to letters" have "neural systems that perceive the phonemes in our language [that] are less efficient than in other children," and that "our NICHD studies have taught us that the phonological differences we see in good and poor readers have a genetic basis" (par. 10). Will this be the explanation for those children who, despite every attempt to improve their phonological processing capabilities, are still unable to read? If so, we are guaranteed to see the return of Jensenism in academic discourse and social policy.

In addition to bringing down science, the new Lysenkoism is inflicting its own collateral damage. For example, the *Journal of the American Medical Association* published an article in which it pointed to the growing concern among a number of prominent child and adolescent psychiatrists about the rising levels of anxiety and depression under the new classroom climate of high-stakes testing (Mitka, 2001).

The National Association of School Psychologists also reported on the psychologically harmful effects of the new school climate:

> As teachers and administrators are pressured to implement policies designed to "end social promotion," students are threatened with retention if they do not meet academic standards or perform above specified percentiles on standardized tests. It is unclear if this threat is effective in motivating students to work harder. However, this pressure may be increasing children's stress levels regarding their academic achievement. Surveys of children's ratings of twenty stressful life events in the 1980s showed that, by the time they were in 6th grade, children feared retention most after the loss of a parent and going blind. When this study was replicated in 2001, 6th grade students rated grade retention as the single most stressful life event, higher than the loss of a parent or going blind. . . . This finding is likely influenced by the pressures imposed by standards-based testing programs that often rely on test scores to determine promotion and graduation. (Anderson et al., 2002, par. 8)

To the extent that they are true, these graphic comments raise serious questions about whether a branch of the NICHD has placed the health needs of children behind the profit needs of corporate America.

Chapter 15

Academic Imperialism Versus Academic Freedom

In their March, 2002 *Scientific American* article entitled "How Should Reading Be Taught?," authors Keith Rayner, Barbara R. Foorman, Charles A. Perfetti, David Pesetsky, and Mark S. Seidenberg lamented that student teachers are not receiving proper instruction in "the vast research in linguistics and psychology that bears on reading" (p. 91). They argued that, if the education community provided student teachers with a "modern, high-quality course on phonics," classroom teachers would then "not have to follow scripted programs or rely on formulaic workbooks" (p. 91). Reiterating that "reading must be grounded in a firm understanding of the connections between letters and sounds," and that "youngsters who are directly taught phonics become better at reading, spelling and comprehension," they concluded that "educators who deny this reality are neglecting decades of research" and that "they are also neglecting the needs of their students" (p. 91).

In other words, linguists and psychologists are in possession of a body of scientific knowledge so relevant to our understanding of reading, that it behooves the education community to study it carefully, in order to be more competent and effective in the classroom. Choosing to ignore this body of knowledge, therefore, is tantamount to ignoring the educational needs of children. And, to the extent that such educational malpractice occurs, society has no choice but to teacher-proof the classroom with scripts and formulas.

This is, quite plainly, an extremist polemic, because the proposed solution to a perceived crisis in the teaching of reading comes at an extreme cost: the deprofessionalization of teachers. Educators who have their own ideas about what teaching is supposed to be, who feel that it is more than test preparation and assembly-line discipline, are, quite simply, being pressured into promoting something they do not believe in. This is a violation of academic freedom, plain and simple. And it applies equally to classroom teachers and university professors.

But Rayner et al. (2002) defend this undemocratic position in their leveling of serious charges against the education community, stating that the latter is neglecting relevant research, that this neglect is willful (educators are "denying" the research), and that such willful neglect is harmful to our children. The authors thus popularized the arguments that have been used to justify government entry into the classroom with laws that coerce educators into behaving in ways they may not agree with pedagogically. This is nothing short of legal weaponry aimed at forcibly displacing the culture of educational research with that of one version of theoretical linguistics and psychology. In the present context, this can accurately be called "academic imperialism." And, to the extent that they are successful, the academic imperialists will have carried out an academic cleansing, one social consequence of the scientific counterrevolution.

The appeal of this academic infantry lies in the background sense of urgency that is highlighted by the possibility that what they are saying is actually correct, that there truly is a literacy crisis affecting our children that is being made worse through the willful neglect by educators of linguistic and psychological science. The "applied" field, we are being told, has not learned the lessons of research in the "theoretical" fields. Therefore, the force of the state must be recruited in order to save our children. The greater good justifies the curtailment of democracy in the classroom.

But there is a huge difference between "neglecting" research in linguistics and psychology, and "rejecting" such research. There is simply no reason to doubt that educators who have not bought the NRP line about the importance of intensive phonics, or the government's line about legally coercing teachers to teach intensive phonics, have rejected, rather than neglected, their arguments. And they have every right to reject them, without their professionalism being compromised and called into question.

Indeed, there is also a "vast research in linguistics and psychology" that supports a pedagogy of reading that emphasizes meaning construction over decoding and information processing, and knowledgeable educators refer to such research in defending their behavior in the classroom. This research includes miscue analysis, text linguistics, speech act theory as applied to written language, print awareness, and the psychology of meaning construction and visual perception. It is research that is presented and debated at teachers' and educators' conferences nationally and worldwide, alongside research on phonics and other isolated skills.

Rayner et al. (2002) insisted that educators accept a linguistics of phonics that has, quite simply, never been adequately elucidated, despite all the loud trumpeting of its virtues. A random collection of this or that phonics rule does not constitute a scientific analysis.

The *Scientific American* article (Rayner et al., 2002) is an unfortunate collection of factual errors, errors of reasoning, and half-truths. For example, Rayner et al. claimed that whole language, a meaning-centered pedagogical paradigm based on Goodman's (1967, 1970, 1994) work on reading, is the historical successor to the whole-word approach to reading (also referred to as the "sight-word" approach). But the only thing whole language and whole word have in common, other than the word *whole*, is that they both point out problems with a strict phonics approach to reading. Whole-word advocates (cf. Chall, 1967 for discussion) pointed out that there are numerous words in English whose recognition cannot be easily accomplished by simple letter-sound conversion. Whole-language advocates (Goodman, 1986; Edelsky, Altwerger, & Flores, 1990; Krashen, 1999; Weaver, 2002) claimed that word recognition is not the key issue.

However, strict phonics and whole word share a fundamental understanding of reading, and how it should be taught. Each emphasizes that elements on the printed page, whether letters or whole words, need to be *recognized* as such.

In the field of reading, the psychology of recognition was initially couched in the terminology of behaviorist psychology, where the appropriate behavioral response indicated that the reader accurately recognized and identified the stimulus.

With the paradigm shift from behaviorism to cognitive psychology, propelled, as we have seen, by Chomsky's (1957, 1959, 1965, 1972) revolutionary insights about language, advocates of strict phonics and whole word could no longer present convincing arguments by using the terminology of stimulus-response models. Now, the rallying expression, provided by cognitive psychology, was "information processing." Mechanisms of the cognitive mind process information on the page in order ultimately to recognize and identify it. Ink squiggles are processed and recognized as letters, letters are processed and recognized as equivalent to sounds, sounds are processed and recognized as components of words, and so on.

In this way, advocates of strict phonics and whole word could retain their belief in the significance of these behaviorist-inspired aspects of reading, while claiming to operate in the new paradigm of cognitive psychology. But the truth is that they are merely operating in the behaviorist closet still present in the house of cognitive psychology. The notion of information processing, as it has been applied to reading, does not go beyond the manipulation of observable "stimuli" on the page.

Whole language is thoroughly and fundamentally different. Rather than conceiving of meaning as derived from the processing of pieces of information that appear on the printed page, whole-language advocates base the reader's interpretation of text on a psychology of meaning construction. The reader brings meaning-laden systems, such as prior knowledge and beliefs, to the page in the task of testing tentative hypotheses about the author's intended meaning. Meaning is present right from the outset, revised and refined as it seeks to accommodate newly arriving text. The psychology of meaning construction is fundamentally stimulus free, and more in keeping with the spirit of the Chomskyan revolution in linguistics.

Elsewhere in their article, Rayner et al. (2002) claimed that "accomplished readers mentally sound out words" (p. 90) as evidence in favor of phonics as pedagogy. But such claims, even if true, are largely irrelevant to the issue of how reading should be taught. The same authors cited evidence that readers exhibit certain patterns of eye movement during reading. But they certainly did not propose that children be given lessons on how to move their eyes appropriately in order to become accomplished readers.

Rayner et al.'s (2002) error of reasoning is based on a lack of appreciation (a willful neglect?) of the independent contributions of educational science, which has long recognized that the need to learn *x* does not entail the need to teach *x*. Setting up an appropriate environment where *x* is learned incidentally may be all that is necessary. This applies no less to phonics than to any other aspect of reading, even if reading is regarded primarily as a task of phonological processing. This is a matter to be investigated empirically, not settled *a priori.*

Rayner et al. (2002) referred to high-tech neuroimaging studies that claim to have identified frontal regions of the brain as the primary locus for reading. They noted that such frontal regions also control speech production, and concluded that vocalization plays a central role in reading. But they failed to point out that neuroimaging studies of reading typically use tasks of letter-sound conversion. Therefore, it is only by equating reading with letter-sound conversion that such neuroimaging studies can be called studies of reading. Their argument is therefore tautologous and circular. To make matters worse, Rayner et al. failed to mention other neuroimaging studies, noted earlier, that claimed to have found semantic processing in the same frontal regions (Demb et al., 1999, p. 263).

Rayner et al. (2002) referred to the U.S. government's National Reading Panel (NRP), claiming that its supposedly rigorous scientific meta-analysis of intensive phonics instruction supports the claim that this method of teaching reading does lead to improved reading ability in elementary-school children. They failed to mention that the NRP made this claim only in its short summary report, the one more readily accessible by teachers and the media, and that its lengthy, unabridged report acknowledged that "there were insufficient data to draw any conclusions about the effects of phonics instruction with normal developing readers above first grade" (*NRP Report,* cited in Garan, 2002, p. 57). As noted earlier, numerous discrepancies of this sort between the NRP's full report and its short summary report have been documented in Garan's important work.

Rayner et al. (2002) referred to a "vast research in linguistics and psychology" (p. 91). In fact, it is even more vast than they seem to imagine, because they clearly omitted from consideration studies on topics cited earlier, namely, miscue analysis, text linguistics, print awareness, speech act theory as applied to written language, the influence of reading on oral language development, and classroom ethnography. In general, these studies have not been very friendly to intensive phonics. But by whose definitions do they not also count as linguistic and psychological studies that bear on reading? Only an overly narrow view of what constitutes linguistics and psychology could justify dismissing the "vast research in linguistics and psychology" that supports meaning-centered reading pedagogy and opposes intensive phonics. Yet, this seems to be precisely the position that Rayner et al. took.

For example, Rayner et al. (2002) approvingly referred to a 1995 letter, addressed to the Massachusetts Commissioner of Education, and signed by 40 Massachusetts linguists and psychologists, including Rayner and Pesetsky themselves, in which the signers expressed their concern over the state's proposed draft curriculum on education in the support it gave to whole-language principles, and in its rejection of certain aspects of phonics. (Rayner et al. failed to mention that Noam Chomsky *refused* to sign their letter.) The letter was distributed by conservative education personality Samuel L. Blumenfeld in his November, 1995 *Blumenfeld Education Letter.* Blumenfeld also printed a cover letter and a follow-up letter to the Massachusetts Commissioner of Education, both signed by David Pesetsky and Janis Melvold.

The group letter criticized the document for claiming the following:

> Research on language has moved from the investigation of particular 'components of language—phonological and grammatical units' to the investigation of 'its primary function—communication.' These supposed developments in linguistic research are used as arguments for a comparable view of reading. We are entirely unaware of any such shift in research. (Blumenfeld, 1995, p. 1)

Instead, they stated, "language research continues to focus on the components of language, because this focus reflects the 'modular' nature of language itself. Written language is a notation for the structures and units of one of these components. Sound methodology in reading instruction must begin with these realities" (p. 2).

To the letter signers, linguistics is the narrowly conceived study of grammar, and nothing counts as legitimately linguistic unless it can be related to a module of grammar. Psycholinguistics is the real-time construction of grammatical representations, language learning is the longitudinal development of grammar, historical linguistics is the diachronic change of grammars, and so on. Accordingly, reading theory is not linguistically valid unless it is also somehow related to grammar. The letter signers asserted this relationship by declaring the central role of the alphabetic orthography in reading, and its supposed status as a notation for one of grammar's modules, namely, the phonological one.

But what they do not recognize is that the study of language is more than grammatology. Those interested in broader aspects of language have had to look beyond the narrow confines of grammatology-based linguistics departments and their journals for rich and satisfying discussions of actual linguistic performance: to literary criticism, for the study of culturally and psychologically based interpretive strategies of written and oral discourse; to anthropology, for the study of the role of language in the production and interpretation of cultural symbols; to sociology, for the study of socially significant groups and how language contributes to their identification; to biology, for the study of the evolution and anatomy of language; and, not least of all, to education, for the study of conditions and methods that promote language learning.

That is to say, the study of language is distributed among a variety of disciplines. The letter signers' version of linguistics is really just the narrow field of "grammatology," however interesting a field it may be. But taken all together, there is no doubt that, following an initial Kuhnian revolution in linguistics, in which the grammatical studies of Noam Chomsky (1957, 1965) helped lay the foundation for a rejection of previous behaviorist-dominated linguistics, a shift has indeed occurred.

Linguistic competence, or knowledge of the formal system of grammar, underlies the capacity for linguistic performance, the use of this knowledge in concrete situations (Chomsky, 1965). Crucially, and to clarify the letter signers' misrepresentation, it is grammar, or linguistic competence, that is modular, not "language," or linguistic performance. This point is most important. The construction of formal semantic representations by a grammar on the basis of phonological, morphological, and syntactic structures is an aspect of linguistic competence. But the real-time construction of contextually appropriate meanings, of which reading is but one example, is an aspect of linguistic performance.

No shift in research focus detracts from Chomsky's (1957, 1959, 1965) cognitive revolution in linguistics. Whereas the study of grammar, or linguistic competence, is what initially revolutionized the field, the shift has occurred in the associated and complementary area of linguistic performance, itself also freed from behaviorist constraints by Chomsky's work, and which could now justifiably pursue "stimulus-free" explanations of language use.

Thus, whereas alphabetic letters were previously viewed as the indispensable primary stimuli of reading, and their associated sounds as the desired responses (Bloomfield, 1942/1961), the construction of meaning from written text could now be investigated by asking whether it could be directly constructed, and whether good readers in fact do this. This became a new empirical question within the framework of Chomsky's (1965) competence-performance distinction.

As such, the meaning construction that occurs in reading may proceed on the basis of a variety of meaning-laden systems, including other knowledge and belief systems, as well as principles of language in use, which include turn taking, conversational implicatures, speech act typology, and so on. Indeed, this applies equally to the real-time construction of meaning in oral language. As an aspect of linguistic performance, there is no *a priori* reason why such systems cannot directly construct meanings, or meaning fragments, prior to consulting the rules of grammar. In such a situation, grammar functions as a kind of *post hoc* formal confirmation of the language user's mental representations of meaning.

The exact relationship between the construction of meaning during reading and the use of grammatical modules is a strictly empirical question. Yet the cover letter (Blumenfeld, 1995, p. 3) characterized the conversion of orthography to phonology as the "common sense view" of reading. Echoing the behaviorist-inspired views of Bloomfield (1942/1961), Pesetsky and Melvold (Blumenfeld, 1995) wrote:

> Written language is a way of notating speech. The basic principles of alphabetic writing systems guarantee that letters and letter groups correspond quite well (even in English) to the fundamental units of spoken language. To become a skilled reader, a learner must master this notational system, learning how the sounds and oral gestures of language correspond to letters and letter groups. Once this happens, the same system that 'constructs meaning' from spoken language will quite naturally 'construct meaning' from written language, and the learner will be a reader. (p. 3)

Of course, to call something a "common sense view" is to acknowledge implicitly that it is based on an assumption for which empirical support is lacking. Only a lack of appreciation of the stimulus-free complexity of meaning construction, and of the empirical research that has looked at this question, along with an uncritical acceptance of the "common sense" behaviorist roots of phonics, could prompt the remark that decoding itself is "common sense."

Likewise, the position of Rayner, Pesetsky, and the other letter signers (Blumenfeld, 1995) that the "direct construction of meaning" is "a surprising view" can only derive from not having investigated the matter. There is ample empirical evidence on the issue, and, to that extent, the "direct construction of meaning," a characteristic of linguistic performance, has far greater scientific support than the "common sense view" that written language must first be turned into spoken language before meaning can be constructed. "Vast research" in the analysis of oral reading miscues has clearly demonstrated that good readers use their knowledge of morphology and syntax, as well as extralinguistic epistemological and belief systems, to predict upcoming words, and that an overreliance on phonic decoding is precisely what characterizes poor reading. (See Brown et al., 1994, for an extensive bibliography; see also Goodman, 1965, 1967, 1985; Goodman & Marek, 1996.)

Still, there is no inherent contradiction between miscue analysis, understood as a method for studying one type of linguistic performance, namely oral reading, and grammatical theory of the type that Rayner et al. (2002) advocated, just as there is no inherent contradiction between linguistic performance and linguistic competence. Indeed, an unfortunately neglected area of research is the investigation of how competing theories of grammar might characterize oral reading miscues. If carried out, there is little doubt that our understanding of the psycholinguistics of reading would be enhanced dramatically, and would amplify exponentially the "vast research" on linguistics and reading.

In fact, miscue analysis, as far as it goes, follows contemporary linguistic methodological principles quite neatly, such as those used in the widely respected work of Merrill Garrett and others in the investigation of "errors" of oral speech (Garrett, 1990, 1984). Garrett looked at spontaneous speech errors occurring, not in controlled settings, but in natural contexts, where language is used purposefully. Garrett's nonexperimental, descriptive analysis of these errors demonstrated how speech production makes use of the various types of grammatical structures and modules proposed in contemporary linguistic theory.

In looking at oral reading errors, Goodman (1965, 1973, 1976) utilized "authentic" texts, that is, literature written for ordinary linguistic purposes, such as communication of a story, not for the purpose of teaching certain letter-sound correspondences. Such authentic written texts are the analogue of oral texts produced in spontaneous, natural, purposeful settings.

As is well known, Goodman (1965, 1973, 1976) compared the observed oral readings (what the reader said aloud) to the expected oral readings (what the author actually wrote) in terms of phonological, morphological, and semantic relatedness, quite analogous to the methodology of Garrett (1990, 1984). Goodman too found that good readers make use of the full complement of modules of linguistic competence, and, furthermore, that letter-sound decoding holds no privileged status.

In fact, Goodman's (1965, 1973, 1976) methodology is not only an accepted methodology of contemporary linguistic science, it *improves* on it. In Garrett's (1990, 1984) analysis of spontaneous speech errors, it is, in principle, impossible to identify semantic errors that do not produce contextually inappropriate meanings. Thus, a speaker who meant to say, "Here is the laundry detergent" but instead says, "Here is the laundry soap" may not self-correct, nor be challenged by interlocutors. And the scientific observer will have no reason to suspect a semantically based error. However, a reader who says "soap" for "detergent" will be readily identified as having manipulated lexical-semantic relationships in such a way as to produce one word rather than another. In other words, Garrett's methodology vastly underestimated the incidence of semantically based errors, unlike Goodman's.

The flaws in the Rayner et al. (2002) article go on. As discussed previously, the authors referred to the meta-analysis of phonics instruction carried out by the NRP (2000). One of the authors of the Rayner et al. article, Barbara Foorman, in fact played a central role in the NRP meta-analysis. According to Garan (2002, p. 78), Foorman was the sole reviewer of the phonics section of the NRP study, which investigated other aspects of reading instruction as well. Of the 38 articles reviewed in the phonics section, Foorman was an author of 4, that is, more than 10%. In essence, she was a reviewer of her own research.

Foorman has replied that she was not a reviewer, but rather a "technical advisor" (Foorman et al., 2003, p. 719). So, she "technically advised" on her own work.

This was not the only serious problem with the integrity of the meta-analysis. The NRP (2000) pooled together research articles from the entire, worldwide English-speaking database, over a period of nearly 30 years. It came up with a grand total of 38 articles that it deemed "trustworthy" enough to meta-analyze. Its conclusions about phonics instruction, along with the government's claims to have a right to legislate phonics, and to punish teachers and students whose phonics is not up to par, was based on these 38 articles.

James Cunningham has remarked that the NRP "first denigrates, then ignores, the preponderance of research literature in our field" of reading (2001, p. 327). But even if its exclusionary criteria were legitimate, the fact that it could only find 38 acceptable articles on phonics instruction from an initial pool of more than 100,000 articles means that this topic was not considered all that important or urgent among reading researchers and practitioners. Thus, it was inevitable that the government would find itself having to legally force phonics on the population in order to deal with the literacy crisis of its corporate benefactors.

The NRP report (NRP, 2000) claimed to have used a "medical model" of research for its meta-analysis:

> The evidence-based methodological standards adopted by the Panel are essentially those normally used in research studies of the efficacy of interventions in psychological and medical research. These include behaviorally based interventions, medications, or medical procedures proposed for use in the fostering of robust health and psychological development and the prevention or treatment of disease. (p. 5)

But this claim is ludicrous. Medical research on new drugs, for example, always looks at both the benefits and the risks of the drug. No matter how beneficial the drug may be, if the risk of adverse reactions is too high, it will not be approved. Or if the risk is moderate, it will be approved with precautions clearly spelled out. And, most importantly of all, no patient is ever forced to take a medicine against his or her wishes, no physician is ever forced to prescribe a certain medicine, and no patient is ever punished for "failing" a blood test.

In their purportedly "medical model" of phonics instruction evaluation, the NRP (2000) never once discussed the potential side effects of too much phonics, such as the certainty that some, perhaps many, children will simply be turned off to reading by this utterly boring and meaningless activity. The NICHD, despite calling for a scientifically trustworthy approach to reading instruction evaluation, and a medical model at that, never once studied in a scientific fashion the risks and benefits of high-stakes reading tests, though it is on public record as supporting it. Information is not lacking on the increasing incidence of anxiety, depression, and somatic symptomatology associated with these tests. Such psychiatric problems are known risk factors for adolescent suicide.

The growing fight against such high-stakes testing is the pivotal rallying cry for proponents of democracy in science, in teaching, and in learning, and has the potential to defeat neophonics by means of a democratic mass movement.

Proponents of democracy in learning see a standardized curriculum as reflecting the needs of certain interest groups, and not necessarily those of the students themselves. High-stakes testing presupposes "core subjects" that will decide the educational fate of children. It devalues "non-core subjects" such as art, music, and physical education. On a view of human nature that respects the phenomenon of stimulus-free creativity, one could easily argue that these should be the core subjects, if there are to be any at all. Protests against high-stakes testing inherently demand an education system that addresses the needs and talents of individual students, and that has no tolerance for promoting poor self-esteem as an untoward side effect of assessment.

The struggle against high-stakes testing in reading and elsewhere is a defense of democracy in teaching, a form of academic freedom, because it recognizes that curriculum is a joint undertaking among teachers, parents, and students, and that judgment, not script, plays the key role in deciding on the flow of a classroom lesson. In the setting of high-stakes testing, teachers see students in an oppositional light, as everything depends on how well they perform on the tests. The supportive and caring relationship between teacher and student that is a prerequisite for an unthreatening learning environment is sabotaged and undermined by the testing climate. In the setting of high-stakes testing, teachers feel pressured to teach to the test, which means the test defines the curriculum. And in this setting of pathologic pedagogy, teachers may even feel it is their moral obligation to look aside when civil disobedience takes the form of "cheating."

Finally, the struggle against high-stakes testing is a defense of democracy in science, because it challenges the notion that a single scientific viewpoint should be sanctioned by the state. Neophonics relies on state support for its very existence. The Reading Excellence Act (1998) and No Child Left Behind (2001) place experimental design in a privileged position, when it has no more claim as a tool to discover empirical truths than descriptive design or intuitions about well-formedness.

The struggle for democracy in general proceeds via struggles for particular democratic rights. The neophonics counterrevolution makes it clear that the struggle is far from over. Many important rights have been won, and need to be defended. But many more lie ahead. They can be won if natural allies—scientists, education researchers, teachers, parents, and students—join together to demand an end to state definitions of science and reading, and an end to high-stakes testing.

Postscript: A Formal Approach to Phonics

This postscript is an initial proposal on defining and characterizing the technical terms and principles that figure into the system that converts letters of written words into the sounds of their oral equivalents. Further empirical investigations using this, or alternative proposals, constitute the scientific study of letter-sound relationships.

Investigations based on the data of letter-sound relationships in English reveal the existence of rules that turn letters into sounds, and sounds into sounds, and that assign to some words the status of being an exception to a particular letter-sound or sound-sound conversion. Therefore, it is not possible to say that individual phonics rules are entirely responsible for turning the letters of a word into the word's pronunciation. Rather, it is the system as a whole, utilizing individual rules and principles that govern their interaction, that accomplishes this feat.

In general, a rule of the phonics system has the form $X \rightarrow Y$. The term X is the input to the rule, and the term Y is the output of the rule. The arrow signifies that the rule turns the input X into the output Y.

The simplest phonics rule converts a single letter into a single sound, and does so without requiring the presence of any additional material in the input, such as other letters or syntactic category. Examples of such simple rules are the following:

$D \rightarrow$ [d]
$d \rightarrow$ [d]
$p \rightarrow$ [p]
$u \rightarrow$ [u]

By convention, a letter is written in italics, and a sound is enclosed in square brackets.

The effect of a phonics rule is to convert the input into the output. Thus, the rule *d* → [d] will take a string containing the letter *d*, such as *dig*, and turn it into [d]*ig*. When each letter of a spelled word has been turned into a sound, and when no additional rules can apply, the spelled word has been converted into a representation of its spoken form. In this way, written *dig* is converted to spoken [dIg].

The formally simplest input and output consists of a single symbol for each, as in *d* → [d]. However, more complex inputs and outputs also exist. An input can consist of two symbols, as in *ph* → [f]. An output can represent two sounds, as in *x* → [ks]. An input can consist of a string of several symbols, but where only some, not all, of the symbols undergo a change, as in *steak* → *st*[ey]*k*.

The symbol or symbols that actually undergo a change are the *target* of the rule, and what it turns into is its *value*. In *d* → [d], *d* is the target, and [d] is its value. In *steak* → *st*[ey]*k*, *ea* is the target, and [ey] is its value.

Any part of a rule's input that is not part of the target is called the *alphabetic context*. In *sew* → *s*[o]*w*, *e* is the target and *s-w* is the alphabetic context. The target *e* turns into its value [o].

If the input of a rule consists of a single-symbol target and no alphabetic context, the rule is called a *default rule*. The rule *d* → [d] is such a rule. Otherwise, it is a *nondefault rule*, such as *ph* → [f] and *sew* → *s*[o]*w*. If the value of the target is [ø], the rule is a *silent rule*. Examples of this include *wh* → *w*[ø] and *mb* → *m*[ø]. If the target is a pair of letters, as in the *ph* rule, it is called a *digraph*.

The output of a phonics rule may consist of a formal expression that denotes that the rule's input is an exception to another phonics rule. For example, in *ind* → *{*i* → [I]*nd*}, the asterisk indicates that the string of letters *ind* is an exception to the short-vowel rule for the letter *i*. A shorthand notion for this is *ind* → *short-vowel rule.

The inputs to phonics rules may be strings that consist of outputs of previous phonics rules. In other words, they may contain phonemes, in addition to, or instead of, letters. Clearly, however, the *initial input* string for any phonic conversion consists entirely of letters, as it is a written word with a spelling. Thus, *dog* and *cat* are initial input strings, but [d]*og* and [k]*at* are not. Nor are [m][I]*nt* and *st*[ey]*k*.

In many words, each individual letter undergoes its own phonic conversion. The word *so*, for example, undergoes *s* → [s] and *o* → [ow].

In other cases, such as when the target is a digraph, more than one letter will together undergo a single phonics rule. In *Phil*, for example, the letters *ph* together convert to [f], according to the phonics rule *ph* → [f]. Furthermore, this word does not undergo *p* → [p] and *h* → [h]. Observing that the string *p* and the string *h* are each *properly included* in the string *ph*, the principle that selects the *ph* rule over the *p* rule and *h* rule can be readily formlated as:

> Definition: The *length* of a string is the number of symbols it contains.
>
> Definition: String *S properly includes* string *S′* if *S′* an be found in *S*, and the length of *S* is greater than the length of *S′*.
>
> The Principle for Competing Phonics Rules: If a string of letters that satisfies the input requirements for phonics rule *R* properly includes a string of letters that satisfies the the input requirements for phonics rule *R′*, then rule *R′* is blocked from applying at the point where rule *R* applies.

Mixed or hybrid strings arise as a result of a sequential application of phonics rules to an initial input. In this case, some, but not all, of the letters have been converted to sounds, so rules need to continue to apply. A sequential application of phonics rules is a necessary consequence of the Principle for Competing Phonics Rules, because this principle can prevent letters in an input string's alphabetic context from converting to sound at the same point at which the target is undergoing a change.

For example, the input string *mint* undergoes *m* → [m] and *int* → [I]*nt*. The letters *i*, *n*, and *t* do not yet undergo *i* → [ay], *n* → [n], and *t* → [t], because each of these targets is included in the string *int*, and blocked from applying at the point where the short-vowel rule for *int* applies. Therefore, the conversion of *mint* to [mInt] must proceed through a stage that includes the hybrid [m][I]*nt*. At this point, *int* no longer exists, so *n* → [n] and *t* → [t] can apply. Obviously, *i* → [ay] cannot now apply, because there is no longer a target letter *i*.

The sequential phonic conversion of written *mint* to oral [mInt] is shown in Fig. P.1. In the first stage of this phonic conversion, [m][I]*nt* is produced from the initial input. In the second stage, the final output [mInt] is produced.

Therefore, the existence of hybrid representations follows from the piecemeal conversion of a written word to sound, and this follows from the existence of rules that contain an alphabetic context and that obey the Principle for Competing Phonics Rules.

When an initial input contains only target letters for the phonics rules of the language, and no alphabetic contexts, the Principle for Competing Phonics Rules may still obtain, as it does for words with consonant digraphs, like *she*. But there will be only a single stage of application of the rules, and

Initial Input	*m i n t*	
STAGE 1.	[m] [I] *n t*	*m* → [m], *int* → [I]*nt* (*i* → [ay], *n* → [n] and *t* → [t] blocked)
STAGE 2.	[m] [I] [n] [t]	*n* → [n], *t* → [t]
Final Output	[m I n t]	

FIG. P.1. Sequential phonic conversion of written *mint* to oral [mInt].

no hybrid will be created. Thus, the form *she* undergoes *sh* → [š] and *e* → [iy] at the same point in the phonic conversion of the word:

s h e	input
[š] [iy]	*sh* → [š], *e* → [iy] (*s* → [s] and *h* → [h] blocked)

Because the input to the *sh* rule and the input to the *e* rule share no letters, the one does not block the other. They apply simultaneously. Such simultaneous application of rules is in accordance with the *Principle for Noncompeting Phonics Rules*: Unless prevented from applying to a form because of the Principle for Competing Phonics Rules, all applicable phonics rules apply simultaneously.

It is now immediately obvious that the phonics system is an abstract system, because its representations include some, namely the hybrid ones, that are never found in actual language use. In their physical manifestations, words are either spelled or pronounced. Hybrid forms are internal mental representations only.

References

Adams, M. (1990). *Beginning to read: Thinking and learning about print.* Cambridge, MA: MIT Press.

Allington, R. L. (2002). *Big Brother and the national reading curriculum: How ideology trumped evidence.* Portsmouth, NH: Heinemann.

Altwerger, B., & Strauss, S. L. (2002). The business behind testing. *Language Arts*, *79*, 256–263.

Anderson, G. E., Whipple, A. D., & Jimerson, S. R. (2002, October). Grade retention: Achievement and mental health outcomes. *National Association of School Psychologists* [On-line]. Available: www.nasponline.org.

Augustine, N. R. (1997, July 2). A business leader's guide to setting academic standards. *Business Roundtable* [On-line]. Available: www.brtable.org.

Augustine, N. R., Lupberger, E., & Orr, J. F., III. (1996, July 2). A common agenda for improving American education [On-line]. Available: www.brtable.org.

Berliner, D. C., & Biddle, B. J. (1995). *The manufactured crisis: Myths, fraud, and the attack on America's public schools.* Reading, MA: Addison-Wesley.

Bloomfield, L. (1961). Teaching children to read. In L. Bloomfield & C. L. Barnhart (Eds.), *Let's read: A linguistic approach* (pp. 19–42). Detroit: Wayne State University Press. (Original work published 1942)

Bloomfield, L. (1994). *Language.* New Delhi, India: Motilal Banarsidass. (Original work published 1933)

Bock, B. (2000). NICHD panel recommends methods to teach reading. *The NIH Record LII* [On-line]. Available: www.nih.gov.

Blumenfeld, S. L. (1995). Forty Massachusetts professors of linguistics and psycholinguistics blast whole language. *The Blumenfeld Education Letter, 10,* 1–7.

The brain reads sound by sound. (1997, November 3). *The Baltimore Sun,* p. 1B.

Brown, J., Marek, A., & Goodman, K. S. (1994). *Annotated chronological miscue analysis bibliography* (Occasional Papers No. 16). Tucson: University of Arizona, Program in Language and Literacy.

Bub, D. N., Black, S., & Howell, J. (1989). Word recognition and orthographic context effects in a letter-by-letter reader. *Brain, 36,* 357–376.

Bush, G. H. W. (1990, July 17). *Decade of the brain: Presidential proclamation 6158* [On-line]. Available: www.loc.gov.

Business group is force in education. (1998, January 31). *The Baltimore Sun,* p. 1B.

Business Roundtable. (2002, December 11). The No Child Left Behind Act: Where we stand after one year [On-line]. Available: www.brtable.org.

Business Roundtable. (2001a, April 25). Press release: Education reform: Senate faces ultimate test [On-line]. Available: www.brtable.org.

Business Roundtable. (2001b, January 23). Press release: The Business Roundtable offers support for Bush administration, Congressional efforts to raise K–12 student achievement [On-line]. Available: www.brtable.org.

Business Roundtable. (2001c, December 11). The Business Roundtable calls conference report a vital step forward for American education [On-line]. Available: www.brtable.org.

Business Roundtable. (1999, June 2). Press release: Business leaders make gains in improving nation's schools, but more work lies ahead [On-line]. Available: www.brtable.org.

Business Roundtable. (1998a, January 1). Fact sheet: Strengthening your child's academic future [On-line]. Available: www.brtable.org.

Business Roundtable. (1998b, November). Building support for tests that count [On-line]. Available: www.brtable.org.

Business Roundtable. (1998c, December 9). Press release: Business leaders build support for tougher tests in school [On-line]. Available: www.brtable.org.

Business Roundtable. (1998d, January 1). Fact sheet: Keep the promise campaign [On-line]. Available: www.brtable.org.

Business Roundtable. (1998e, October 8). Press release: Coalition of nation's top business and education leaders launch hard-hitting PSA campaign to raise academic standards [On-line]. Available: www.brtable.org.

Business Roundtable. (1997, July 2). Press release: Baseball, business, policy leaders and teachers launch ad campaign to promote education excellence [On-line]. Available: www.brtable.org.

Business Roundtable. (1995a, January 1). Press release: Continuing the commitment: Essential components of a successful education system [On-line]. Available: www.brtable.org.

Business Roundtable. (1995b, May). Continuing the commitment: Essential components of a successful education system [On-line]. Available: www.brtable.org.

Business Roundtable. (1993, August 1). Workforce training and development for U.S. competitiveness [On-line]. Available: www.brtable.org.

Business views of assessments and accountability in education: Hearings before the Subcommittee on Education Reform, Committee on Education and the Workforce, U.S. House of Representatives. (2001, March 8). (Testimony of E. Rust) [On-line]. Available: edworkforce.house.gov.

Carnine, D., & Meeder, H. (1997, September 3). Reading research into practice. *Education Week,* pp. 41–43.

Chall, J. (1967). *Learning to read: The great debate.* New York: McGraw-Hill.

Children's literacy: Hearings before the Committee on Education and the Workforce, U.S. House of Representatives. (1997, July 10). (Testimony of G. Reid Lyon) [On-line]. Available: edworkforce.house.gov.

Chomsky, C. (1970). Reading, writing, and phonology. *Harvard Educational Review, 40,* 287–310.

Chomsky, N. (1975). *Reflections on language.* New York: Pantheon.

Chomsky, N. (1972). *Language and mind* (Enlarged ed.). New York: Harcourt Brace Jovanovich.

Chomsky, N. (1965). *Aspects of the theory of syntax.* Cambridge, MA: MIT Press.

Chomsky, N. (1959). A review of B. F. Skinner's *Verbal behavior. Language, 35,* 26–58.

Chomsky, N. (1957). *Syntactic structures.* The Hague: Mouton.

Chomsky, N., & Halle, M. (1968). *The sound pattern of English.* New York: Harper & Row.

Clowes, G. A. (1999). Reading is anything but natural: An interview with G. Reid Lyon. *School Reform News* [On-line]. Available: www.heartland.org.

Coles, G. (2003). *Reading the naked truth: Literacy, legislation, and lies.* Portsmouth, NH: Heinemann.

Coles, G. (2000). *Misreading reading: The bad science that hurts children.* Portsmouth, NH: Heinemann.

Coverdell, P. (1998). Testimony of Paul Coverdell [On-line]. Available: www.thomas.loc.gov.

Crystal, D. (1995). *The Cambridge encyclopedia of the English language.* Cambridge: Cambridge University Press.

Cunningham, J. W. (2001). The National Reading Panel report. *Reading Research Quarterly, 36,* 326–335.

Curtiss, S. (1977). *Genie: A psycholinguistic study of a modern day "wild child."* New York: Academic Press.

de Saussure, F. (1966). *A course in general linguistics.* New York: McGraw-Hill. (Original work published 1922)

Demb, J. B., Poldrack, R. A., & Gabrieli, J. D. E. (1999). Functional neuroimaging of word processing in normal and dyslexic readers. In R. M. Klein & P. A. McMullen (Eds.), *Converging methods for understanding reading and dyslexia* (pp. 243–304). Cambridge, MA: MIT Press.

Dressing, H., Obergriesser, T., Tost, H., Kaumeier, S., Ruf, M., & Braus, D. F. (2001). Homosexual pedophilia and functional networks: An fMRI case report and literature review. *Fortschritte der Neurologie-Psychiatrie, 69,* 539–544.

Druckman, D., & Lacey, J. I. (1991). *Brain and cognition: Some new technologies.* Washington, DC: National Academies Press.

Edelsky, C., Altwerger, B., & Flores, B. (1990). *What's new in whole language?* Portsmouth, NH: Heinemann.

Education research and evaluation and student achievement: Quality counts: Hearings before the Committee on Education and the Workforce, U.S. House of Representatives. (2000, May 4). (Testimony of G. Reid Lyon) [On-line]. Available: nichd.nih.gov.

Foorman, B. R., Francis, D. J., & Fletcher, J. M. (2003). Correcting errors. *Phi Delta Kappan, 84,* 719–720.

Foorman, B. R., Francis, D. J., & Fletcher, J. M. (1997). NICHD early intervention project [On-line]. Available: www.Interdys.org.

Foorman, B., Francis, D., Novy, D., & Liberman, D. (1991). How letter-sound instruction mediates progress in first-grade reading and spelling. *Journal of Educational Psychology, 83,* 456–469.

Garan, E. (2002). *Resisting reading mandates: How to triumph with the truth.* Portsmouth, NH: Heinemann.

Garrett, M. F. (1990). Sentence processing. In D. N. Osherson & H. Lasnik (Eds.), *An invitation to cognitive science: Language Vol. 1* (pp. 133–176). Cambridge, MA: MIT Press.

Garrett, M. F. (1984). The organization of processing structure for language production: Applications to aphasic speech. In D. Caplan, A. Roch Lecours, & A. Smith (Eds.), *Biological perspectives on language* (pp. 172–193). Cambridge, MA: MIT Press.

Gell-Mann, M. (1978, June 27). Letter to the editor of the Oxford English Dictionary [On-line]. Available: www.duke.edu.

Goodman, K. S. (1994). Reading, writing, and written texts: A transactional sociopsycholinguistic view. In R. B. Ruddell, M. R. Ruddell, & H. Singer (Eds.), *Theoretical models and processes of reading, 4th ed.* (pp. 1093–1130). Newark, DE: International Reading Association.

Goodman, K. S. (1993). *Phonics phacts.* Portsmouth, NH: Heinemann.

Goodman, K. S. (1986). *What's whole in whole language?* Portsmouth, NH: Heinemann.

Goodman, K. S. (1976). Miscue analysis: Theory and reality in reading. In J. Merritt (Ed.), *Proceedings of the fifth IRA world congress on reading* (pp. 15–26). Newark, DE: International Reading Association.

Goodman, K. S. (1973). Miscue analysis: Windows on the reading process. In D. Goodman (Ed.), *Miscue analysis: Applications to reading instruction* (pp. 3–18). Urbana, IL: NCTE.

Goodman, K. S. (1970). Psycholinguistic universals in the reading process. *Journal Typographic Research, 4,* 103–110.

Goodman, K. S. (1967). Reading: A psycholinguistic guessing game. *Journal of the Reading Specialist, 6,* 126–135.

Goodman, K. S. (1965). A linguistic study of cues and miscues in reading. *Elementary English, 42,* 639–643.

Goodman, K. S., & Goodman, Y. M. (1979). Learning to read is natural. In L. B. Resnick & P. W. Weaver (Eds.), *Theory and practice of early reading: Vol. 1* (pp. 137–154). Hillsdale, NJ: Lawrence Erlbaum Associates.

Goodman, Y. M., & Marek, A. M. (1996). *Retrospective miscue analysis: Revaluing readers and reading.* New York: Richard C. Owen.

Graham, L. R (1974). *Science and philosophy in the Soviet Union.* New York: Vintage.

Grice, H. P. (1975). Logic and conversation. In P. Cole & J. Morgan (Eds.), *Syntax and semantics: Vol. 3* (pp. 41–58). New York: Academic Press.

Halle, M. (1959). *The sound pattern of Russian.* The Hague: Mouton.

Harris, Z. S. (1951). *Methods in structural linguistics.* Chicago: University of Chicago Press.

Hart, J. (1968). *An orthographie, 1569.* Menston, England: Scolar Press.

Haskell, D., Foorman, B., & Swank, P. (1992). Effects of three orthographic/phonological units on first-grade reading. *Remedial and Special Education, 13,* 40–49.

Herrnstein, R. J., & Murray, C. (1999). *Intelligence and class structure in American life.* New York: Free Press.

Howard father pushes reading reforms. (1997, November 19). *The Baltimore Sun,* p. 1B.

H.R. 2614 (The Reading Excellence Act). (1998). *U.S. House of Representatives* [On-line]. Available: www.thomas.loc.gov.

Jackendoff, R. (1983). *Semantics and cognition.* Cambridge, MA: MIT Press.

Jensen, A. (1969). How much can we boost I.Q. and scholastic achievement? *Harvard Educational Review, 39,* 1–123.

Kahn, D. (1978). Syllable-based generalizations in English phonology. Unpublished doctoral dissertation, Massachusetts Institute of Technology, Cambridge.

Katz, J. J. (1981). *Language and other abstract objects.* Totowa, NJ: Bowman & Littlefield.

Kertesz, A. (1982). *Western aphasia battery.* San Antonio, TX: Psychological Corporation.

Kiparsky, P. (1973). Elsewhere in phonology. In S. R. Anderson & P. Kiparsky (Eds.), *A festschrift for Morris Halle* (pp. 93–106). New York: Holt, Rinehart & Winston.

Krashen, S. D. (1999). *Three arguments against whole language and why they are wrong.* Portsmouth, NH: Heinemann.

Krasuski, J., Horwitz, B., & Rumsey, J. M. (1996). A survey of functional and anatomical neuroimaging techniques. In G. R. Lyon & J. M. Rumsey (Eds.), *Neuroimaging: A window to the neurologic foundations of learning and behavior in children* (pp. 25–52). Baltimore: Paul H. Brookes.

Krol, J. A. (1998, January 1). Statement on voluntary national testing [On-line]. Available: www.brtable.org.

Kuhn, T. S. (1996). *The structure of scientific revolutions* (3rd ed.). Chicago: University of Chicago Press.

Labov, W. (1969). The logic of nonstandard English. In J. E. Alatis (Ed.), *Georgetown Monographs on Language and Linguistics 22: Linguistics and Language Study: 20th Roundtable Meeting* (pp. 1–31), Washington, DC: Georgetown University Press.

Lenneberg, E. (1967). *Biological foundations of language.* New York: Wiley.

Levelt, W. J. M. (1989). *Speaking: From intention to articulation.* Cambridge, MA: MIT Press.

Liberman, I. Y. (1971). Basic research in speech and lateralization of language: Some implications for reading disability. *Bulletin of the Orton Society, 27,* 71–87.

Liberman, I. Y., Shankweiler, D., & Liberman, A. M. (1989). The alphabetic principle and learning to read. In D. Shankweiler & I. Y. Liberman (Eds.), *International Academy for Research in Learning Disabilities Monograph Series: Number 6. Phonology and Reading Disability: Solving the Reading Puzzle* (pp. 1–33). Ann Arbor, MI: University of Michigan Press.

Lyon, G. R. (2002, November 18). Remarks presented at forum of the Coalition for Evidence-Based Policy entitled: Rigorous evidence: The key to progress in education? Lessons from medicine, welfare and other fields. Miami, FL. Available: www.excel.gov.org.

Lyon, G. R. (2001, July 27). *White House Early Childhood Cognitive Development Summit: Summary* [On-line]. Available: www.Education.News.org.

Lyon, G. R. (1998). Why reading is not a natural process. *Educational Leadership, 55,* 14–18.

Maryland Business Roundtable for Education. (1997, Fall). Business works to ensure that students are prepared for workforce of 21st century. *MBRT Highlights,* Baltimore, MD.

Maryland Business Roundtable for Education. (1996). *Annual Report.* Baltimore, MD.

Mead, M. (1961). *Coming of age in Samoa.* New York: William Morrow & Company.

Measuring success: Using assessments and accountability to raise student achievement: Hearings before the Subcommittee on Education Reform, Committee on Education and the Workforce, U.S. House of Representatives. (2001, March 8). (Testimony of G. Reid Lyon) [On-line]. Available: edworkforce.house.gov.

Medvedev, Z. A. (1969). *The rise and fall of T.D. Lysenko* (I. M. Lerner, Trans.). New York: Columbia University Press.

Meyer, R. J. (2001). *Phonics exposed: Understanding and resisting systematic direct intense phonics instruction.* Mahwah, NJ: Lawrence Erlbaum Associates.

Mitka, M. (2001, May 23/30). Some physicians protest 'high-stakes' tests. *Journal of the American Medical Association (JAMA), 285,* p. 2569.

National Council of Teachers of English. (1999). Position statement on reading [On-line]. Urbana, IL. Available: www.ncte.org.

National Council of Teachers of English. (1998). A statement of opposition to the Reading Excellence Act: Endorsed by the National Council of Teachers of English, the National Reading Council, the National Conference on Research in Language and Literacy, and the Conference on College Composition and Communication [On-line]. Urbana, IL. Available: www.ncte.org.

National Institute of Child Health and Human Development. (2000a, April). *Report of the National Reading Panel: Teaching children to read, an evidence-based assessment of the scientific research literature on reading and its implications for reading instruction—reports of the subgroups.* Washington, DC: NIH Publication No. 00–4754.

National Institute of Child Health and Human Development. (2000b, December). *Report of the National Reading Panel: Teaching children to read, an evidence-based assessment of the scientific research literature on reading and its implications for reading instruction—reports of the subgroups (Summary Report).* Washington, DC: NIH Publication No. 00–4769.

National Institute of Neurological Disorders and Stroke. (2000, June 8–9). 21st century prevention and management of migraine headaches [On-line]. Available: www.ninds.nih.gov.

Navarro, V. (1993). *Dangerous to your health: Capitalism in health care.* New York: Monthly Review Press.

The No Child Left Behind Act of 2001. (2001). *United States Public Law 107–110* [On-line]. Available: www.ed.gov.

Orton, S. (1939). *Reading, writing, and speech problems in children.* New York: Norton.

Overview of reading and literacy initiatives: Hearings before the Committee on Labor and Human Resources, U.S. Senate. (1998, April 28). (Testimony of G. Reid Lyon) [On-line]. Available: www.readbygrade3.com.

Phonics paves Christian way. (1998, March 1). *The Baltimore Sun,* p. 2B.

Pitman, J. (1969). *The initial teaching alphabet.* London: Pitman.

Ponnuru, R. (1999, September 13). Fighting words, *National Review.* pp. 34–38.

Posner, M. I., & Raichle, M. E. (1994). *Images of mind.* New York: Scientific American Library.

Presentation of the National Reading Panel Report: Hearings before the Subcommittee on Labor, Health and Human Services, and Education of the Senate Appropriations Committee. (2001, April 13). (Testimony of Duane Alexander) [On-line]. Available: www.nichd.nih.gov.

Rayner, K., Foorman, B. R., Perfetti, C. A., Pesetsky, D., & Seidenberg, M. S. (2002, March). How should reading Be taught? *Scientific American,* pp. 85–91.

Read, C. (1975). *Children's categorization of speech sounds in English.* Urbana, IL: NCTE.

Reading bill full of flaws. (1997, November). *The Council Chronicle,* p. 1.

The Reading Excellence Act. (1998). *United States Public Law 105–276* [On-line]. Available: www.thomas.loc.gov.

Rosenberger, P. B., & Rottenberg, D. A. (2002). Does training change the brain? *Neurology, 58,* 1139–1140.

Sampson, G. (1985). *Writing systems: A linguistic introduction.* Stanford, CA: Stanford University Press.

Shaywitz, S., Shaywitz, B. A., Pugh, K. R., Skudlarski, P., Fulbright, R. K., Constable, R. T., Bronen, R. A., Fletcher, J. M., Liberman, A. M., Shankweiler, D. P., Katz, L., Lacadie, C., Marchione, K. E., & Gore, J. C. (1996). The neurobiology of developmental dyslexia as viewed through the lens of functional magnetic resonance imaging technology. In G. R. Lyon & J. M. Rumsey (Eds.), *Neuroimaging: A window to the neurologic foundations of learning and behavior in children* (pp. 79–94). Baltimore: Paul H. Brookes.

Simos, P. G., Fletcher, J. M., Bergman, E., Breier, J. I., Foorman, B. R., Castillo, E. M., Davis, R. N., Fitzgerald, M., & Papanicolaou, A. C. (2002). Dyslexia-specific brain activation profile becomes normal following successful remedial training. *Neurology, 58,* 120–1213.

Smith, F. (1994). *Understanding reading: A psycholinguistic analysis of reading and learning to read.* Hillsdale, NJ: Lawrence Erlbaum Associates.

Strauss, S. L. (2003). Challenging the NICHD reading research agenda. *Phi Delta Kappan, 84,* 38–42.

Strauss, S. L. (1999). Learning a first language for the second time: 'Goodman contexts' and 'Vygotskyan zones' in recovery from aphasia. In A. M. Marek & C. Edelsky (Eds.), *Reflections and connections: Essays in honor of Kenneth S. Goodman's influence on language education* (pp. 403–419). Cresskill, NJ: Hampton Press.

Sweet, R. W. (1996). Illiteracy: An incurable disease or education malpractice? [On-line]. Available: www.nrrf.org.

Taylor, D. (1998). *Beginning to read and the spin doctors of science: The political campaign to change America's mind about how children learn to read.* Urbana, IL: NCTE.

Temple, C. A., Nathan, R. G., & Burris, N. A. (1982). *The beginnings of writing.* Boston: Allyn & Bacon.

Transcript of the second presidential debate. (2000, October 11). *ABC News* [On-line]. Available: www.abcnews.org.

Traub, J. (2002, November 10). What works? *The New York Times Education Life Section,* pp. 24–28.

Twenty-First Century Workforce Commission. (2000, June). *A nation of opportunity: Building America's 21st century workforce.* Washington, DC: National Alliance of Business and U.S. Department of Labor.

Underwood, A. (2001, May 7). Religion and the brain. *Newsweek,* pp. 52–57.

U.S. Department of Education, Office of Vocational and Adult Education. (2001). Biography of Hans Meeder [On-line]. Available: www.ed.gov.

Venezky, R. L. (1999). *The American way of spelling.* New York: Guilford.

Warrington, E. K., & Langdon, D. W. (2002). Does the spelling dyslexic read by recognizing orally spelled words? An investigation of a letter-by-letter reader. *Neurocase, 8,* 210–218.

Warrington, E. K., & Shallice, T. (1980). Word-form dyslexia. *Brain, 103,* 99–112.

Weaver, C. (2002). *Reading process and practice* (3rd. ed.). Portsmouth, NH: Heinemann.

World Health Organization. (2000, June 4). Press release: WHO issues new healthy life expectancy rankings: Japan number one in new 'healthy life' system [On-line]. Washington, DC and Geneva, Switzerland. Available: www.who.org.

Author Index

R

S

T

U, V

W

Subject Index

M

N

P

R